PRAISE FOR
THE LONGEST RACE

"Kara's story is inspiring and powerful, and she shares it with vulnerability and honesty. This book has something for everyone, whether you're a seasoned runner, just starting out, or don't think you have any interest in running at all. A must-have for your bookshelf, it leaves you motivated, empowered, and ready to take on the world. Thank you, Kara, for sharing your story and reminding us all that we are stronger than we know."

— **ALLYSON FELIX**, seven-time Olympic gold medalist
and twelve-time World Championship gold medalist

"Stunning in its honesty and intimacy, *The Longest Race* is one of the most important athlete memoirs of its generation. Kara Goucher takes us inside a breathtakingly complex world, showing us the love and beauty of sport as well as its gruesome abuses of power, callous cruelty, and disregard for the athlete—specifically the female one."

—**KATE FAGAN**, *#1 New York Times* bestselling author
of *What Made Maddy Run: The Secret Struggles
and Tragic Death of an All-American Teen*

"Kara Goucher's journey is dramatic and alarming. Beyond that, she and Mary Pilon have put together a stellar work of investigative journalism. *The Longest Race* will break your heart and blow your mind."

—**JAMES ANDREW MILLER**, *#1* bestselling author of
Those Guys Have All the Fun: Inside the World of ESPN

"A lightning-quick runner who would go on to become a two-time Olympian and the face of Nike, Kara had no idea that her seven years with the Oregon Project would elevate her career to soaring new heights—and drag her into one of the darkest chapters of her life. In her explosive new memoir, Kara opens up about how she and [her husband] Adam helped expose Salazar—the once-beloved coach they regarded as a father figure."

—*PEOPLE*

"This must-read memoir for running fans is as interesting as it is important. Told from Kara's vantage point as a distance-running star, it also serves as a call to action for women and girls to tell their stories of abuse and power imbalances—hard as that may be—so they can give each other strength, push back as a flock, and make things better for the next wave."

—**MOLLY HUDDLE**, two-time Olympian, American record holder in the half-marathon and 5,000 meters, and coauthor of *How She Did It: Stories, Advice, and Secrets to Success from Fifty Legendary Distance Runners*

"*The Longest Race* is a striking reminder of the importance of using your voice. Kara's courage to stand up against the powers that be has helped pave the way for change. Her book is essential reading for anyone who wants to make sports safe and fair for everyone."

—**MARY CAIN**, Founder of Atalanta NYC and 2014 World Junior Champion in the 3,000 meters

"Both books—Goucher's and [Lauren] Fleshman's—should be victory laps for two celebrated runners. But that's not the sort of book either woman set out to write. Each has produced something much grittier: a close-up look at the uncertain and often unhealthy climb toward stardom for women in organized sports."

—*THE WASHINGTON POST*

"In her new memoir, Goucher says for the first time publicly that she is the woman behind the sexual assault allegations that led to her former coach Alberto Salazar to be banned from the sport for life in 2021."

—*GOOD MORNING AMERICA*

"The world silver medalist's memoir lays bare why female athletes may never realize their full potential under systems still rife with inequity, abuse, and harassment. . . . Goucher reveals just what she endured in order to achieve as much as she did in her running career . . . her transparency about so much of her career is what elevates this memoir as perhaps the most important contribution she'll ever make to women's sports."

—WOMEN'S RUNNING

"Goucher is finally telling the whole story of her experience at the Oregon Project in her book *The Longest Race*, written with sports journalist Mary Pilon. . . . The details around how sexual and emotional abuse can be so expertly intertwined to convince victims not to seek help, and even question their own experiences, is a chilling but necessary story."

—SPORTS ILLUSTRATED

"*The Longest Race* is a fearless self-examination of Goucher's life and career. . . . The book has resonated within the athletic community as women's sports continue to face a necessary reckoning and remake themselves."

—DULUTH NEWS TRIBUNE

"Reducing *The Longest Race* to the single story of assault would be a huge mistake . . . [it's] a rare look inside the highest levels of the sport and its players . . . there are Olympic moments, inside scoops, sports industry revelations. . . . Yes, athletes will love this book, but it's also a memoir for anyone who has put their heart on the line."

—OISELLE

"The distance runner's new memoir details years of abuse and indignities in her sport. . . . Goucher has much to be proud of, on and off the track. Perhaps we'll remember her most for the voice she found to hold others to account, so that all of us, her son included, could believe in the sport she loved."

—THE STAR TRIBUNE

"A track-and-field star pulls the lid off the big money behind corporate sponsorship of sports. Goucher makes a strong case against a powerful sports machine."

—KIRKUS REVIEWS

"[Goucher] shares her history of money and transitioning from running for fun to running for money . . . and then the triumphant battle back to running for joy. It's a story about greed, power, disturbing abuse, and more (doping, NCAA violations . . .), and yet is still an uplifting, empowering story."

—STACKING BENJAMINS

"*The Longest Race* is an eye-opening read into the inner workings of professional road and track racing at the highest level, and also the pressures that go along with it."

—THE BOULDER DAILY CAMERA

THE LONGEST RACE

Inside the Secret World of
Abuse, Doping, and Deception
on Nike's Elite Running Team

Kara Goucher

with Mary Pilon

Gallery Books

New York   London   Toronto   Sydney   New Delhi

G

Gallery Books
An Imprint of Simon & Schuster, LLC
1230 Avenue of the Americas
New York, NY 10020

First Gallery Books trade paperback edition March 2024

Simon & Schuster: Celebrating 100 Years of Publishing in 2024

GALLERY BOOKS and colophon are registered trademarks of
Simon & Schuster, LLC

For information about special discounts for bulk purchases,
please contact Simon & Schuster Special Sales at 1-866-506-1949 or
business@simonandschuster.com.

The Simon & Schuster Speakers Bureau can bring authors
to your live event. For more information or to book an event,
contact the Simon & Schuster Speakers Bureau at 1-866-248-3049 or
visit our website at www.simonspeakers.com.

Interior design by Lexy East

Manufactured in the United States of America

10 9 8 7 6 5 4 3 2 1

Library of Congress Cataloging-in-Publication Data has been applied for.

ISBN 978-1-9821-7914-4
ISBN 978-1-9821-7915-1 (paperback)
ISBN 978-1-9821-7916-8 (ebook)

This book is dedicated to the believers,
and those who find power in writing their own stories.

"When a woman tells the truth, she is creating the possibility for more truth around her."
—Adrienne Rich

CONTENTS

THE
LONGEST
RACE

INTRODUCTION

When Kara Goucher reached out to me in November 2019 to ask if I would consider helping her tell her story, I thought the request would be easy to shrug off.

I had long known Kara's name, having covered running as a journalist on *The New York Times* sports desk from 2011 to 2014, then having written about sports for *The New Yorker*, *Esquire*, and *Vice*, among other publications. I knew that she was one of the grittiest American distance runners of the twenty-first century, a podium finisher on the track at the World Championships and the New York City and Boston Marathons. I knew that she had made her second Olympic team in 2012, barely a year after giving birth to her son, a relatively novel occurrence at the time.

I also knew that in recent years, she'd become something of a pariah. In 2015, she and her fellow Olympian husband, Adam Goucher, had publicly accused their former coach, running icon Alberto Salazar, of pushing the limits of anti-doping rules. Kara and Adam had been coached by Alberto at the Nike Oregon Project, an elite, secretive, lavishly funded team based out of the headquarters of the world's largest athletics apparel brand. In September 2019, just two months before Kara reached out to me, Alberto received a four-year ban from coaching from the U.S. Anti-Doping Agency. Kara, who had provided evidence in the case, wasn't implicated in any wrongdoing, though neither were her teammates Galen Rupp and Mo Farah.

Word of the Salazar ban was still fresh, but my reaction when Kara reached out was: *This feels like old news.* I was born and raised in Eugene, Oregon, Nike's birthplace and the self-proclaimed track and field capital of the world. Nike runners had godlike status in my home state. For years, on regular visits back, gossip about whether Alberto, Galen, Kara, and other Oregon Project runners were doping was nearly constant, not only on the lips of my sports-obsessed family, but at local coffee shops and bars.

Everyone wanted to know if Alberto and his runners only pushed the edges of doping rules, or crossed them. More recently, people questioned how Kara's claim that some people on the tight-knit Oregon Project team could be dirty, and others clean, could be true.

My feeling was that the sport was tarnished, and had never been squeaky clean in the first place. One idol after the next had been accused to have been cheating over the years—from Marion Jones, to Justin Gatlin, to countless Russian track and field athletes—and the motivations were clear. (Jones has admitted to taking performance-enhancing drugs. Gatlin, who has tested positive for banned substances twice and was served bans in 2001 and 2006, had denied that he doped until 2017, when he apologized for "any wrongdoings or black eyes I've brought onto the sport," according to *Sports Illustrated*.) If you could take something to become richer, stronger, and more famous, and knew you were unlikely to get caught, would you do it? What if you knew that many of your competitors were doing it already? Factor in that you have a very limited window to earn the income you'll be living off of for a lifetime, and the knowledge that with a single injury, your career could be over. This didn't make doping right, but I felt I understood the very real and potent incentives to cheat. More to the point, I wondered how much the question of who did and didn't cross the lines even mattered.

By 2019, my focus had shifted away from covering sports in a traditional sense. I had just released an audio series about Larry Nassar and the institutional failures and cover-ups that had allowed him to abuse young gymnasts for decades. Once I started reporting on serial pedophiles and systemic corruption, I found it hard to care as much about athletes trying to shave a few seconds off their finish times with some shady supplements. I was asking questions about complicity, enablement, and trauma. I was interested in the resilience and bravery of the young women who spoke out, brought their abuser to justice, exposed troubled institutions, and changed the way America thinks and talks about survivorship.

So, as I got ready for what I was certain would be a quick call with Kara, expecting to hear about steroids, supplements, testosterone creams, and intravenous infusions, I was already brainstorming a polite response. The Nike Oregon Project story had been well covered. Alberto was banned. Life moved on.

Then, she started talking, and everything changed.

I couldn't type fast enough. Running and doping were part of the story, but there was so much more—things that she had never spoken about, except to a few of her closest family members, and to the investigators at the myriad sports and law enforcement agencies pursuing Salazar's case. The dynamics from inside the Nike headquarters were beyond what I ever had imagined. As with the Nassar scandal, Kara's story was about abuse both subtle and overt, the culture in which it transpired, a chain of command that allowed it to proliferate, and the risks faced by those who spoke out. Kara, the runner who had appeared on billboards and in glossy magazine spreads for nearly a decade, depicted by Nike as the perky Olympian mom from the Midwest, had lived a double life that reminded me of John le Carré thrillers, rife with secrets, lies, and threats.

Her story was exactly the sort that I was interested in, and that I wanted to help tell. As we kept talking—conversations punctuated by barking dogs, walks to school, caretaking for older relatives, the drumbeats of our respective lives—we established two basic ground rules. 1) No questions were off-limits. 2) Kara would provide documents, photographs, logbooks, medical records, texts, emails, arbitration transcripts, contracts, and access to her contacts—including her family members and people in the running world—so I could verify her claims. She delivered on all counts.

Kara's story is one that only a very small handful of people have ever heard before. It contains details about sexual abuse and doping, exploitation of power and corporate corruption, alcoholism and disordered eating. (In the back of this book, you'll find resources to learn more about these topics and gain assistance if you or someone you know needs help.)

To write this book, I had to ask Kara to relive some of the most painful moments of her life. After years of holding herself back from looking too closely into what had happened—for reasons of self-protection, among others—she was opening up all of the doors and windows. There were moments in our conversations where it almost felt like she was stepping back into memory as if awakening from a dream, reentering the experiences as she understood them at the time. One of my favorite memoirs is *The Night of the Gun*, by my late friend and mentor David Carr, which wasn't just about the facts of David's addiction, but how his relationship to his reality had changed over time. Kara's book is similar in that it's the story of someone coming to terms with inconvenient truths that she struggled for years to compartmentalize and put away. It's about exposing the facts, and also how her relationship to them has, and continues to, evolve. It is her love story with running, the sport to which she has devoted her life. It is the type of memoir she and I wish that we had read in the past and want to see more of on bookstore shelves now.

And it's all true. Inspired by David's application of journalistic rigor to the memoir genre, I reviewed thousands of pages of documents. Kara subjected herself to hundreds of hours of interviews over a four-year period and dozens of other sources were interviewed. I retraced Kara's steps in Colorado, Oregon, Los Angeles, Boston, and New York. I built a forty-page timeline of Kara's story. My notes encompass more than 550 pages and several notebooks.

I suspect that many people, women in particular, will find pieces of Kara's story all too relatable. I know that I did. The sports media world shares some uncomfortable parallels with the companies, like Nike, that sponsor the athletes it covers. In 2021, 79 percent of sports editors were white men. When I asked for a raise at *The New York Times*, a masthead editor met me with rolled eyes and said, "I'm tired of women coming in here for their 'lean in' moment." I had my story ideas reassigned to men on the sports desk without my permission, and once had a reporter respond to my inquiries about taking an overseas post with questions about my fertility. But, like Kara at earlier points of her life, I largely stayed quiet about my frustrations, seeing it as a tax I had to pay to do what I loved, putting everything that I could into the page and blowing off steam on the running trail. Nike, unlike many S&P 100 companies, doesn't release official data about its demographic makeup, but has faced outcries from investors and employees about its lack of diversity. Though they've made splashy announcements about how they're increasing representation, Nike's board of directors recommended that shareholders vote down a proposal to publish more detailed reports about diversity and inclusion measures in 2021. (A 2018 memo that leaked also quoted Monique Matheson, an executive vice president of global human resources at Nike, saying that Nike had "failed to gain traction" in hiring and promoting more women and people of color.)

At its core, this book is about power. Historically, stories like Kara's get swept under the rug, and that seems to be precisely what Nike attempted to do. The company has felt so threatened by Kara's claims against Alberto that it has allegedly spent millions of dollars to fight them. Nike and many of the powers in the sports world don't want you to hear it, but you need to know this story. If you've ever bought a shirt or pair of shoes with a swoosh, you need to know this story. If you've ever tuned in to watch an Olympic final, a World Series, a Super Bowl, or any other professional sporting event, you need to know this story. Kara and I have spent four years of our lives trying to make that happen.

Along the way, I've often found myself wondering, *Why did Kara speak out? Why did she keep going, in the face of death threats and lawsuits? How does a person summon the courage to take on an abuser, a company, an industry, with such dismal odds of winning any sort of justice?*

Thanks to Kara, I now know the answer.

—*Mary Pilon, Los Angeles, June 2022*

AUTHOR'S NOTE

In legal documents and proceedings, Nike's lawyers have denied claims surrounding alleged abuse and doping at the Nike Oregon Project. In 2015, Nike said it conducted an internal investigation into Alberto Salazar and Galen Rupp and found nothing. In August 2021, they removed Alberto's name from a building on their Beaverton campus. "This change follows the SafeSport decision to permanently ban Alberto from coaching," a Nike spokeswoman said in a statement to employees, which was obtained by *Willamette Week*. "The nature of the allegations and the finding of a lifetime ban make it appropriate to change the name of the building."

Alberto has also denied doping and abuse claims, both in legal proceedings and in a lengthy blog post. He has said he followed USADA and WADA protocols and that he never forced athletes to take prescriptions illegally. He wrote, "Let the haters hate; we're going to keep winning through hard work, dedication, and fair play."

Galen and Mo Farah, too, have denied all allegations that they took any banned substances or otherwise violated doping protocols or any NCAA rules. Neither the NCAA nor USADA has served either of them a violation or reported a positive test result.

PREFACE

I was six years old when my grandpa, Calvin Haworth, took me to my first running race.

The one-mile jaunt was part of the 1984 Hermantown Festival, an annual summer celebration that took place near our home in Duluth, Minnesota. The festival was like countless others that take place across the country in the summer: kids running around, parents chasing them, the smell of hamburgers and hot dogs in the air, local businesses handing out key chains and brochures, some faces you knew, some that you didn't.

It also included a footrace open to both kids and adults. Papa, as my two sisters and I called him, held my hand at the starting line. I wiggled among the cluster of arms and legs, dancing between excitement and fear, waiting for the starting gun. Today, such a race would be the very definition of a "fun run" for me, but as far as I was concerned that afternoon, it may as well have been the Olympics, it felt so special to be there. No one else from my family or my first-grade class was around. It was just me and Papa.

Papa stood tall with wire-rimmed glasses and snow-white hair that he kept dutifully cut short. He had a charm evocative of the actor Jimmy Stewart, and spoke with a similarly endearing drawl. That voice carried, too—he could shake the snow from a fir tree. He voted Republican, listened to Rush Limbaugh, and believed that his daughters and granddaughters had just as much potential as his son and grandsons.

Papa always had me and my two sisters outside and on the go. In summer, he took us with him for tractor rides and out on his pontoon boat. In winter, we would sled in his yard. In and around town were miles and miles of wooded trails that he led me and my sisters through on walks, the same ones that my mother had traveled when she was a child. Duluth felt like the middle of nowhere and the center of the universe.

Papa *loved* running. The miles he covered on foot made up a sort of cartography of our family life. It was about sixteen miles from his and

Grandma's house on Fredenberg Lake to our mom's house. For a short jaunt, he could go the one mile from our mom's house to the restaurant that he and Grandma owned. Between shifts, usually in the late afternoon, he took my mom out for jogs on the nearby roads while Grandma watched me and my sisters.

I ran, like most kids, as part of a game or as a way to get from one spot to another, but in the Hermantown Festival race, there were stakes. A first-, second-, and third-place finisher would be awarded. My time would be written down somewhere and saved forever. I thought of it as a stage, where I was being asked to perform, with hundreds of strangers watching. I was focused, and present.

Off we went. A rush went through my entire body. I pushed faster and faster, hurtling through space. I was hyper-aware of my breath, taking big gulps of air.

Then, *THUD*.

My knees, then palms, hit the asphalt. I had barely started the race, yet I'd gone over the edge, pushing so fast that I tripped over someone else's legs. When I pulled my head up, I could see the other runners getting away.

Small, bright red dots appeared on my knees. My grandpa had stopped next to me, looking worried, wanting to help. He assumed I wouldn't want to continue the race.

I surprised him. Without thinking, I just got up, showing a burst of competitiveness that he didn't know I had. I started running again, with him smiling and striding beside me. Off we went.

When we crossed the finish line—nowhere near first, second, or third—I was sweating and my tiny chest was pumping up and down. Streaks of blood made their way down my legs in small red lines. Papa was so proud that I had finished, and that I had done it on my own terms. I was proud, too. My love story with running had begun.

In time, the sport would bring me money and medals, but also death threats. FBI agents would show up at my door. I'd witness violations of anti-doping rules. I'd experience abuse. I'd have dreams of going to World Championships and Olympics come true.

If I could talk to that little girl at the finish line in Hermantown, I'd tell her to buckle up for the ride of a lifetime.

Like any love story, this one is a bit crazy.

CHAPTER ONE
Patty and Mirko

I'm here because of an unlikely romance that bloomed next to a college soccer field.

My mother, Patty Haworth, was born in 1953. Her dad, Cal Haworth (aka Papa), had come back to his home state of Kansas after World War II, having served for three years in the army as a military policeman, including twelve consecutive months in a war zone. He worked as a chemist for a short time, and then in radio broadcasting, which took him and his young family—his wife, Ola Jean, my mother's older sister, Susan, my mother, and her younger brother, Brent—to live for stints in various Midwest towns: Russell, Kansas; Webster City, Iowa; Salina, Kansas; Waukegan, Illinois. Through all of the moves, Ola Jean was unflappable. She managed to stay calm and get everything done, from baking a loaf of banana bread to getting the kids off to school on time. She wasn't afraid to offer a dose of sass or crack a joke when needed, either. Eventually, the Haworths landed in Duluth when my mother was in eighth grade.

The scenes as described to me from my mother's childhood feel like something out of *Little Women*: pastoral, rural, kind, loving, dashed with grit and resilience. The Haworths were outdoors people. They skied, hiked, and boated. They saved and tended to abandoned or harmed critters and brought sick ones back to health: snakes, birds, dogs, anything that needed help. My mother was voted "biggest flirt" by her high school classmates, made the junior varsity cheerleading squad her junior year, and then varsity her senior year, one of the few athletic opportunities available to girls at the time. She continued to rescue animals.

She enrolled at Ottawa University in Ottawa, Kansas, the same small private Baptist school that both of her parents and her sister, Susan, had attended. It was where my grandparents had met, and on that same campus, near the soccer field, during my mother's freshman year, she met my father,

Mirko Grgas, a senior on the soccer team. They began to date off and on as a seemingly unlikely and surprising match. Their backgrounds were a study in opposites.

How my dad ended up in Kansas is a cinematic tale of its own. He was born in 1948 in Zablaće, a part of Šibenik, Croatia, a small and scenic collection of villages in the Dalmatia region on the country's southern coastline. Though naturally beautiful, it was a harsh place to be in the aftermath of World War II. Some thirty concentration camps had been constructed in Croatia by the occupying Nazi, Italian, and Ustashe (Croatian fascist) forces during the war, including at least two that held only children. Bruno Grgas, my father's father, had fought in the resistance against the German and Italian occupiers during the war. My dad—whose name, Mirko, means "the peaceful one" in many Slavic languages—and his older brother, Tony, and little sister, Davorka, came of age in a country that was trying to rebuild and recover.

When my dad was four years old, Bruno boarded a ship for America. He lived in Queens, New York, and began working and saving up all the money that he could to bring his family with him. Two years later, he sent for Tony, but due to financial constraints and a discriminatory quota system that limited legal immigration from Eastern Europe, it took until my dad was thirteen before he, Davorka, and their mom, Jerka, could come. In Queens, the family was reunited.

My dad spoke no English upon arrival in the U.S., but picked the language up within six months. He thrived in school, and soared as a soccer player. His skills in high school landed him in the famed *Sports Illustrated* "Faces in the Crowd" column and he earned a scholarship to play at Ottawa University. His teammates remembered his fierce competitiveness on the field, good sense of humor, kindness, and generosity. He became a three-time All-American, and received a write-up in the 1970 edition of *Outstanding College Athletes of America*. His senior year, his team made it to nationals. That was also the year he met my mother.

After graduation, he played semipro soccer and was even drafted to play in a professional league, but he passed on the opportunity due to the low paycheck and traveling lifestyle. Instead, he played soccer recreationally and joined the family business. Bruno had set up a company, based in

Queens, that installed building insulation. The Brothers Insulation Company, as it was called, was taking off, and the work allowed my father to build up a stable life with his now-fiancée, who had gotten a degree in elementary education. The company even laid some of the insulation for the Twin Towers at the World Trade Center and in the renovation of the Chrysler Building.

My parents married in 1973 and lived in a split-level house in Queens. Three years later, my older sister, Kelly, was born. In July 1978, I arrived. Just before my fourth birthday, in 1982, my little sister, Kendall, came along. (The K names weren't initially a strategy on the part of my parents, but after naming me Kara, they decided to roll with it.) My mom worked toward her master's degree so she could be certified to teach in New York State.

Running her family in a home in the city got my midwestern-raised, outdoorsy mom wondering if we could move to a happier medium: a place near enough to New York for Dad's work, with some green space. Also: still *close* to the extended Grgas family, but maybe not *so* close. We moved to a house in Waldwick, New Jersey, a commuter town just outside the city, in July 1981.

This was my parents' American dream fully realized: three cute kids, stable income from the family business, and a literal white picket fence in a lush, green suburb. That was supposed to be our life.

When the time came for the Haworth family reunion in Duluth in the summer of 1982, the plan was that my mom would take us girls out first for a few days, dad would finish some work, then he'd fly up to meet us. Kelly was five, I was three, and Kendall was five weeks old, looking like the baby doll Kelly and I treated her as. My mom packed our toys, diapers, and clothes up, and off we went.

On July 1, my mom, sisters, and I were at Papa and Grandma Ola Jean's house in Duluth. It always smelled like cinnamon there, coupled with whatever other baked good Grandma was concocting. It had a front porch, sprawling lawn, and cozy country decor—clunky shelves that Papa had made by hand, candles (which were never lit), flowers, a garden's worth of plants inside, and framed photos, some of travels to national parks, most of grandchildren smiling for school portraits.

Kelly remembers that we were in the yard playing. Then, she says, we came into the house and saw Mom holding on to the phone. Grandma was near her.

"Go back outside," my mother told us.

We knew immediately that something was wrong, not by what she said, but how she said it.

Papa came back to the house from the restaurant earlier than usual and went inside. Kelly isn't sure if she overheard what the adults were talking about, or somehow knew through intuition.

She started crying. Through the tears, she said: "My daddy is dead."

———

The details were sparse to me, but I knew that my father had been in a car accident, hit head-on, and was gone.

We all flew to New Jersey as quickly as possible. Papa identified my father's body so that my mother wouldn't have to. A funeral was held. Our friends, neighbors, and family were packed into the church. Kelly remembers sitting in the second row of the pews, staring at a giant soccer ball wreath near the closed casket. I couldn't really process the fact that he wasn't coming back. On some level, I thought Dad's car would pull down our street again, that he would walk in the house, sweaty from a soccer game with a smile.

My mother later said that she was glad to have been nursing Kendall at the time because going through the motions of attending to her baby gave her purpose.

Beyond that, she said, "I had no idea what I was going to do."

She had spent more than ten years building a vision of a life together with my father, and within days she had to completely rewrite it. She sold the home in New Jersey and we moved to Duluth. Papa helped her find a house in town, about a twenty-minute drive from where he and Grandma lived on the outskirts. The line between our new home and my grandparents' home blurred, though, as Papa and Grandma Ola Jean became critical caregivers for me and my sisters, and features of our daily lives.

We adjusted to our new reality. Papa made Russian tea with sugar and orange flavoring for us at his house. Every afternoon, he and Grandma sat in their rocking chairs on the screened-in porch, looking over Fredenberg Lake, and drank Mountain Dew. Papa and Grandma owned and operated a cozy neighborhood restaurant called Somebody's House. It backed into the woods and almost looked like a ski chalet, with large picture frame windows. We ate there at least once a week, the staff doting on us, the dining room feeling like an extension of our own. There was a helium tank in the front; I always requested a pink balloon, my favorite color, and tied it to my chair as we ate. Burgers were the signature dish on the menu, with standard add-ons like bacon, barbecue sauce, or a fried egg, but also outlandish and delicious ones like the Napoli Burger with tomato sauce and mozzarella, and the Blizzard Burger topped with a dollop of sour cream.

At our house, we played with Cabbage Patch dolls, tore around in the yard, fed deer, and stayed up late watching movies on VHS. My sisters, my mom, and I were extremely close. There was a hole—a cavern, really—in our hearts, but we shared a steel bond.

What impeded the healing of our wounds were the details of the crash that had killed my father, which emerged over time.

I learned that the morning of July 1, 1982, had been scorching and humid in New York City. It was eight days before my fourth birthday. My dad had gotten in their bike on and he had driven the route that he knew by heart, going south on the Harlem River Drive, the bustling ribbon of road along the eastern perimeter of upper Manhattan. He was near 142nd Street, the Harlem River and buildings of the Bronx were to his left, while the towering upper Manhattan skyline of massive concrete and brick apartment buildings stood tall to his right. He stayed in his lane, and obeyed the speed limit. His was one of the millions of anonymous cars making their way along the New York City streets to start the day.

But a car in the northbound lane lost control. Within seconds, it jumped the divider and "became airborne," as police later said. That vehicle bounced first off the hood of another car in the southbound lane and then smashed into my father's car. The driver of the erratic car was uninjured.

Two other people were injured and taken to the hospital. They survived. My father did not. Looking at the police account of what happened, it was a miracle that more people didn't die that day.

My father was thirty-four. The driver who killed my father was thirty, and drunk. He was charged with drunk driving and manslaughter. He was sentenced to nine months in jail, and served only six.

These facts were painful, and senseless. My mother was completely baffled and infuriated. But Papa told her: "This will not be in vain." He helped her harness her anger, reminding her of a core value that he always taught. If you see something wrong, make a plan to make it better. In his words, "If you don't like it, fix it."

A Mothers Against Drunk Driving chapter didn't exist in Duluth, so with Papa's assistance, my mom spent a year organizing the paperwork and navigating the bylaws to create one. She turned our kitchen table into a war room. She researched the laws and science around drunk driving. She met with local judges, law enforcement officers, church groups, political leaders, and grieving families. She retold our family's story, on one victim impact panel after another, humanizing the problem. She proved to be so effective that she was hired by the county to work with survivors.

Through the MADD chapter that she started, she received support in her grieving, and gave it to others. She found a group of mothers, many of them raising children on their own. She built a world for herself, and her daughters. We watched. We noticed.

At home, she read us *Anne of Green Gables* and the Little House on the Prairie books, got us to the bus on time for school, and cooked our dinners. We watched and sang along with *The Sound of Music*. We dog-eared the American Girl catalogue as soon as it landed in our mailbox (I had Samantha and Felicity) and rearranged the furniture in our dollhouses with precision.

As normal, and even idyllic, as things could often feel, grief had a way of reappearing. On the way back from one trip to swim at the local YMCA, I started crying and said, "I miss Daddy."

My mom placed one of the few photographs we had of me and him together in my room. The picture gave me a sense of what he looked like, but I wondered: *Was my hair color exactly the same as his, or did it just look that way in the picture? What would he do if he was here right now? What would our lives have been like if the car accident hadn't happened? What was he really like?*

I didn't know, or couldn't remember, how his voice sounded. How his body moved. How tall he seemed in person. What he smelled like.

I was so young when he died, I couldn't help but feel that I barely knew him.

CHAPTER TWO
Dreams of Jennings

When I learned in 1985 that Mom might remarry, I was elated.

My mom had met Tom Wheeler at church, and they'd gotten to know each other for a few months before she introduced me to him after my gymnastics class at the YMCA. I liked him, and, at six years old, I was thrilled by the idea of having a dad and three new stepsiblings in our house. Tom had a daughter, Carrie, who was five years older than me; a son, Nathan, who was two years older than me and in the same grade as Kelly; and another son, Andy, who was six months younger than me and a grade below.

Tom was well regarded in the community, with family roots in the Duluth area stretching back to the nineteenth century. He worked in insurance and financial planning. He was a sports nut who had played hockey at Hamilton College. Tom also had a prior marriage that had ended tragically. On a pristine, clear September afternoon in 1983, Tom's wife, Dale, a tennis buff and jogger, got on her bicycle for a ride and left a note saying that she would be back in time for dinner. The rest of the family went off to church. Always punctual, when she didn't return home by mid-evening, they called the police.

A citywide search ensued, and the next morning an angler found the handlebars of her bicycle along an overgrown, shrubby section of the Lake Superior shoreline. Her body was recovered nearby, dressed in the same workout clothes that she had worn when she had left her house. Her wallet and checkbook were scattered within two hundred feet of the crime scene, and a year later, her purse was found three miles away. Some cash had been taken from the wallet, but nothing else, making the cops doubtful that it was a mugging or robbery. There were no fingerprints. She was thirty-three years old. Police struggled in their investigation and no suspect was charged. Speculation ran rampant. Was it a serial killer on the loose in the otherwise pastoral woods? Someone close to her?

For two families that had endured such dramatic losses, when my mother and Tom decided to marry on June 2, 1985, just before I turned seven, by outward appearances it looked like a beautiful next act of rebuilding. Tom and his kids moved into our house. It was like a 1980s version of *The Brady Bunch*, two families merging under one roof, six kids and two adults. My mom, who had gone by Patty Grgas, even took Tom's last name, as did my sisters and I. We started calling him "Dad" right away. We were now the Wheelers.

But inside the house, it was far from a sitcom. We quickly learned about Tom's fits of anger. "Walking on eggshells" is the only way to put it, as none of us ever knew what would set him off yelling. It could be him coming home to the toys being left on the floor of the playroom, or something inconsequential missing from a kitchen drawer. His face reddened, his voice bellowed, and doors were slammed. My mom never left us three girls alone with him.

There were no photographs of Tom's first wife anywhere in their house and I don't remember Tom ever talking about her. Sometimes, her relatives visited, and they were always very nice to us and our half siblings, but even from them, Dale's name was not mentioned. My father had lived on a bit through my mother in part because of her work with MADD, but that didn't happen for Dale, even though I knew her children missed her dearly. Aside from her work with MADD, my mother didn't talk about the loss of my father to us directly when she was married to Tom. No one really knew how to handle the grief. So, for the most part, we just pretended the losses weren't there.

What was clear was the role that sports played as a way to earn Tom's attention. Athletic achievement ran deep for him. Tom said that I was "too fragile" for hockey, a sport that his children played, though Kelly was somehow deemed strong enough to play. Kelly was also a spitfire on the soccer field. I played soccer, but wasn't as good. I needed something that I could excel at, and running—unclaimed by the other kids in the house—seemed promising. After the Hermantown Festival event with Papa, I had started to run in a couple of races every year that allowed kids.

Sporting events were where everyone came together. Tom attended our competitions and Papa and Grandma Ola Jean were like Beatles fans at

Shea Stadium in their enthusiastic support. My grandma further incentivized us with homemade banana bread when we were done.

I'm grateful for how normalized and integrated my experience as an athlete was with that of my stepbrothers. Then, and still today, when a little girl expresses ambition, be it starting a lemonade stand or running in a race, so often she's told that it's "cute." When a boy does, the narrative is often about his prodigious talent or drive. Papa, in particular, always took me and my sisters seriously.

So seriously, in fact, that he became my first running coach. He kept a notebook and pen in one hand and a stopwatch in the other, logging splits with precision. His observation skills were keen, his eyes peering, often from underneath the visor of a baseball cap. Papa and I set goals together, like a specific time or distance, and then he would plan out what I needed to do to get there. This was Papa's recipe for mastery: breaking things down into smaller pieces and putting in the sweat equity.

In sixth grade, I found out that I was set to compete against Scott, the great love of my late elementary school life, in the 440-yard race. (We were a known pair, despite never having so much as kissed or held hands.)

It was one thing to race against boys, but I had no idea how to handle racing against Scott. If I let him win, it would be disingenuous. If I beat him, his feelings would be hurt.

In the race, I questioned whether I should pass him or not. I will, I thought, as I crossed the finish line in first place. I turned to face Scott, expecting him to be embarrassed, only to find his face covered in a smile. He congratulated me and seemed genuinely impressed and pleased. Today, there's lots of talk about how to raise and empower girls. That matters. But when I think about how we need to raise boys, I think of Scott and how he handled being beaten by his sixth-grade girlfriend. As I progressed through middle school and got more into organized running, I had the confidence to believe that I could kick a guy's butt on the track and he would high-five me at the end. All teenagers should be so fortunate.

Running became my obsession. When I wasn't running, I was thinking about when and how I would run again. The chaos of my family life seemed to dissolve when I ran.

When I was twelve and in seventh grade, I raced in the Duluth Middle School Cross Country City Championship and won the title.

Due in part to budget cuts in middle school sports, the track coach at Duluth East High School had asked me and my friend Amy Hill to run on the high school team when we were still middle school students. Amy and I were lunch buddies and also played in the school band, me on the French horn, she on the trumpet. Amy was taller than me, lanky, blond, and always working on something: homework for the hardest classes, an extra-credit project, practicing for another sport. Maybe because Amy and I both had older siblings, the idea of competing alongside kids that were potentially on the other side of puberty didn't intimidate us as much as perhaps it should have.

It did make for some awkward moments, though. As a seventh-grader, I had to run against my former babysitter, then a senior in high school. During one race, I ran behind her, determined not to pass her. At the time, it felt disrespectful to run past someone who seemed so much older and like an authority figure, even if I had more fire in my legs that day.

She could feel me on her shoulder. "Pass me," she said.

I hesitated.

"It's okay," she assured me.

I did. Her grace in losing stuck with me, as did the idea that competition is about who is the best on any given day. As with Scott, it was another formative moment that made me feel safe expressing myself on the track.

I needed that external support. At the house, Tom continued to get in loud fights with my mother. He threw things, slammed doors, then shoved *his* foot in the door if anyone tried to close one on *him* without his permission. It was all the more reason to devote myself to track, and spend as much time as possible outside of the house. At the same time, I was also desperate to please him, and thought that succeeding at running could do just that.

In eighth grade, I grew to just over five feet tall, and began winning high school races. I won half of the events I entered and finished second in the rest, except at the state meet where I finished third. I really started to feel pressure, that everyone expected me to win. With the success came a new feeling: a pressure against my chest before competitions, a difficulty catching my breath. An inner voice told me: *At some point you're not going to win.*

As soon as the starting pistol went off, the anxiety stopped. The race itself was still safe territory, where my body and brain found a natural presence.

At the core of my panicky spiral was a nugget of truth. As an eighth grader, I made it to the 1991 Minnesota State Cross Country Championships, an annual competition taking place in early November, where I went up against Carrie Tollefson, a phenom a year older than me from the small town of Dawson, about four and a half hours from Duluth. Carrie beat me by 23.2 seconds. Amy finished right behind me. Carrie's high school changed classification annually, meaning some seasons I wouldn't have to race against her, but the threat of someone that dominant in the state loomed large.

I knew that comparing myself to Carrie was a painful thing to do, but I couldn't help it. She was also a truly nice person, which in a way, made it worse. She would ultimately win five cross country titles, which was a national record for the most consecutive titles and still stands today.

The summer before my freshman year of high school was the summer of the 1992 Olympics in Barcelona. My siblings and I parked it on our couch, our eyes glued to the television. I was mesmerized by the pomp and pyrotechnics of the Opening Ceremony, the precision of the gymnasts, and the raw power of the swimmers, but nothing compared to track and field. Tacked up on my bedroom wall were pictures of Olympic track athletes including Carl Lewis, Florence Griffith Joyner, Jackie Joyner-Kersee, and Gail Devers.

When the women lined up for the 10,000-meter race, the sheer fact of the distance sounded crazy to me. I was a serious runner already, but the fact that they were about to run 25 laps around the track was mind-blowing. I fixated on Lynn Jennings, the American, as the gun went off and she circled the track with the other runners, one after the other. I held my breath for the last lap, as the runners in front sped up even *more*, then began to all-out sprint. The fans in the stadium were on their feet going wild. *How can they run this far, this fast?* I marveled. *This is what running could be?*

Derartu Tulu came in first, becoming the first Black African woman to win an Olympic gold. Elana Meyer of South Africa darted in right behind Tulu for silver. And in the battle for the bronze, I watched Jennings win out, setting a new American record in the distance. I loved how she looked doing it, too, laying out every ounce of effort in her red, white, and blue running uniform, her short hair bobbing around.

I didn't tell my mom, Papa, Tom, or my siblings, but it was then, at age fourteen, that I decided: I, too, would go to the Olympics.

Running as a career, especially distance running, was still a revolutionary notion for women. It had only been eight years since the women's marathon was added to the Olympic program, in 1984. For decades, deranged arguments had been made about why women shouldn't compete in strenuous athletic contests, including the ludicrous idea that they might displace their uteruses if they ran too far or too hard. Yet here was Jennings, actually doing it.

I carefully thumbtacked a picture of her kicking away from everyone else at the 1992 World Athletics Cross Country Championships on my bedroom wall, where she took pride of place among the others.

———————

My freshman class at Duluth East had about four hundred kids, big enough to make us feel like being at the high school was a Big Deal, but small enough that most of the faces were familiar, especially since many of us had survived kindergarten through middle school together. At the time, the school was on 4th Street, a few blocks away from the shores of Lake Superior. With its brick facade, it looked like a set for a John Hughes film. The neon fashion palette worn by the students inside, of scrunchies, leggings, and sweaters, wasn't far off from that, either. REM's *Out of Time* and *Monster* got the most use in my cassette player.

My freshman year, in 1992, I was the overwhelming favorite in the state meet, having gone undefeated all year. I felt so much pressure to win that I mentally broke down in the 3,200-meter race and struggled to finish in fifth. But because that was still a high overall finish, Amy ran well, and our other teammates performed well, too, our Duluth East High School team won the overall State Championship. It felt incredible.

My sophomore year, my results from a regional qualifying meet in Wisconsin made me eligible for the biggest race of them all: the 1993 national Foot Locker Cross Country Championships. This meant flying to San Diego in mid-December to line up against the best runners in the nation, including Carrie Tollefson, of course.

While my mom and Tom and Kendall got settled at the hotel, I went out onto the beach for a short prerace jog, known as a "shakeout run," with some of the other girls in the competition.

There, against the azure of the Pacific Ocean and the bright pale sand, a type of comparison I hadn't made before led to a new flavor of panic in me.

The other girls wore sleek spandex shorts and sports bras with no shirt. They marked their times with high-tech digital watches. They were toned like fitness models twice my age. I wore baggy Umbro shorts, a loose T-shirt, and fidgeted with the Swatch on my wrist. I felt completely out of place and intimidated, like a little girl who had snuck into a big-kid party.

In the race, there were TV cameras positioned throughout the course, adding to the pressure. I tried to remind myself that my times had landed me here, that I belonged, that my family and coaches were so proud of me just for qualifying. I raced hard and ended up finishing ninth out of 32 girls. Carrie came in fifth. A ninth-grader named Erin Davis from Saratoga Springs, New York, won. On the boys' side, a twelfth-grader from Colorado Springs named Adam Goucher won the title. We met very briefly. Boys weren't a focal point for me then. I was focused on running. I wanted to come back the next year, faster. I was happy with my time, but it opened my eyes to how many faster runners were out there.

On the flight home, I looked over at my mom, thinking of the winter holidays, just a couple of weeks away.

"Mom," I asked, "can I have a Timex running watch and some Nike running outfits for Christmas?"

CHAPTER THREE
Changes

My junior year, I raced well enough to finish second at the State Championships, behind Carrie, and help secure our third-straight team championship for the Duluth East girls. I placed fifth at regionals and once again qualified for the Foot Locker National Championships.

This time, instead of focusing on the sleek clothes the other girls were wearing, I noticed their thinness. I had gained weight, but some of the girls had lost so much from the year prior that I barely recognized them. When I lined up for the race, I overheard coaches, most of whom were men, using words like "lean" and "trim" to describe them, in reverent tones.

I finished in 17th place, a big drop from the previous year. I was a little disappointed, but I also ran a much faster time on the same course. I had actually gotten better, but so, too, had the girls around me.

When it came to comparing my weight and body to the other girls, I got really lucky, because I had Amy and the rest of my teammates as friends. I talked to Amy about it, and we made a pact: we were going to be healthy eaters and encourage each other to do so. We had a teammate who was in and out of the hospital for an eating disorder. It scared us. We rebelled against the temptation to believe we needed to restrict our calories to be competitive. We wanted something different for ourselves and the other girls on the team. Hell, we wanted something different for our sport's culture.

I channeled some of my frustrated energy into righting a wrong at my school. Unlike the boys' hockey team, who had gotten a rousing "welcome home" assembly the year before when they won their state tournament, our *three-peat* cross country championship winning team had never gotten so much as a round of applause. I complained to my mom about it and she told me nothing would change if I didn't say something. So, I gathered my courage and talked to the principal, and after that, all teams received a send-off assembly to state meets and a welcome home if they won.

In December of my junior year, I got my period. It had come much later than for all my friends, but it still took me by surprise, and I wasn't happy: it felt like a huge hassle. My mother never used tampons, so I found myself running races in what felt like a diaper. Hair showed up in places that it hadn't been before and the shape of my face rounded out. Hips appeared, and breasts, too. I felt like I was getting fat, clumsy, and slow. I hated my body. I struggled to adjust to it. My little sister, Kendall, also started running and immediately showed promise, appearing to me as what I'd once been: younger, and puberty-free.

This was an era when rail-thin women lined the pages of magazines and billboards. "Body positive" didn't exist as a mainstream concept and thin was the ideal, on runways and just about anywhere else you looked. I'm not typically a fan of flowery platitudes, but puberty feels like the time to lay them on thick, to counteract so many other messages telling girls the opposite of what they need to hear. When girls' bodies change, I wish we would say to them: "This is normal. This won't last forever. What's happening to you right now is magic because female bodies are designed to do incredible things. There is nothing wrong with you. Feel what you need to feel. Keep with it. You are great just the way you are."

Like true Minnesotans, Amy and I both competed on our school's cross country ski team in addition to the track and cross country teams.

Our skiing results were strong enough that we were both invited our junior year to a week-long biathlon training camp in Lake Placid, home of the 1980 Winter Olympics. We had never actually competed in biathlon, but the thinking was to take top high school skiers and train them to shoot and become biathletes.

Obscure in the United States but huge in Eastern Europe, the biathlon is one of the Winter Olympics' nuttiest and most delightful sports. As a combined cross country skiing and rifle shooting event, it requires a mixture of raw cardiovascular power (skiing as hard and fast as you can) with precision and focus (hitting a bull's-eye target while struggling to catch your breath).

While in Lake Placid, the national biathlon officials offered me a spot with the junior training program there, basically a boarding school where I'd live and train, and a potential pipeline to the Olympics.

I thought of my wall of running heroes and wondered if maybe I had it wrong this whole time, that biathlon could be my way to the Olympics, rather than running. But after thinking it through, I turned down the opportunity. Growing up where I did it sounds crazy, but I didn't want the biathlete's life of deep-cold weather. And though I loved to ski, I didn't get the same joy from it as running. I was also an unapologetic homebody; the idea of leaving my mom, sisters, and friends in Duluth and moving to upstate New York was terrifying.

During my senior year of high school, I couldn't help but wonder if I'd made the wrong choice. I felt like I kept putting more effort into my running, and the results kept moving in the wrong direction. I was running 5 to 10 seconds slower in the mile. None of my clothing fit anymore. It was maddening.

That fall, Kendall, as an eighth-grader, was running for the high school varsity team and was like a rocket; she seemed to have springs of some kind in her small feet. In one race, I could feel her running off my shoulder, just behind me. I pushed hard to try and break free from her, but I knew in my gut that she was holding back so she wouldn't beat me. The scene was familiar.

I yelled at Kendall, "Pass me!"

I could sense her hesitation. I thought back to the respect I felt for my babysitter when she did the same for me.

"It's okay," I told her. I watched Kendall's chestnut ponytail soar past me and cross the finish line.

I knew I had done the right thing, but her defeating me was a huge bruise to whatever was left of my self-pride.

My mom drove me home from the meet, knowing I needed some extra love and letting me avoid the team bus. I cried, feeling like a shell of the middle schooler who had once beaten the bigger kids—though I did have a new wave of empathy for my former opponents.

"Get it all out," my mom told me, as I sniffled and wiped tears away. "And when we get home, we're going to celebrate Kendall."

I finished in third place individually at the State Championships that year, with Carrie Tollefson out of high school and the competition not quite as stiff. My friend Amy came in a few spots behind me, and Kendall finished just behind Amy. It was enough to secure our team our fourth consecutive title.

I was thrilled about the team win with Amy and Kendall by my side, but crushed because at regionals I had failed to qualify for the Foot Locker Championships. Even worse, I had dropped out of that race, the first time I had ever done so, because I was so far behind, I knew that I wasn't going to place high enough to make the cut. In the end, running is an individual sport. On the drive home with my mom, I felt like a failure and wondered whether if I stopped eating, I could be skinny like the other girls who had made it. The thought came to mind that if I was lighter, I'd be faster, even though I risked losing muscle and making myself injury-prone. Thankfully, this idea didn't stick with me for long, and my eating quickly returned to normal.

At home, Tom's childlike outbursts continued. He and my mother began to fight more intensely and frequently. He made it repeatedly known during those shouting matches that he didn't love her anymore.

The Haworth side of the family always celebrated Christmas with fervor, and on Christmas Day my mom went all out. She made a turkey dinner, decorated a large, lush tree with treasured ornaments, and bought thoughtful gifts for every single person in the home. While opening presents, it became clear that Tom didn't get her anything. Not even a card. I was disappointed and furious.

That's when my mom and Tom told us all that Tom was moving out. That day.

What this meant for my (already complicated) relationship with Tom and my stepsiblings was uncertain. In under a year, I hoped, I would be leaving home for college somewhere. Carrie and Nathan, Tom's two oldest kids, had already moved away for college. Kelly had, too. But would Andy, Tom's youngest, stay with us, or go with Tom? And where would Tom go to live? Was he still my dad? Had he ever been? The loss of Tom tugged at the central loss of my father, reminding me of that grief. Tom wasn't perfect, but he had been a father figure, and now he was going away. "Why are you doing this?" I pleaded with him. I didn't get an answer.

My mother later said that part of why she hung on to the relationship for so long was precisely because she didn't want her daughters to suffer the loss of another father figure. She and Tom had tried couples counseling, but he had said that he just wanted medication without therapy, a notion the therapist shot down.

Tom's moving out on Christmas Day felt like a cherry on top of an F.U.-milkshake of a year. My body had transformed into one that I felt I no longer knew. In spite of my best efforts, I was slower than ever. As a result, the college recruiters who had been eagerly watching me before seemed to have vanished. My dream school, Stanford University, may as well have been Mars. And now my family structure as I knew it was slipping away.

With recruiters having disappeared, I went out on my own to try and find a spot on a strong university track team. My target list included Georgetown, the University of Colorado at Boulder, Notre Dame, Alabama, and Montana State. Meanwhile, Kelly was off at our father's alma mater, Ottawa, crushing it on the soccer field and basketball court.

My mom and I tracked down phone numbers for coaches and I left messages on answering machines. I had a pitch memorized, mentioning that I was a two-time Foot Locker finalist, that I'd had some injuries (true: a stress fracture, shin splints) but had a big future ahead.

After hanging up, I'd clutch the phone, wondering if the coaches who would determine my fate were actually listening, or if I was telling my story to the wind.

When a coach at the University of Colorado at Boulder returned my message and asked me if I wanted to come and visit, I was part relieved, part thrilled. The CU Buffaloes (they reversed the U and the C in their acronym in the 1920s, seemingly to distinguish it from the University of California's) were a consistently strong team that boasted a number of top national runners, including Adam Goucher, the boy I'd briefly met at the 1993 Foot Locker Championships, Kelly Smith, Alan Culpepper, and Shayne Wille. (Alan and Shayne were a couple.)

Amy had hoped to ski in college, but ended up taking a full scholarship to run at the University of Wyoming, which meant that although we'd no longer be teammates, we would often get to compete against each other.

At Boulder, I would receive a 20 percent scholarship, not quite the full ride often touted to high school athletes as the big carrot, nor was it as generous as other offers that I received from schools where running wasn't as much of a focus, but CU had such a good team, and I felt like even if I never returned to being a great runner individually, maybe I could help them win a national cross country title. I would wear the black and gold singlet, race for a Division I running school, and build myself up again, in pursuit of my dreams, on my own terms. Boulder would be my shot at a new beginning.

CHAPTER FOUR
Boulder

From the moment I arrived in Boulder in the fall of 1996, I was in love. I felt as though I had teleported into a place that combined the best elements of the things I wanted: it was beautiful and outdoorsy but still had a bustling side with lots going on. Most people seemed absurdly fit, trotting and biking around in the crisp, high-altitude air. As I strolled along Pearl Street, I saw hippies for the first time.

Tom and my mother were attempting to reconcile, so the three of us made the thousand-mile drive together. Perhaps unsurprisingly, it didn't last. After dropping me off at school, they got in a huge fight on the sixteen-hour drive home, and, eventually, that was that.

After they pulled out of town, I felt a preemptive pang of homesickness set in, and went for a run up the canyon into the mountains. It calmed me down and grounded me instantly. The view took my breath away. I thought, *This, THIS is why I came here.*

In school, I declared myself a psychology major and looked forward to learning from brilliant professors. When it came to the running team, I would be in the hands of coach Mark. Wellington.

Mark loved the writer Ken Kesey, and could have easily been mistaken for one of Kesey's Merry Pranksters. He was tall and thin with hair that started short my freshman year, but didn't seem to get cut after that. He had been the men's distance coach since 1992—his team consistently placing well in its conference—and had just taken over the women's program for the start of the 1996 season, my first at CU. While he was tough and competitive, he was known mostly for a calm, methodical, creative, and freethinking approach to coaching. He liked letting his runners set their own goals and take ownership of them. He could be stern, but never lost his temper. He expected a lot from his athletes, and reciprocated that dedication.

Together, we charted a plan to increase my mileage slowly, build confidence, and not burn out. Having lost a race to my eighth-grade sister less than a year before, it was just what I needed. I committed to the plan, and it paid off. I made friends on the team. I felt my self-belief recovering one workout at a time. With it, my times improved.

Papa and Grandma Ola Jean schlepped to any collegiate race that they could drive to. Papa continued to cheer me on at the top of his lungs, his stopwatch still in hand. I knew that I was living a life beyond what he'd ever had the opportunity to do. He'd been prevented from running in college by having to work to help support his family, then later going off to war. I was so grateful to be where I was, and to have his support.

———————

The thoughts about food and weight that I'd managed to keep in check with Amy's help in high school emerged again with more force during college.

My self-worth was tied up in my running times—a dangerous, double-edged sword. When I ran well, I felt at one with the universe, that everything in life was going exactly how it should be. When I didn't, my ego crashed with my race results, and something as silly as literally running around in circles on a track would force me to question my entire framework around life's meaning. Controlling my eating seemed like a way to gain control over the ups and downs of life.

I made up new rules out of thin air to change my eating habits, with the goal of losing weight. No more than 700 calories before dinner. Only drink water, never soda or juice. On Fridays and Sundays, and only then, I could eat what I wanted, making me long desperately for the end of the week. I suffered from stomach pains and diarrhea, but I also received compliments as I lost weight, and found that I liked the attention. I'd never been known as one of the "skinny girls" before. I was intoxicated when I stepped on the scale and saw the numbers drop to new lows, the same way I relished lowering my times on the track.

I was far from the only one on the team timidly poking at my salad greens, and taking baby-sized sips of tomato soup. Though we all knew the stories about female runners in our college conference being hospitalized with eating disorders, we didn't talk about it. A nutritionist came by at the start of the season, but it was up to us to decide if we wanted to seek their guidance. I never did, and I can't remember hearing about any of my teammates doing so. It was a culture.

Though I often felt tired in training, it was easy for me to justify my choice, because in the spring of 1999, I finished a surprise second at the NCAA Championships in the 3,000 meters (to Carrie Tollefson, of course, who was now at Villanova). I was a junior in college but because I hadn't run any races for CU in 1998 due to extreme lower leg pain that resulted in surgery, I was in my second year of NCAA eligibility. The partial-ride scholarship I had received was bumped up to a full one. In the fall of 1999, I was featured in the "Faces in the Crowd" column in *Sports Illustrated*, the same column my dad had appeared in as a college soccer player. It was surreal.

I was getting noticed, but what people didn't see was that I was obsessively measuring my oatmeal in the morning. An indulgence would be an Odwalla bar for lunch with some fruit. It wasn't enough food for anyone, and certainly not for someone running 10 to 12 miles a day.

In February of 2000, my mom came to visit and was waiting for me on a day when Mark sent me home early from practice to get some rest after I bombed out of a workout. She asked about my fatigue.

"I've been pooping my brains out for months," I told her. This was true, but of course not the whole truth. We went to the doctor and I received a diagnosis of gastritis, an irritation of the stomach lining that can be a precursor to ulcers and even cancer. It meant my body wasn't absorbing the nutrition that it needed. I wasn't putting in enough to begin with, and I was anemic and dehydrated. A doctor prescribed me medication to prevent ulcers that I took for three months.

I didn't want to tell my mom that the gastritis wasn't the sole reason for my weight loss. I wasn't ready to give up the control I felt I'd gained over my eating. I continued to drop a lot of weight. On my 5'8" frame, I got down to a frightening 113 pounds my junior year.

A month after my mom visited, my friendship with my former teammate Adam shifted into dating. Adam was three years older than me and had graduated in December 1998. He was tough but silly, which I loved, and had a deep respect for strong women. His father, Richard, and his mother, Lois, divorced when he was in fifth grade, and he'd spent most of his childhood with his mother and two older sisters, his dad visiting once a month. Recently, he had reconnected with his father, a Vietnam War veteran, and forged a more positive relationship. He was also an incredibly hard worker. His running scholarship hadn't been enough to cover his expenses in college, so he'd done odd jobs, including as a janitor. Even then, he still had loans to repay.

When Adam graduated, he'd done so with one of the best college running careers in CU history behind him. He had gone to the Olympic Trials in the 5,000 meters in 1996, won the NCAA indoor track title in the 3,000 meters in 1997 and 1998, won the 5,000 meters NCAA outdoor track title in 1998, and won the NCAA cross country title in 1998. He, along with Mark Wetmore and our teammate Chris Severy, were the main subjects of a book written by Chris Lear about the 1998 season called *Running with the Buffaloes*.

Since graduating, Adam had turned pro, having gotten a contract from the athletics apparel company Fila. He continued to use Boulder as his home base and train with Mark. He also volunteered as an assistant coach for the CU team.

As I started to spend more time with Adam in early 2000, my fourth year on campus, I became perplexed by his relationship with food. It seemed so . . . *normal*. He was one of the fastest men in the country that year and he just ate when he was hungry. He didn't follow a rigorous diet but ate a balanced mix of protein, veggies, dairy, and carbohydrates. He ate sweets when he felt like it. He cared about what he was putting in his body, but it didn't obsess him. His example planted the idea in my head that not only could you be one of the best runners and still eat, but in fact, not starving all of the time may actually help your running.

My cooking skills in college had consisted of grabbing a piece of bread on my way to the track, until Adam taught me how to really prepare food. He showed me how to stuff a bell pepper, roast a zucchini, and transform a heap of produce into a delicious stir fry. Before our relationship, I had never *eaten* a bell pepper or a zucchini. My grandparents owned a restaurant, but their idea of a vegetable was a potato, carrot, or a sweet pickle soaked in sugar. Adam and I began to cook well-rounded, nutritious meals together composed largely of things from the produce aisle rather than a box. It was the budding of our runner-nerd romance.

One night around March 2000, I realized that we needed to stop by the grocery store to grab some ingredients before we could begin preparing dinner, and made it known that I was starving. Adam offered me some Doritos to tide me over until we were done shopping and cooking.

A Dorito? I thought. *He must be crazy.* I could feel the anxious thoughts building up, quick and harsh. If I ate the Dorito, I would be losing control of my diet. If I lost control of my diet, I would lose control of my running and all of my dreams would crumble. My future as a runner and perhaps worth as a human being, it seemed, were wrapped up in the need to reject that neon-orange triangle.

Adam looked at me. He looked *through* me. Somehow, I knew he was putting it all together—the dropped pounds, my picky habits.

"I don't want the Dorito," I told him.

"Eat the Dorito," he said playfully.

I didn't budge. He popped one in his mouth, then another, showing me that he wasn't asking me to do anything he wasn't willing to do himself. Eating a Dorito wouldn't make or break me. Starving myself would.

"Eat the fuckin' Dorito," he said, extending the crinkly bag.

I reached in and grabbed a single chip, the orange powder coating my fingertips.

Crunch.

I would love to say that I felt empowered and triumphant as I ate it, but the truth is that I was scared. I hated Adam in that moment. I despised the Dorito and hated the fact that its calories were now working their way through my body.

Even though it wasn't an instant transformation, it took more than a year until my relationship with food was really normalized—that lone Dorito was the turning point. Slowly, I came to think about nutrition holistically, about the importance of protein, vegetables, hydration, balance. I realized that a glass of red wine or a chocolate bar wasn't going to make everything I worked for collapse. Considering the mileage I was running in college, eating an entire cake probably would have been fine.

The problem wasn't the calories, it was the scarcity mindset, the idea of deprivation being a path to victory and heroism. I would never encourage a friend to pursue deprived eating, yet I had no problem cheerleading myself into its clutches of false security. I credit Adam, as well as my mom, for holding up a mirror to me and showing me that the obsession with weight loss wasn't in my best interest.

The truth is, running often attracts a personality type that gets high off extreme discipline. On the upside, this kind of discipline can help us stick with rigorous training, but it can also go hand in hand with the numerology of an eating disorder. I've trained with runners, men and women both, who weigh their food by every single gram and count their calories multiple times a day. It's important for runners and other elite athletes to monitor what goes in their bodies and when, but only for the sake of being healthy.

The idea that I could control my life, or even my race results, by controlling my eating was an illusion. It wasn't "mastery" over something in a world of chaos. It was harmful to my brain and body. It could have killed me.

———————

In spring 2000, my results got even better. Mark's approach—simple, steady, chill—was clicking. We set the goal of me beating the school record of 16:18 in the 5,000 meters. Prior to that year, I'd mostly run the 3,000, and had only raced the 5,000 one time at a conference meet, so my current PR (personal record) was 16:30. If I took well to the distance, the secondary goal was 16:04, which would automatically qualify me for the NCAA Championships. The third, and long-shot, goal was to run sub-16. That sounded nutty.

At the Mt. SAC Relays, an annual race in Walnut, California, in mid-April, I felt great. I started passing people in the 5,000 and all of a sudden I could hear Mark shouting "71! 72!" In practice, I had run 78-second laps around the track. The idea of running splits that fast was far beyond my expectation. If I hit the times Mark was calling out, I would break the record and qualify for NCAAs easily.

When I crossed the finish line, I looked at the numbers, stunned. *15:28?*

I hadn't just qualified for the NCAA Championships, and run sub-16. I had run fast enough to qualify for the Olympic Trials.

That race turned something on in me that I couldn't ever turn off again. All of the wondering in high school and college, all of the uncertainty about whether I was on the right path, vanished. That night, even with my floppy, tired limbs, I couldn't go to sleep. I stared, wide awake, at the popcorn ceiling of my hotel room in total disbelief about what had happened. I was going to the Olympic Trials.

The next weekend, full of newfound confidence, I ran a personal best in the 3,000 meters at another race in California. I went on to become the NCAA outdoor champion in the 3,000 and 5,000 meters, and then the NCAA cross country champion in the fall of 2000, nearly mirroring Adam's medal haul. We had become a Serious Couple by then, and had agreed to move in together. There would be two champions in the house.

CHAPTER FIVE
What Next

To make the U.S. Track and Field team for an Olympic Games is straightforward but unforgiving. First, you have to hit the qualifying standard time for your event. (These standards are set and updated by the USATF and are released about a year ahead of each Olympics.) Then, you have to race at the Trials, make it through your heats, and finish in the top three in the final event. That's it. In the end it all comes down to one day, one race. You're a defending gold medalist who wakes up on the wrong side of the bed on Trials day, or with an injury? Too bad. You're a college kid no one has heard of? If you meet the standard time in your event, get through heats, then deliver the goods on race day and land in the top three, the spot is yours.

Some athletes argue that because of this, Trials are more stressful than the Games themselves. Whatever you do at the Olympics, you're still an Olympian forever and have the experience of a lifetime. If you flame out at Trials, you've missed the opportunity to *have* that opportunity. Years of training can conclude with an anticlimactic thud.

At the 2000 Trials in Sacramento in July, I was starstruck. Gail Devers had climbed out of the magazine photo on my childhood bedroom wall and was *in the same warm-up area as me*. Anne Marie Lauck, who I had watched in the 1996 Atlanta Games from my couch in Duluth, was in my heat in the 5,000 meters. Even weirder, I beat her in that heat, coming in fourth to her sixth place, which put us both in the final and made me the youngest runner there.

Adam had qualified for the Trials in the 5,000 meters, too, and then made it to the finals even though he was battling an injury. His race was before mine, so I was at the warm-up track getting ready while he ran, trying to focus but also unable to stop from looking over and cheering. I was glad I watched, because I got to see him *win*, finishing in first place and earning his Olympic spot.

I didn't have the same success in my finals, and finished in eighth. Lauck finished fifth. It meant we had both fallen short of making the Olympic team. It hurt, but I was deeply proud of myself too. It meant that my dream wasn't such an insane notion, after all. Far from it. I was only seconds away.

When Adam and I got back to our hotel that night in Sacramento, I started crying in the shower. I was so proud of Adam, knowing how much work he'd put into his training, and didn't want to show him the part of me that was jealous. Regular shower criers know the efficiency of this move, as your face is already wet and the sound of the water pounding down drowns out most of the noise. It's a private, cleansing ritual, an ideal venue when you feel you can't do it in front of someone, in this case someone I lived with, trusted, loved, and wanted to have his well-deserved moment.

As I came to the end of my NCAA eligibility, I was faced with the question of how I'd pay my bills. I wanted to keep running, and turn professional, but it's not like being a baseball, basketball, football, or hockey player. There's no league, draft, guaranteed contract, or even union. The money mostly comes from shoe companies, who sign individual runners to sponsorship deals. Other sponsors, like food or supplement companies, could come along, but shoe contracts are the professional runner's lifeline.

Nike, which had sponsored our athletic department at Boulder, was by far the biggest company out there, but competition had emerged during the 1990s from Adidas, Saucony, Fila, Brooks, and others. Contracts from these companies could range from around $20,000 a year to millions. (All of that before agent fees of 10 to 15 percent, and federal and state income tax.) Most sponsors also offered performance bonuses of varying amounts for hitting metrics like winning medals or setting national or international records. Adam's current Fila contract had a base salary of $50,000 a year, for example, but also a generous bonus structure. Because he ran so well during his first year and exceeded expectations, he'd earned $185,000 (a welcome windfall that helped him pay off some student loans). The double-edged sword of the performance piece of contracts, however, was that in addition to bonuses, contracts sometimes included performance *require-*

ments. That meant if you didn't hit certain metrics, you could lose money, or forfeit your deal altogether.

Besides Adam, there were a few other former University of Colorado runners who had made the transition to professional, notably Alan and Shayne Culpepper, who had gotten married in 1997 shortly after Shayne had graduated. In 2000, Shayne made the Olympic team in the 1,500 meters and Alan in the 10,000 meters. Seeing them strike out as professionals reinforced the notion that it was something within reach for me.

Because of my fifth-year senior season (and the cost of plane tickets), I wasn't able to make the trip to see Adam compete in Sydney at the 2000 Olympics. We sent each other emails while he was there and occasionally managed a quick call with the time difference.

He made it to the 5,000 meters final, which was held on the last night of competition. He ran a great race but finished 13th, a blow to his expectations. Talk of the pervasiveness of steroids and hormones, especially erythropoietin, or EPO, was flitting around.

During my final cross country season as a Buffalo, in the fall of 2000, I started racing under the name Kara Grgas-Wheeler. Though Tom often still showed up at my races, he and my mom had gotten divorced. I wasn't sure how he fit into my life anymore. While I didn't drop his name altogether, I was ready to reclaim my roots. I was eating healthily, returning to my baseline weight. And I had a fantastic season, culminating in becoming the women's NCAA cross country champion. As a team, we also won the first ever national cross country title in CU history.

At the 2001 NCAA Outdoor Track & Field Championships in Eugene, Oregon, at the beginning of June, I knew shoe sponsors would be there watching. It was my final official competition as a Buffalo. I went in as defending champion with the fastest qualifying time in the 5,000 meters, but I had a knee injury, and also struggled mentally. A lot of women stormed past me, and at the end of the race I didn't even know what place I had finished in (it was seventh). I felt I'd given the sponsors nothing to see.

I was convinced it was high school all over again. This time, instead of my hope of going to Stanford fading away, it was my hope of turning pro, and instead of recruiters disappearing, it was agents. It seemed no one wanted to represent me, and I couldn't blame them. I didn't know when my knee would heal. I had no recent, significant results to point to. I applied for and received a postgraduate scholarship and considered pursuing a master's in psychology.

That's when Nike called.

CHAPTER SIX
Love and Injuries

At Hayward Field in Eugene, where I raced my final NCAA Championships, there's a spot right off the track nicknamed "Cap's Corner." It's where John Capriotti, known to most as "Cap," had his perch. As the executive at Nike in charge of recruiting and paying track and field athletes, his eyes—peering from behind thick-framed glasses—and his Nike-stamped checkbook were the most important in the business.

Cap had watched me from his corner during the June 2001 Championships. Though I'd faltered in the final, he knew I was a defending champion: he later told me that he had seen me win the NCAA Cross Country Championships in November 2000, and was just waiting until after the spring 2001 Championships to talk to me, as NCAA rules prohibited recruiters from professional sponsors from doing so earlier. I signed a four-year contract with Nike for $35,000 per year, and by late June was donning my Nike singlet for the first time at the USATF Outdoor National Championships in the 5,000 meters. I was elated. The salary felt like a small fortune to me and I couldn't believe that anyone, let alone the apparel company I had worn and revered since childhood, was paying me to run. As a kid, I always made a beeline for the Nike shelf at Duluth's running store, Austin-Jarrow, shrugging off the kind folks working there who suggested that maybe I try on some other brands. This was the company with running in its DNA, founded by onetime University of Oregon runner Phil Knight and his coach, Bill Bowerman.

There was much to be thankful for in my personal life, too. Adam and I had gotten engaged. Our wedding was planned for September 16, 2001.

Five days before our wedding, I watched the terrifying image of planes crashing into the World Trade Center on television. I thought of the people in the buildings, how their families believed they were going off to work on a day like any other, just like my family had thought my dad was doing the day he died. The buildings represented something else to my family, too, as the Brothers Insulation Company had worked on them, a major point of family pride.

My aunt and uncle still lived in New York, and my uncle was out that morning on an installation job. None of us could get ahold of him all day. Thankfully, by that afternoon, we learned that he was safe and sound.

Adam and I had no idea what to do about our wedding. We were living in a townhome in Superior, Colorado, a more affordable suburb of Boulder, and the wedding was meant to be at the Lionscrest Manor, an event space with a big yard and indoor reception area in Lyons, Colorado, about thirty minutes north of Boulder. Many of our guests were local, including Adam's father and stepmother, two hours away in Colorado Springs, his mother in Nederland, thirty minutes outside of Boulder, and our running friends from college. But many others were planning on flying in, a prospect that now felt impossible.

We decided to go forward. To me, it felt like the only thing that made sense at that moment was marrying Adam. I was less interested in the wedding itself; I cared more about the transformations it represented in our lives.

Among them was changing my name from Kara Calean Grgas-Wheeler to Kara Calean Goucher. Calean was a combination of my Haworth grandparents' first names Cal and Ola Jean, which was a legacy I wanted to keep. And while I was sad to lose my father's name, I'd only recently started using it again, and very few people knew me by it. I was excited to be a Goucher.

The rehearsal dinner was in the yard of Adam's mom's house under a tent. Adam stayed with his groomsmen in a cabin near the wedding venue and led them all on a shakeout run the morning of the ceremony to calm his nerves.

In my daily life, I never wore makeup—I didn't begrudge women who did, it just wasn't my thing. Some of that was practical: I could walk out the door looking like a model and after a lap or two on the track have creepy clown mascara and eyeliner running down my face. I also wasn't a morning person, so making the effort to doll up, whether I was going for a sweaty run or not, didn't feel like a good use of my limited energy early in the day.

Yet for my wedding, I had my hair and makeup done. I was actually a bit excited to have my hair styled, a pile of sprayed-in, sculpted curls held up with a metalwork of bobby pins. When it was done, people kept saying that they didn't recognize me.

Weddings can be difficult for anyone who has lost a parent, whether to death or estrangement. At best, it can be an affirmation of the new world you're building, a rebirth even. At worst, it's yet another reminder of a thing that a lost loved one isn't there to share with you. It was impossible to not miss my dad in the planning and on the day itself. I was the first of the three sisters to get married, and I know we all felt our father's absence.

Tom came to the rehearsal dinner and introduced himself to the room as "Kara's father" as prelude to reading a rhyming poem he had written. In his booming voice, Papa said "No you're not" loud enough for it to be awkwardly heard by most in attendance.

"Not right now," Grandma quickly shushed him.

Like a lot of what came out of Papa's mouth, there was some truth to what he said. Tom wasn't my father and I knew that I didn't want him to walk me down the aisle. I knew precisely who I wanted by my side.

I had asked Papa if he was up for the task. It was the rare instance when he choked up. "It would be the honor of a lifetime," he had told me.

I wore a sleeveless white dress with my inevitable sports bra tan line proudly displayed, and walked arm in arm with him.

At the reception, we did run to a lingering reunion which came at the expense of eating. My mom was savvy enough to have stashed some cake in our getaway car, finding a way to see to my needs before I could. Adam and I inhaled it in the car, a solid first official act of being a married couple. To think that just a couple of years earlier we had argued over a Dorito.

Back in our room at the Hotel Boulderado, Adam spent forty-five minutes helping retrieve the bobby pins from my hair sculpture (maybe some are still in there?). The next morning, we gorged on chocolate chip pancakes, opened a few gifts, and left for our honeymoon in Fiji. I was twenty-three, and Adam was twenty-six. We were too young to realize how young we were. We just knew that we were joyful.

We had never spent the kind of money before that we did on those plane tickets. When we landed, we were overwhelmed by the shockingly clear blue water, the lush, green tropical beach landscape, and the seemingly endless skies that stretched into forever. Other hotel guests, also on their honeymoon, asked if Adam and I were siblings, which we thought was hilarious. Then came the bad weather and Adam's violent stomach sickness. We upgraded our tickets on the flight home so that he could sit closer to a bathroom. We laugh about it now, but Adam was beyond miserable.

I knew I could drive Adam crazy and he could do the same to me. We weren't *always* happy with each other, even in our early stages of dating. We recognized that in many ways we were different. Adam was fiery and not afraid to say something inappropriate or stand up to someone. I tended to avoid confrontation. But we also knew we were the right partners for one another. We balanced each other out. We could safely disagree, without fear. When we had a big fight, we said "I love you" at the end of it. We were committed to working through any problems that arose. We were best friends, and trusted each other more than anyone else.

I felt lucky in love, but like a loser on the track.

I had the financial and psychological support of my Nike contract, but was injured. In October 2001, soon after Adam and I returned from Fiji, I had surgery to scrape out a worn-down part of my patellar tendon, which helps connect the knee to the shinbone, and part of my kneecap. I was not prepared mentally or physically for how long the recovery would be. My confidence went with the knee. I couldn't race and I could barely train. The poet Rainer Maria Rilke wrote, "No feeling is final," but when I was in this injury funk, it felt as though there was no end in sight.

I was spending a lot of time at home watching soap operas, then got hooked on watching the 2002 Winter Olympics in Salt Lake City. When I wasn't on my couch, I had it on at my massage therapist's office. One day while I was lying on the massage table I looked up at the screen and gasped.

"I know them," I said, sounding feeble.

The women racing in the biathlon, in their spandex suits, rifles hitched over their shoulders, skis gliding along the trails, were some of the same ones I had trained with in Minnesota and Lake Placid. They'd made it.

They were Olympians. *Good for them*, I thought with genuine pride. I also wondered: *Did I blow it?*

My injury slump doubled down on me. After recovering from the patellar tendon surgery, I got a stress fracture in the shaft of my femur. It showed up on an X-ray—unusual for that type of fracture, and evidence of just how pronounced it was.

Back into soap operas with the Winter Olympics over, when I wasn't trying to numb my brain with love triangles and overacting, I thought about how much I despised running. The positive memories I had of the sport felt like a montage from a movie of someone else's life. At that moment, I hated that I had ever been good at it. It had hooked me, addicted me, and now wouldn't let me go.

Adam struggled, too. Though he pushed himself and had a decent race in Europe not long after the Winter Olympics, he wasn't consistent and didn't feel very good. While I watched soaps, he spent a lot of time drywalling a basement.

I worked with a therapist, Dr. Stephen Walker, off and on about depressive thoughts, particularly around this recurring feeling that I wasn't good enough. It didn't seem to matter what times I hit in practice. I hadn't made the Olympics. I hadn't accomplished my goal. My thought patterns seemed stuck in place.

Dr. Walker listened and helped me break down my insecurities and explore where some of the feelings came from. We talked about Tom's anger, my relationship with my father, his too brief life and death. He prescribed me a low dose of Zoloft, an antidepressant that I stayed on for a few months while we worked together, and he encouraged me to put my thoughts, particularly those about Tom, into letter form. It was empowering to have someone help me integrate, digest, and rethink my own story.

As far as my Nike sponsorship went, Cap was being very kind. Despite my injuries and struggles to get back to competition, and the fact that my contract was microscopic relative to the multimillion-dollar endorsement deals that the company brokered, Cap pledged his continued support. My contract did have basic clauses that would allow Nike to reduce my pay if I didn't compete, but Cap let me know in an email that they would keep my pay the same. It helped deter any feeling that my feet would be held to the fire.

2003 ticked by, then early 2004, and I finally got healthy enough to consistently work out. I began to claw my way back to fitness, one practice session at a time, and then onto the scoreboard at races. My confidence slowly returned.

Adam and I both ran fast enough that year in the 5,000 meters to make it to the 2004 Olympic Trials in Sacramento. Perhaps that alone should have felt like an accomplishment but I was bitterly disappointed when I not only failed to make the team, but I didn't even make it through the heats to the final race. Adam struggled as well, and didn't make his final. I wondered how we could put so much work into a single effort and feel as though we were going nowhere, or maybe even backward.

We left Sacramento with our hearts and egos shook, but reminded ourselves that we still had time, the dream wasn't over. The 2004 Trials had featured even more people we knew and had raced against, including Carrie Tollefson, who made the Olympic team in the 1,500 meters, and Shayne Culpepper, who made it in the 5,000 meters. (Alan Culpepper also snagged a spot at the Marathon Trials.) In my more competitive, hopeful moments, this invigorated me. It gave me the sense I belonged. On lower-self-esteem days, I felt completely unworthy.

Adam and I shifted our focus to the 2008 Beijing Olympic Trials and the World Championships leading up to it. We were ready to try something new when it came to training, and were willing to move away from Boulder as part of that.

We made a trip to Madison, Wisconsin, in late July 2004, and met with coaches Jerry Schumacher and Peter Tegan. Jerry had turned the University of Wisconsin Badgers men's program around, and Peter was the long-standing coach of the women's team. If we moved to Madison, we'd be only a five-hour drive from my family in Minnesota. I was impressed with Jerry's and Peter's dedication to the sport and drawn to the idea of being closer to my family. When Adam told Papa that we were likely relocating to the Midwest, he was overjoyed.

Just when we thought we had decided, someone working with Cap at Nike told us of an opportunity in Beaverton that might be of interest to me and Adam called the Oregon Project. Adam had become a Nike-sponsored runner at the start of 2003, switching from Fila when Fila decided he was making more money in bonuses than they were willing to pay him. Although he hadn't made the 2004 Olympic team, he had made it in 2000 and was still considered by some to be the Next Big American Star. (No pressure.) Nike was paying him $90,000 a year. They were being nice to make it sound like the opportunity in Oregon was for us both equally, but Adam's times were far more intriguing and promising than mine, and no one had to tell me that by "Adam and Kara" they more likely meant "Adam . . . Maybe Kara, too."

The Oregon Project was a team coached by the famed Alberto Salazar. It sounded secretive and exciting, like an invitation to a Special Forces unit, or Hogwarts. Cap got us flights to Portland. We boarded the plane, eager to find out more.

CHAPTER SEVEN
Valhalla

Clutching our bags and strolling down the long, wide corridors of Portland International Airport in September 2004, Adam and I looked around, thinking we might see a junior-level Nike representative in a telltale swoosh tracksuit, or a driver holding a card with GOUCHER written on it.

We were surprised when we spotted Alberto Salazar himself standing there—alone, unassuming, and seemingly unrecognized by anyone else.

Just under six feet tall, he kept a lean, wiry figure though it had been decades since he had competed. He was clean-shaven, with graying hair cut close to his head. He met us with a wide smile and a warm demeanor.

Alberto was a legend in the running world. The son of Cuban immigrants, he grew up in Massachusetts and tore through the high school running circuit there before joining the University of Oregon's storied team during the American running boom of the 1970s. At Oregon, he built a reputation as one of the most cutthroat and ruthless competitors in sneakers, piling up titles in cross country, the 5,000, and the 10,000 meters. He was an Olympian in 1980 in the 10,000 meters and 1984 in the marathon, but it was in the Boston and New York City Marathons where he cemented his legacy. In 1982, he outkicked Dick Beardsley in the last 50 yards of the Boston Marathon in what became known as the "Duel in the Sun" showdown. He crossed the finish line setting a new Boston record, then collapsed and was rushed to a hospital to get an IV drip of six liters of saline solution. He won back-to-back-to-back New York City Marathon titles—in '80, '81, and '82—in a similarly punishing fashion. In the 1990s, after being snakebitten by a series of injuries (which some speculated were due to his brutal training methods) he transitioned into coaching. In 2001, he founded the Nike Oregon Project—the same year he was inducted into the National Track & Field Hall of Fame. He was known for preaching the same philosophies as a coach he'd adhered to as a runner: train with high volume, calculate every detail of your plan, run as if it's going to be the last race of your life, and push yourself to the absolute limit.

Now here he was, ready to be our taxi driver.

I was intimidated and surprised as he walked us across the teal geometric carpet toward the airport exit, telling us how eager he was to show us around Portland and the Nike campus. He was charming, kind, approachable, welcoming. Immediately, he made me and Adam feel like we were the center of his attention; when either of us said anything at all, his eyes and body language were totally focused on us. For the first time, I wondered if instead of us trying to woo Nike on this trip, maybe it would be the other way around.

Alberto jumped right into the story of the Oregon Project. At the 2000 Boston Marathon, he explained, he and Tom Clarke, a Nike vice president, watched in distress as American runners failed to finish anywhere near the front of the pack. No American man or woman had won in Boston since Lisa Rainsberger (known then as Lisa Weidenbach) in 1985. In New York, it was worse: Alberto was *still* the last American male winner, from 1982, and an American woman hadn't won since 1977. In 2000, no American finished in the top 15. Frustrated, he and Tom began to brainstorm the idea that would become known as the Oregon Project.

The notion was simple but ambitious. The Oregon Project would be an elite team of only American distance runners, built from the ground up, funded by the biggest sporting goods company in the world, training on Nike's amenity-rich campus in Beaverton, and coached by one of the icons of the sport. If Nike could create distance running's next Tiger Woods or Lance Armstrong, they'd not only be heroes in the running world, but would stand to make huge profits in shoe and apparel sales.

We stepped out of the sliding airport doors into the clean, crisp air, and loaded into Alberto's black BMW. As he drove along the wide highways, surrounded by fields and Douglas firs, he started talking about one of his former athletes, Mary Decker Slaney. Slaney, a world champion in the 1,500 meters and 3,000 meters, and a world record setter in the mile, 5,000, and 10,000 meters, was the subject of a doping scandal in 1996 when, while being coached by Alberto, she tested positive for elevated levels of testosterone. Alberto told us in a clear and authoritative manner that even though Slaney had received a two-year ban, all of the stories about her doping were hogwash. He explained that the testosterone test at the time had proven unreliable for women in their late thirties on birth control, as Slaney was. (Slaney has denied using any banned substances.)

Soon, the fields outside the window gave way to Portland's tangle of bridges and rivers, and Alberto was dropping me and Adam off at our hotel downtown. As soon as Adam and I were in our room, we looked at each other and started talking about how much we admired Alberto's forthrightness in diving right into the Slaney controversy, and addressing it head-on. His explanation of what happened sounded fair to us both, and if he had done anything wrong, surely Nike wouldn't have risked its reputation by hiring him and giving him free rein over its program to build the world's best running team.

With Alberto, we felt like we were in the presence of greatness. It was contagious.

The next day, Alberto, smiling and warm, greeted me and Adam at our hotel and drove us to Nike's large and lush campus in Beaverton, just west of Portland. It was well buzzed about as being the finest sports-training facility in the world. I had been to the campus once before, when Nike invited me after my senior season in college, but lots of people got those invitations. Going for a tour as a prospective member of the Oregon Project was different. Approaching the secured and beautifully landscaped perimeter, I felt the sense of exclusivity. You could only pass through the secure entrance with a badge, or the blessing of someone who had one, giving the place a kind of Fort Knox–meets–national park vibe.

Alberto guided us around the campus's sacred soil. It seemed no window had a smudge, no blade of grass was too tall. Set into the woods was the five-lane Michael Johnson running track. There was a wood chip running path through the trees. The landscape swept me away and reminded me a bit of the Duluth trails where I had run so joyfully as a kid. There was an actual creek, called Cedar Mill Creek, winding through the trees and around the modern steel, glass, and concrete buildings, which were named after Nike-backed athletes. Alberto had one of those buildings, inside of which his Boston Marathon laurel wreath and three New York

City Marathon medals were carefully preserved behind museum glass. Not far from that was the Joe Paterno Child Development Center. There was also the "Dream Six" maintenance building named after the 1992 Olympic Dream Team; the Cristiano Ronaldo soccer field; and a structure honoring Mia Hamm.

The glass-walled, supermarket-sized Lance Armstrong Center, known as "the Lance," would be the central workout space for the Oregon Project, Alberto explained. He led us inside, where trophies, photos, and bright yellow artifacts paying tribute to the famed cyclist lined the hallways and rooms. There was the Linda fitness studio, named after Lance's mother, and Luke's Landing, a perch overlooking an eleven-lane swimming pool, named for his son. There was a massive gym, lounge space with a couch and a TV set, and ice baths, among other amenities. It wasn't just that Nike had the best facilities in the world—it had training tools that Adam and I had *never even heard of.* Off campus, in Northwest Portland, there was the Nike House—where we could opt to live—featuring gadgetry including underwater treadmills and a filtration system to simulate life at a high elevation, as studies had shown that it could increase red blood cells and performance. To Adam and me, it sounded like we were talking about NASA at peak Space Race, but for running. Access to all of it, along with expert massage therapists, and all of the Nike gear one could want, came with your spot on the Oregon Project.

All of this was incredibly enticing, but the single most attractive prospect was being coached by Alberto. He was more committed to making his runners into winners than anyone we'd ever met. He had a swoosh tattooed on his left bicep. He told us that he had the personal backing of his billionaire friend and fellow Oregon track alumnus, Nike CEO and cofounder Phil Knight, to make the Oregon Project a success.

I began to envision me and Adam trotting along the pristine, tree-lined track, lifting the shiny new weights at the gym, driving our car along the smooth and spacious roads every morning. As the magnetic Alberto described it, Nike was a way of life, a religion. It represented a collection of people with a strongly defined culture and sense of purpose. As much as I relished the opportunity to be close to my family in Wisconsin, and even though it gave me the slightest pause to hear that I'd likely be the only woman at the Oregon Project, as men's distance running had been

Alberto's sole focus to date, there was no comparison to what Alberto was offering.

"Give me six months," Alberto told us. "If you hate it, you can leave, no hard feelings." He even offered to cover our moving expenses from Colorado to Oregon, and our first few months of rent, since we didn't plan to live in the Nike House.

We were sold.

CHAPTER EIGHT
Welcome to "the Nike Family"

On October 30, 2004, Adam and I moved to Portland. We signed a lease on a narrow townhome with two bedrooms and an office near the Nike campus. We had our photos taken for keycards to get in and out of parts of the campus in Beaverton and received instructions for how to access the Nike House in Northwest Portland (which were to find the key under the mat if no one was home), and how to use the underwater treadmills in the backyard. Everything we'd need to win was at our fingertips— equipment, massages, medical care, coaching—and if it wasn't, we could ask for it. It felt like we'd won the lottery. We were giddy to be part of what many in the running world were touting as the most ambitious endeavor in our sport's history. As we drove onto the campus for our first day of training, I thought: *Oh God. I'm actually here!* And then: *Did they make some kind of mistake?* There was a whiff of impostor syndrome. I was about to be at the popular kids' table.

The wunderkind and already undisputed star of the Oregon Project was the eighteen-year-old, Portland-raised Galen Rupp. Adam and I met him a few days after arriving. Blond, cherub-faced, and soaftspoken, Galen had already demolished American high school running records and racked up two state cross country titles, plus three more on the indoor track. In 2003, he had finished second at the Foot Locker Cross Country Championships, the same race where Adam and I had competed as young talents. In 2004, Galen was named the *Track & Field News* High School Boys Athlete of the Year. When we arrived, Galen had graduated from high school but was delaying entering college to focus exclusively on training and competing under Alberto, who he'd been working with since he was fourteen.

From the start, it was clear that Galen held a special place in Alberto's heart. Alberto said that he considered Galen to be more like a son than an athlete. Galen also quickly became like a (very fast) little brother to Adam and me.

The other runners on the Oregon Project when we arrived were Mike Donnelly, Dave Davis, and Dan Browne. Mike was a former All-American at Providence College, a couple years older than me, who had finished fourth at the 2004 Olympic Trials in the 10,000 meters. It was quickly apparent how hard he worked, and how kind he was—he helped us get our feet under us in Portland and became our first real friend in town. Dave was also very nice and passionate about improving, but extremely quiet and not someone Adam or I got to know very well. Dan held the notable distinction of being the first Oregon Project athlete to make the Olympics, having finished third in Trials in the 10,000 meters and the marathon, and having competed in both events in Athens just months before we arrived.

As a training group, we all had our sights set on the 2008 Olympic Trials. Between now and then would be practices upon practices, high-altitude training camps, regular tune-up races, and major competitions. My personal goal was to run under 15 minutes in the 5,000 meters, a feat that only a handful of American women had accomplished.

As we settled into life in Oregon, Alberto often took me and Adam for lunch at the Mia Hamm building on campus. The building housed his office, along with all of the sports marketing offices, and cafeterias. He usually took us to the smaller upstairs café, which he preferred to the main cafeteria because it was quieter. Most times, I felt like the third wheel, sitting there as Alberto carefully broke down Adam's training plans. At one of these lunches, he mentioned that he could modify a training program he had used for high school boys for me. I couldn't tell if he meant it to be genuine, but it left me with the sense that he had low expectations of me. I was desperate to show him that I could do more than he thought I was capable of.

———————————

The Nike Oregon Project's thrilling mission was to be ahead of the competition in every sense. To do that, Alberto told us we needed to be innovative, push the edge. We were following in the philosophy that was core to Nike's history, dating back to when cofounder Bill Bowerman famously used a waffle iron to make the soles of some of the company's first running shoes.

One of the earliest innovations Alberto introduced us to was an altitude tent to sleep in at night. The contraption looked like a giant cylinder which surrounded our bed. The idea was to simulate the lower oxygen levels of a high-altitude environment, thus causing the body to produce more red blood cells and increase oxygen-carrying capacity. When we returned to lower altitude—in this case, just on the other side of our tent—the expectation was that we would be able to run longer and faster. We started using the tent right away, exhilarated at the notion that even when we were asleep, we were still doing something to make ourselves better. There was no such thing as being "off" at the Oregon Project, we quickly learned: full commitment was the only way to achieve our goals. (Later, we paid to have entire rooms of our house in Portland sealed off for altitude, and had tents shipped to us at hotels when we traveled for competitions, or even to Minnesota when we visited my family. We learned to assemble them with the alacrity of Everest climbers.)

When Kelly came to Portland for a visit and saw me in my altitude tent, watching television, beads of sweat running down my face, she couldn't believe it. (The sweat was due to the fact that the tent was always hot and stuffy. Sometimes Adam would use a shoelace to MacGyver up a fan; I was afraid it would fall down and chop up my face, but the cool breeze felt incredible.) "Weird," was Kelly's assessment. When Kendall later came out for her first visit and saw the tent, she said it looked like we were in a "running film."

Maybe we looked ridiculous. But if that was one of the details that could tip us from whether or not we made it onto a podium or an Olympic team, we were going to accept it. Sprinters, whose fates are determined by a hundredth or a thousandth of a second, usually get the press for precision (and to be fair, they are often detail-obsessed), but the middle- and long-distance runners are typically Type A, too. It's all about sweating the small stuff, and sweating with your spouse while eating carefully selected proteins and watching sitcoms in a sweltering tent.

Though I wanted nothing more than to prove to Alberto and everyone else at the Oregon Project that I was fast and I belonged in the club, I had a hard time doing so because for my first few months after joining, I was fighting through an injury in my right shin. It was frustrating. I thought it might be a stress fracture, but did my best to push through the pain. My sense of the Oregon Project culture was that you had to live the ethos that nothing could stop you. You had to tough it out.

Alberto sometimes invited his runners to his home in the Portland hills to use some of the team equipment he had set up in his garage, including an anti-gravity treadmill called an AlterG. Alberto also had a gadget popular for recovery with athletes that uses radio waves to create heat inside your body called a TECAR machine.

Alberto's kids were in their teenage and college years, and when Adam and I were at the house we'd exchange friendly greetings and catch up with small talk about their various interests. I loved Mark Wetmore, but I had never had a coach open his home to athletes the way that Alberto was doing. It was something Adam and I were especially grateful for, being far from our home states and loved ones. Alberto's wife, Molly, even made us spaghetti—a meal my mom had always cooked for me. Alberto referred to us as being part of "the Nike family" nearly as soon as we came to Portland, and we felt that.

After a run at his house one day in January 2005, when my right shin had been particularly bothersome, he told me that he had an idea. Rather than have me see an orthopedist or sports medicine doctor, he'd give me a treatment that he'd heard was used on racehorses. His daughter competed in equestrian events, but to the best of my knowledge, Alberto didn't work closely with any horses or have a background in equine health or performance, so I didn't know where he was getting that from. But he seemed confident that the idea he had would work, and I was happy to try.

Alberto crushed up aspirin pills into a powder, then mixed them with an over-the-counter cream that's easily absorbed by the skin called DMSO (typically used to help alleviate injuries and heal pains including osteo-arthritis, burns, and scar tissue). Alberto explained that by applying the powdered aspirin as a cream to the hurt body part, the medicine would be more effective. He applied the cream concoction to my right shin, then locked it in with plastic wrap. I sat there for a couple of minutes. My shin began to tingle. Then burn.

I have a relatively high pain tolerance, but it progressed into a throbbing, fiery sensation unlike anything I had ever felt, like someone had put kerosene on my leg and lit a match.

I told Alberto: "It's burning."

He told me: "Leave it. That means it's working."

I bore down for a few more minutes, but the pain was getting worse. "This is *really* hurting," I told him. I was sweating, and could feel the flush and the tears coming to my face.

Alberto told me to leave it on overnight.

I drove home with the wrap still on, gingerly shifting my right leg to tap the gas or brake pedal when I needed to, feeling every centimeter of movement. When I got home, Adam was horrified. He looked at my leg, which was red and blistering. We cut off the plastic wrap and washed off all of the crushed pills and cream. My leg was a raw, miniaturized landscape of red skin and bumps. I had second-degree burns.

When I told Alberto all this, he laughed it off and said something along the lines of "Oops, guess I was wrong on that." I feebly laughed with him. I couldn't wear socks, tights, or have any fabric touch my shin for several weeks, nor could I even aqua jog, a type of cross training where you run underwater from the waist or shoulders down. But hey, Alberto was known as a rogue, someone with bold ideas who got results, and his plan, cockamamie as it was, had been worth a try. Like a mad scientist, he was always experimenting, searching for those tools—whether in training, technology, or recovery—that would make us faster. Part of that approach was the sense that it was okay to risk being wrong. No risk, no reward. I forgave him and let it go.

Beyond his storied résumé and star power, what gave Alberto the standing to try out innovative, edge-pushing approaches was the fact that many of the things he landed on proved to be successful, soon to be copied by other teams around the world. The aspirin and DMSO treatment may have been a miss, but the specific type of treadmills and altitude tents he was so fond of soon proliferated in the sport. He told us to cut holes in our racing singlets for ventilation, which seemed a bit silly, but soon, perforated running gear became ubiquitous. Alberto seemed able to look into the future of performance. We felt lucky to have him guiding us toward it.

With my shin pain unimproved, however, I did go see a doctor. It turned out the problem was actually compartment syndrome in my right calf. Compartment syndrome—which I'd had once before, in 1998—is an issue with blood flow caused when pressure builds in your muscles, which can be brought about by extreme exercise. I got surgery in March 2005 to relieve the pain. Because we were technically independent contractors and not Nike employees, we got our insurance through USA Track & Field, with Adam being the primary account holder and me as his dependent. However, Nike graciously paid for the remaining balance on the surgery bills that my insurance didn't cover. As soon as I recovered, I went right back to training with Alberto.

———————————

Our coach's influence reached far beyond the realm of performance technology. Alberto was friendly with the University of Oregon's athletic director, Bill Moos. Galen was thinking about joining a college program in time for the spring 2005 NCAA outdoor season, and was considering the University of Oregon. In Alberto's opinion, the program had been diminishing in recent years under coach Martin Smith, but Phil Knight and Alberto wanted to sculpt it back into the distance running powerhouse it had been in their time. However, Smith apparently didn't love the idea of bringing on an athlete whose private coach wanted to continue to oversee his training program. It's worth noting here that Nike was the single biggest sponsor of Oregon's athletic department. Alberto talked to Moos and told him that there were many other schools that would be happy to have Galen, including the University of Portland.

In February 2005, Galen won the USA Junior Cross Country title, and in mid-March, he placed 20th at the World Junior Cross Country Championships in France, with Alberto coaching him. Adam went to France, too, running on the senior team, while I recovered from my surgery at home. When Galen returned to Portland, he enrolled at the University of Oregon in time to compete in the outdoor collegiate track season.

In March, Martin Smith resigned and the esteemed Vin Lananna, who had built one of the NCAA's winningest programs at Stanford since 1992, was named associate athletic director. He immediately got to work, not only on improving the track and cross country teams—which he did—but eventually in helping to brand Eugene as "TrackTown USA." He led the effort to get the university's hallowed Hayward Field track named as the host site of the 2008 Olympic Trials, which he successfully accomplished in October 2005. He then started a two-year renovation of the track, with Nike funding. It had the added benefit of giving the university's running teams arguably the best college training facility in the world.

Though Galen was now in college in Eugene, he remained based out of Portland, a two-hour drive away. He continued to train intensively with Alberto and us on the Nike campus. He received massages, training, gear, supplements, plane rides, altitude equipment, hotels at training camps, and other amenities in tandem with what Adam and I received as professional Nike athletes. Some days, he took his college classes online; other days, Alberto drove him south to Eugene for in-person classes on campus so that Galen could relax and not have to waste energy thinking about traffic. Adam and I liked Galen, but this made Adam in particular a bit nuts, as he'd worked to afford his college education and juggle that with his track team commitments and school. Galen's preparation and lifestyle looked nothing like ours had in college, or anyone else's he would race against in a college meet.

Adam and I also knew from our time in Boulder that the NCAA had strict rules regarding amateurism, particularly when it came to student-athletes receiving gifts or money from coaches, boosters, or companies. Valid or not—and we both questioned it—our impression of those rules related to Galen working out with professional runners at a shoe and apparel company's headquarters felt murky to us at best, and at worst a violation. Being around Alberto and Galen as this was all going on gave us an early window into the multilayered influence our coach and sponsor wielded in the sport. It was my opinion that it was an influence that was not only to Galen's benefit, but my and Adam's, as well. As far as I could tell, the NCAA never found Galen guilty of wrongdoing, or sanctioned Galen, the University of Oregon, Alberto, or Nike. We were told by Alberto that as Oregon Project runners, we would never have to worry about getting credentials or invitations to meets. Most were backed by Nike.

CHAPTER NINE
Pushing the Edge

In May 2005, Alberto took me, Adam, and Galen to Park City, Utah, for our first Nike Oregon Project high-altitude training camp. We all shared a condo, which emphasized the familial feelings. (Other runners like Mike Donnelly, Dave Davis, and Dan Browne were part of the team but more intermittently so—some worked full-time jobs in addition to running, others were injured, others came and went—while Adam, Galen, and I became the consistent, core group.) I was healed from my surgery and working out again, and the idea was to put in miles at altitude in a focused, retreat-like atmosphere.

After altitude camp, my fitness improved and my results picked up. I joined Adam, Galen, and Alberto in Europe for races in the summer—my first trip abroad with the Oregon Project. It was both an exciting moment, and a time of confronting some harsh realities. At a competition in Lignano, Italy, I was posing for a photo with the meet director and he let his hand slip to rest on my breast as the picture was taken. I told the guys about it, making light of it even though it had made me uncomfortable. But a few days later, on July 23, at an event in Heusden, Belgium, I set a new PR in the 5,000 meters, 15:17.55.

When we got back to Portland, I found the photograph from Italy and it became a big joke. Alberto "comically" re-created the scene, putting his arm around me and letting his hand fall onto my breast. I knew that it was wrong, I felt uneasy, but I didn't tell that to anyone. Alberto was always encouraging me to "loosen up," and I didn't want to seem like a pill. With my results picking up, too, I didn't want to question things.

Cap made an offer to extend my contract for another three years at $35,000 a year. I felt so relieved, elated even, and happily accepted: I wanted to stay at Nike, and having been injured on and off for so long and only just now starting to perform well in races, I didn't feel I had much of a case to ask for more.

After I set my PR in the 5,000 meters, Alberto started to take much more interest in my training. I quickly experienced how his reputation for pushing his runners to go further, faster, and harder than anyone else was accurate. One such coaching technique was having us Oregon Project runners do a workout within 15 minutes of finishing a race—like repeats at the warm-up track, or a tempo run. It was unconventional, to say the least.

But I took to Alberto's coaching style, and Adam did, too. We felt certain that if we stuck to his plan, ticking off the boxes, training one day, one workout at a time, it would bring us to where we wanted to go—our shared Olympic dreams. As days rolled around when our brains and our bodies were totally depleted, when we had to say no to a social life and yes to training, we told ourselves that these were mere sacrifices. It was satisfying to know that we were doing exactly what we needed to do. It also meant a lot to feel more integrated into the program, to have my potential beginning to be taken as seriously as Adam's, and to have Alberto's attention focused on my future. Alberto told me and Adam, with complete conviction, that World Championship and Olympic podiums were in reach for us both. I got goose bumps.

It was during this period in summer 2005 that I really became "one of the guys." Two of Galen's friends, one from high school and one from college, had recently started training with us. This further upped the ratio of men to women, a point underscored by the fact that the vast majority of the assistant coaches, team personnel, and executives tied to the Oregon Project at this time were also men. One woman named Caitlin Chock ran with us off and on and was occasionally around, but she seldom raced due to health issues and we rarely overlapped for workouts.

Not wanting to feel like such an outsider, when I sensed that I was at last being welcomed into the boys' club, I was happy to accept. Predictably, this came with challenges. Alberto and other Nike employees didn't hesitate to make sexually charged jokes and offhand comments around me and even *to* me about women's bodies, whether it was about other female runners, or about a waitress at the restaurant we were dining at. The words "fat," "thin," and "hot" were commonly used.

More often than not when this happened, I made the mistake of either trying to change the subject, or laughing along with it. I even cracked my share of dirty jokes. It didn't make me feel good, but the truth was, I wanted to belong in the locker room, and I felt like I had to walk a tightrope to manage that. I liked the feeling of being included with the guys, I liked feeling that they were treating me as "an equal," even if it came at the expense of other women, even if I knew the behavior was repulsive.

When it came to Alberto's advice that I "loosen up," he was often talking about my relationship with alcohol. I had never been much of a drinker: as a way to honor my father, I had promised myself while I was in high school that I wouldn't drink until I was twenty-one. And by the time I turned twenty-one, my college running schedule was so intense that drinking just wasn't a regular feature of my lifestyle, nor Adam's. Some of our teammates at CU could juggle a night out with being sharp enough for Mark Wetmore's practice in the morning, but Adam and I weren't among them. We didn't begrudge them, it was just that running 10 miles at a killer pace while hungover wasn't our idea of fun.

Alberto, however, was a drinker. It was an open joke that at 5 p.m., whether we were on the track or traveling for a competition, it was beer o'clock for Alberto. Oregon Project support staffers talked about it as an endearing quality, a vestige of the era when racing culture wasn't so stodgy and professionalized. It added to his mystique.

So, when Alberto put pressure on me to have a glass of wine with dinner, I'd often have one. Sometimes it felt fun, other times, I did it just to shut him up. Alberto would usually order another round, poking fun at me for not keeping up. I'd shrug him off, but I'd wonder if maybe he was right, maybe I did need to relax a bit.

Massage therapy was another favorite pastime of Alberto's, though it was more for recovery than relaxation. Oregon Project runners received massages after almost every hard workout. This wasn't an innovation—massage therapists had long been known as an athlete's best friend—but what *was* new was having our coach sometimes double as our masseur.

We had trained professionals, some of the best in the world, who typically worked on us, but when they weren't around or when we were on the road, such as at training camp in Park City or at a competition, Alberto would often take over. He wasn't licensed or professionally trained as a physical therapist or masseur as far as any of us knew, but Adam and Galen and I trusted him enough not to worry about that. Alberto seemed to know more about *everything* to do with running than just about everyone else, and this felt no different. It was helpful, yet another way in which he was going above and beyond as a coach, invested in our success.

I often ran in shorts, and when Alberto was massaging me, he would pull my shorts up way high. "I have to get your glutes," he'd sometimes say. There was no more discussion than that, and unlike when the professionals were working on me, he didn't ask before touching. Nor did he drape me with a cloth or towel as a professional would.

I found this unsettling. But these weren't intimate spa massages where it's just two people in a dimly lit, lavender-scented room with a pan flute soundtrack playing in the background. These were done with other runners and staffers around, typically after workouts in spaces where people were congregated, like in the living room of the Nike House, at his house, or in our rental condo in Park City. They were athletic massages, often called "body work"—a good term, as you feel more like a car at the mechanic's shop, getting a tune-up. It's utilitarian, and all about performance. Alberto called his massages "flushes," just a quick fifteen to twenty minutes of work.

As I lay there with most of my ass exposed to everyone who was around, I did worry about how Adam would feel. But I reminded myself that Alberto pulled Adam's and Galen's shorts up, too, when he was massaging them. I would think, *Surely someone would say something if there was anything weird about this.* No one did. Alberto was "just old-school," we all said when we talked about it. He knew how running bodies worked because of his experience as an athlete. He laughed, made jokes, and told us stories as we lay there. It all felt like an extension of our workout, and an opportunity to get in some extra time with the coach.

Alberto believed most doctors didn't understand running. He made comments to the Oregon Project athletes about how physicians didn't understand the sport like he did. As with the aspirin and DMSO cream, he took a personal interest in medication—anti-inflammatories, Imodium, diuretics, and so on—and the ways it could help his runners. He'd been obsessed with running for decades, so what did some squares in white coats think they knew about it?

There was one doctor, however, who Alberto came to like very much. In fact, Adam and I were the ones who told Alberto about him.

Jeffrey Brown was a Houston-based endocrinologist. He had treated a number of Olympians, and was considered one of the best doctors in the country working with track athletes. He had even worked with the national governing body for the sport, United States Track & Field (USATF). In the spring of 2003, Adam was struggling with extreme fatigue. His mother had hypothyroidism, which can cause exhaustion and sleeping issues and runs in families. We had heard of Dr. Brown through Mark Wetmore, who had spoken to another physician involved with USATF, who recommended Dr. Brown. So Adam and I took a trip to Houston. We found Dr. Brown's office in a large concrete building next to a Jack in the Box in a West Houston strip mall. Inside there were piles of papers and books. Dr. Brown proceeded to do a full examination of Adam, including drawing blood himself. We both felt comfortable with him from the outset. He was tall and skinny with legs that he could pretzel into a knot when he sat down, and mostly bald, with small tufts of pewter-hued hair resting on top of his ears. He had a smile fixed on his face and a friendly, bright demeanor that reminded me of the Whos from Dr. Seuss books.

He determined that Adam did indeed have hypothyroidism, and prescribed the hormone medication Levoxyl. He also asked Adam a question that seemed out of left field, initially. He wondered if Adam had ever been to BALCO, a California laboratory that was just starting to make headlines for being a supplier of performance-enhancing drugs for athletes (including sprinter Marion Jones and slugger Barry Bonds). Adam told Dr. Brown that he hadn't. When we left the office, Adam and I talked about the BALCO question and realized that Dr. Brown must have been asking about it to make sure that Adam wasn't looking to break any anti-doping rules.

Dr. Brown took Adam and me out to dinner that night (not at the Jack in the Box), and over the meal it became clear to us just how much he loved running. We went home feeling good about the whole visit, that we trusted Dr. Brown, and he trusted us.

A year later, in 2004, I started feeling generally unwell on top of my spate of injuries. Pretty much all of the women in my family had already been diagnosed with hypothyroidism, including my grandmother, mother, and eventually, both of my sisters. I thought it was worth checking out if my thyroid might be acting up, and scheduled an appointment with Dr. Brown for early May 2004.

He did a similar exam with me as he'd done with Adam—including drawing blood himself, and asking me about BALCO—and the appointment had a similarly personal, informal feel. He asked me about my medical history, and told me that both the history of bladder infections I'd mentioned as well as the diagnosis of polycystic ovary syndrome that I'd received in college were linked with hypothyroidism. As part of his physical examination, he asked me to undress and put on a hospital gown. He opened it and examined my naked body, saying that based on my body hair, he suspected I had slightly higher than average testosterone, probably linked to my polycystic ovary syndrome. I thought back to fifth grade, when a boy named Brandon told me that I had a mustache like an old lady, and felt embarrassed.

Dr. Brown told me that I did indeed have hypothyroidism, and prescribed Levoxyl, the same medication that he'd prescribed Adam and that my mother had also been taking for years. The dose Dr. Brown initially gave me was the same dose my mother took and quickly proved to be too strong—my muscles ached, my heart rate went up, and my hair started falling out—so he lowered the dosage. It wasn't a magic bullet for all things that ailed me, but once the dose was corrected, it seemed to be helping, and I didn't feel any negative side effects.

When we joined the Nike Oregon Project, we discussed our medical histories with Alberto and mentioned Dr. Brown as a reputable person to know about in case anyone on the team was having endocrine-related problems. Alberto reached out to Dr. Brown, and in early 2005, went to visit him. Alberto said he had struggled with his health for a long time and that he had felt tired for years. Given the way he had taxed his body as a runner, this didn't surprise me. When Alberto returned from Houston he was excited about having met Dr. Brown, and reported that he, too, had been diagnosed with hypothyroidism. He said that he wished he had gone a decade ago because his underactive thyroid could have been causing all of his symptoms. Soon after, Alberto returned to Houston, this time taking Galen with him. Galen was diagnosed with hypothyroidism as well.

Adam and I scratched our heads. With Alberto, it seemed like nothing more than an odd coincidence. Hypothyroidism tends to be more common in women, but Alberto described his symptoms convincingly: it easily seemed like something he could have been living with since the end of his professional career. With Galen, Adam and I had a moment of pause, wondering what the chances could really be that he had it, too. But Levoxyl was not a performance-enhancing drug in any way, and it, along with other thyroid medications, were permitted by the U.S. Anti-Doping Agency (USADA) and World Anti-Doping Agency (WADA). Alberto also told us that Galen was on a very low dose. When Galen started crowing about how amazing he felt, two days after starting the medication, we smirked, chalking it up to an impressionable kid on a harmless placebo high. (Galen has denied doping allegations, saying he did not "break the rules.")

CHAPTER TEN
Pros and Cons

For the 2005 winter holidays, Adam and I planned to go to Duluth for Christmas, then spend a couple of days with his family in Colorado. It was a big reward at the end of a tough training schedule and series of races, and I looked forward to it for months. Being part of "the Nike family," so intensely focused on my running goals, meant having less time to spend with my actual family, making these visits more precious than ever.

The whole group was there: my grandparents, my mom, Kelly and her girlfriend at the time, Kendall and her husband, Bret, who she had married in June 2005. We had breakfast together, built fires, and drank hot chocolate. We gathered around a big Christmas dinner.

Though being in Duluth was a break from the normal routine, training never stopped. Alberto gave Adam and me workouts to do on our own over the holidays. I was out for one along the dirt roads at Papa's property, shortly after Christmas, when my Achilles started to hurt. I got back to the house and called Alberto to let him know and seek his advice. He insisted that I come back to Oregon "AJAN" No discussion, debate, or alternative.

I loathed having to tell everyone that I had to leave, cutting my visit home by a day or two and bailing on going to Colorado with Adam. They were bummed by the news, but good sports. They'd met Alberto a couple of times at meets where they'd come to watch me race and loved him, always talking about how he "lit up a room." Alberto had even made a point of calling my mother during my first year in Oregon and saying kind things to her about the job she did raising me, and how much he cared about my progress and Adam's. We all agreed that Alberto knew best, and he was sacrificing some of his own holiday time to tend to one of his athletes personally, even a nonstar like me. We were grateful for his care.

When I landed in Oregon, my Achilles protesting after the long flight, I found Alberto waiting for me, just as he had more than a year earlier when

Adam and I came for our recruiting trip. As he greeted me, I smelled the red wine on his breath and saw the pink hue that it had left on his teeth. He knew that he was picking me up at the airport that night, so I falsely assumed he would have forgone his typical 5 p.m. happy hour.

To my eye, his drinking had increased of late. If we were out on the roads for an afternoon run, he would stop by a corner store for a beer. If he came over to my and Adam's house, he would open up the refrigerator and look for a drink. Sometimes Alberto asked Galen, Adam, me, or whoever else was around to signal to him when he was done with drink number two—the limit he had set himself for the evening. When we did as we were told, he'd say we were "no fun" and keep drinking anyway. "Who are you," he'd say to me after his end-of-second-drink reminder, "my mom?"

As we got in his black BMW in the airport parking garage, my hopes that he was only a little buzzed were dashed. We pulled out of the concrete structure, zigging, zagging, careening back and forth. My limbs tightened; my right hand clenched the handle by the passenger's seat. He insisted that we go to his house first, about a thirty-minute drive, so that he could treat my Achilles with some gadget he had there. Then he'd take me home.

Alberto knew that a drunk driver had killed my father. As we'd spent more time together and built up trust, I'd opened up to him about my life in and beyond running, the struggles I had faced in losing my father so young, my strained relationship with my stepfamily, my insecurities. He listened and offered the occasional pearl of wisdom or story about his own father, a strict Catholic Cuban immigrant who Alberto said was still hard to please.

This is so irresponsible, I thought, as angry at myself as I was at him. Since childhood, I had promised myself that I would never get behind the wheel of a car after drinking, nor would I get into the car of someone who was drunk. It was bad enough to risk your own life or that of your passengers, but no one needed to tell me or my family what the consequences could be when someone was driving intoxicated. Yet, I was also fearful of speaking up, or telling him to pull over. I worried that he would think I was judging him and questioning his choices. I felt trapped. At least it was a quiet, winter night, so there weren't a lot of other cars on the already slow-moving streets. But to get to Alberto's house in the hills, we had to careen up one hairpin turn after another.

Finally, Alberto parked in his driveway. I could feel my heart beating out of my chest. He walked into the house, poured himself a glass of red wine, and told me to lie down on a massage table that he had set up. I didn't see or hear anyone else in the house. He got out the TECAR machine and began massaging my Achilles with it.

In his current state, I was worried about him making my injury worse. The intention of the TECAR machine is to ease inflammation and pain with warming radio waves. When operated correctly, it kind of feels like having a lukewarm iron on your skin, but the machine should be operated by a professional for many reasons, one of which is that if you let it idle, it can burn you.

Alberto kept drinking his wine while using the machine, sometimes pausing to grab his glass while keeping the machine pressed against my body. The amount of heat on my skin was increasing. It soon reached a point where I got really worried. *My Achilles is melting,* I thought. *This could cost me my career.*

I knew Alberto cared very much that the athletes he coached believed in him. He wanted full buy-in. As in the car, I worried about saying anything at all, afraid that he would be mad that I was questioning him. I didn't see Alberto as a yeller or prone to frightening outbursts like Tom, but given his inebriated state, I wasn't sure. I stayed silent.

The clock read 10:30 p.m. I thought, *What am I going to do? How am I going to get out of here?* This was before Uber and Lyft and my pink Motorola Razr flip phone didn't have reception in the hills, so I couldn't call a friend or cab. Because of my anxiety about saying the wrong thing to Alberto, asking to use his landline didn't feel like an option. My spot on the team, Adam's spot, our Nike gigs, all felt in jeopardy if I made the wrong move.

I knew that I was going to get in that car with him again to get home, even though I also knew that it was unsafe. It made me sick. It's a testament to how profoundly confused I was. When it came to Alberto, the gatekeeper to my dreams, I was able to rationalize anything. *I'm lucky to be here,* I thought. *It's not that long of a drive to my house.*

We wrapped up the TECAR therapy, I got in the car with Alberto, and he drove me home, swerving the whole way.

When I got inside, I locked the door behind me, climbed into bed, and collapsed.

How did I live with Alberto's behavior? Why didn't I say anything?

As a kid, I had learned to compartmentalize my feelings. I figured out how to put my feelings about my father's death in a box, thinking that I shouldn't let it impact me. I did the same with Tom's anger—I could tuck away the pain, and still love him. These were handy skills for me as an athlete, allowing me to put bodily pain and mental doubt aside and push myself to the limit. With Alberto, I knew in one part of my mind that his sexist comments and drunk driving and attempts at playing doctor were wrong, but I was able to wall that off from how I felt about him as my running coach.

There was another force at work, too. With my father deceased, Tom Wheeler mostly out of my life, and Papa far away in Minnesota, the father figure position in my life was wide open. It seemed to me that Alberto was eager to fill it. Though Adam had made an effort to get to know his father after years of resentment, to some extent Alberto filled that role for him as well. Alberto, like Adam's father, was Catholic, and Alberto invited us to join him for a few church services. Learning more about Catholicism intrigued Adam. And of course, Alberto was Adam's coach and potential key to athletic success, same as he was for me. This all made it difficult for either of us to see outside of our bubble, or give each other perspective.

Whenever a voice inside me protested that something Alberto had done was wrong, another, louder one counteracted it. *He's a great guy*, it would say. *A father, a churchgoing Catholic.* He was just *"old-fashioned."* If none of that quite worked, a standby that seemed to shut the door to further questioning was: *Nobody is perfect.*

Undergirding all of this was the fact that Adam and I were committed to our running careers and Olympic dreams. In the second half of 2005 both of our running times had gotten faster and more consistent, thanks to Alberto's guidance. I was setting personal records. Adam was racing well. Our dreams were coming closer into focus. It was easy to justify the behavior of a man who was giving us results.

At the USATF Cross Country Nationals in New York City in mid-February 2006, my Achilles was still bothering me, but not enough to keep me out of the race. The top six finishers in each major event would get to go to the IAAF (International Association of Athletics Federations) World Athletics Cross Country Championships and represent our country. Adam won the men's 4k title, proving to everyone that he was a star continuing to ascend to the top of his game as a professional. I came in seventh in the women's 4k, missing the national team by less than one second. And who won my race but Carrie Tollefson. It wasn't the finish I'd hoped for, but given that the Achilles had been hindering me all through practices in the lead-up to the event, it wasn't a bad result.

The week after Cross Country Nationals, I was back at the Nike campus. The late-February day was gray and damp. Aside from the sore Achilles, I was feeling fine, and I had just completed an afternoon cross training session that went well. I hopped in my SUV to drive home, thinking about the birthday gift I had just bought for Adam's sister: Old Navy pajamas that actually had a shot of arriving to her home on time. I was on the highway, heading toward the Murray exit, when I suddenly saw brake lights ahead. I tried to change lanes and slam on my brakes, but it was too little too late.

In what felt like slow motion, my SUV made a stomach-curdling *screech* and then *crunch* as it careened into a semitruck. It then spun, hit the semi again, and swerved into a concrete wall along the highway, before it finally lurched to a stop. The airbag did not go off.

Once the tears started coming, I couldn't stop them. It was an uncontrollable gush. I couldn't catch my breath. I couldn't bring my hands to unbuckle my seat belt. I couldn't process that I wasn't dead.

The driver of the semi climbed down from his rig and a woman from another car approached me. She was a nurse. She took my flip phone and called Adam. I remember how incredibly kind the truck driver and the nurse were to me. I expected the driver of the smashed semi to be mad, but instead he cracked jokes and was sweet.

"You tried to take down a sixteen-ton truck!" he said to me in a folksy drawl. "I've never had someone try and take on my semi before!"

In one of the great miracles of my life, somehow, no one else was hurt. I felt overwhelmingly lucky. I also felt pain in my neck, and along my waist where the seat belt was. Police had been called, Adam had been, too, and I just sat there as the minutes passed, not sure if the shock preventing me from moving was physical or mental.

Then, from the corner of my eye, I saw Adam, with his strong Olympian stride, running down the ramp of the highway at God only knows what pace. He had parked his car off the road near the Murray exit and bolted about a quarter mile over to my car. I tried to assure him between my sobs that I was fine. The police showed up soon after, interviewed witnesses, and tried to tell me over and over again that everyone was safe, that it was going to be okay, that accidents happen.

As it turned out, the shock was mostly mental. I saw a doctor who examined my injuries. I had a sore neck from whiplash, and a bruise from my seat belt, but nothing very serious. The doctor prescribed some painkillers, and ordered me not to run for two weeks. Cap and Alberto were okay with this, and the irony was that the car-accident-induced time off ended up helping my Achilles injury heal. It took a car crash to really give that part of my body the break it needed.

The fear stayed with me longer than the physical pain. Adam did all of our driving for months after the crash. I couldn't stop replaying the moments of impact on loop in my mind, wondering, *Why, in this strange lottery of life, was I spared but my father was not?*

Kelly flew to Portland to try and raise my spirits. We were hanging out at my house one day when I got a phone call from someone at USATF with the news that Lauren Fleshman, a runner who had beaten me at Cross Country Nationals in New York and earned a Worlds spot, was injured. This opened up a place for me on the team. I'd be going to Japan with Adam in April.

I feel bad when any runner injures out of an event—I'd been there— but this was undeniably huge for me. I began dancing around my home like someone on *The Price Is Right* after winning a new car. A friend had recently stayed with us and left behind a case of beer. I grabbed one and pounded it. Then another. Then another.

"What are you doing?" my older sister wisely asked. "You're going to the first World Championships of your life and you're getting shit-faced?"

I puked soon after.

"Get it together," Kelly said.

In Fukuoka, Japan, in April 2006, I watched Adam finish sixth in the world in the 4,000 meters. *Sixth in the world!* It was an incredible race for him. When we went out for dinner that night, Alberto told him that second to Galen setting the junior national record in 2005, this was his proudest moment as a coach. Alberto got so drunk that night that he couldn't find his room at the hotel. A kind employee at the front desk escorted him to the proper door.

I raced the next morning and finished in 21st place, not near the podium, but it gave me exposure to competing internationally on a big stage for the first time, and a chance to suss out the pace of the top female runners in the world. Alberto wrote me a note after my race that said I was "gutsy." It was magical to be at a World Cross Country Championships, with Adam, coached by a legend, all on Nike's dime.

CHAPTER ELEVEN
Jetting

Coming off the World Cross Country Championships, I was healthier than I had been in a long time, running faster, and getting more praise from Alberto. On May 28, 2006, I set a PR of 4:07.50 in the 1,500 meters at the Prefontaine Classic in Eugene. On June 23, I finished second in the 5,000 meters at the USA Outdoor Championships in Indianapolis, running a PR of 15:14. Alberto had always been encouraging, but he started to express a new level of pride about where I was at, and excitement about my future. In turn, my own expectations and hopes of what was possible for me in professional running shifted in a positive direction. After slogging through injuries for so long, then getting in a car crash, I was ecstatic about the change.

Adam and I, both running well and making a name for ourselves as some of the most "rugged" runners in the field for sticking with the sport after so many injuries, began to travel internationally for races more often. The circuit took us to glamorous locales like Berlin and Brussels, where we continued to be asked if we were siblings (and continued to find the question hilarious). In truth, the day-to-day lifestyle was bare-bones sleeping in airport chairs in sweatpants, snacking from vending machines, staying in the tiniest and most basic of European hotel rooms—but it didn't matter. We were in the big leagues, racing in the same competitions as the stars of the Kenyan and Ethiopian national teams, who we revered, like Tirunesh Dibaba, Kenenisa Bekele, and Eliud Kipchoge.

Most of the races, like the Night of Athletics in Heusden, Belgium, were evening affairs. We ran under bright lights before packed houses. There was electricity in the air, and I loved the powerful sense of presence that came with the theater of it all. It felt to me like being in a Formula 1 competition, with my body and brain as the car.

It was also a joy to befriend other female runners, including

Alice Schmidt and Christin Wurth-Thomas, who I regularly saw at competitions—my fellow travelers on this strange trail. Everyone knew what times the other women were trying to hit. Before races, we'd be quiet and focused, but after we'd often celebrate together if one of us achieved a goal. It was easy to get invested in their success, especially when seeing up close how hard they worked.

When I wasn't racing, I was training. I logged about 65 miles a week, up from about 50 a year earlier, plus a daily thirty- to sixty-minute session of cross training. It was more than I'd ever run in my life. Even when I was doing something else, my body seemed to keep thinking about the motion of running, kind of like that sensation you feel when you step off a treadmill and your legs want to keep moving.

Being healthy enough to push myself to go faster and further was validating. I was fine-tuning my ability to recognize the difference between an injury and good fatigue, the line between "something is wrong with my hip" and "I'm sore getting out of bed." There was something a bit sick about being able to brazenly embrace the most obsessive aspects of my personality, but experiencing that tension with the dark space, the voices telling me to stop, pushing through, and coming out on the other side feeling stronger, gave me the sense of inching that much closer to my goals.

About 20 percent of my weekly mileage was done on treadmills, primarily the AlterG. Now these anti-gravity machines can be found around the world, especially in physical therapists' offices, but Alberto got one of the early prototypes in 2005, and the Oregon Project runners were among the first athletes in the world with regular access to one. He kept the machine in his garage while we waited to get proper space carved out for ourselves at the Lance on Nike's campus. Using the machine required wearing a pair of harness-like compression shorts that zipped into a "cockpit," reducing impact and allowing you to log huge numbers of miles with less wear and tear. As much as I loved running in the fresh air of a track or the open roads, the treadmill was a godsend, giving me and the other Oregon Project runners a great workout for the cardiovascular system, while sparing our joints. It allowed us to put in more miles than our bodies could have otherwise handled. The AlterG at Alberto's house was also outfitted with a cube around it that was similar to our altitude tent at home, pushing less-oxygenated air into the space so you could simulate running at higher elevations.

The wetsuit-like shorts that you have to use with the AlterG go over whatever running gear you're normally wearing. They're a tight fit and chafing is common. We only had one pair of shorts at the time, and the order of its use was hierarchical. First, Galen. Then Adam. Then me. Then the four or five other runners who were often around at the time. Alberto made a point of telling us he threw the shorts in the wash every night, but there was no way around the fact that each day, each successive runner was getting the funk-loaded shorts of all those who had used them previously. (Eventually, we got more machines, including on the Nike campus and at the Nike House, and our own pairs of shorts—which we took proud possession of and wrote our names on.)

In the fall of 2006, Kendall and Bret moved to Portland. Bret was a very good runner and had a six-month tryout with the Oregon Project. Kendall took classes to train as a masseuse. Bret's tryout didn't result in him getting a long-term spot on the team, but he got a job at Nike in sports marketing, working mostly on the Nike Cross Nationals, a series of elite high school running meets. His office was in a cubicle in the Mia Hamm building. It was nice to have family around.

———

After my PR of 15:14, Alberto and I set the goal of hitting the IAAF world qualifying standard time of 15:09. (The IAAF world standards are set and updated independently from the USATF Olympic Trials standards, and are typically faster, as was the case in 2007 for the 5,000 meters.) It was just a half second per lap faster than the time I'd already run. If I did that, and also finished in the top three at USATF National Championships in 2007, I would secure a spot to compete at the 2007 IAAF World Athletics Championships in Osaka, Japan. This was the biggest and most important event in track and field outside of the Olympics.

I hit the world standard in the 5,000 in a race in Liège, Belgium, though just barely. I went to watch Adam and Galen race in Heusden, Belgium, and then Alberto, Adam, Galen, and I went to a training camp together in Cologne, Germany. Galen, like us, was competing in Europe that summer.

As long as he didn't collect any money for prizes or appearance fees, NCAA rules allowed him to compete. He was coming off a strong if not amazing 2006 college season: he'd helped lead the Ducks to a Pac-10 Conference cross country title, beating out the Stanford Cardinals, who had won the previous six titles, and finished sixth in the 2006 NCAA Men's Cross Country Championships.

Originally, the plan was for us all to go from Germany to London to run the 5,000 meters at the London Grand Prix, where I'd try to lower my time even further under the world standard. However, the race organizers changed the women's race from a 5,000 to a 3,000 (while keeping the men's 5,000 in place), so it no longer made sense for me to go to London. Alberto began to look for another race I could run.

The fact that he would do this reflected a recent shift. Being in the Oregon Project reminded me of growing up in a house with five other siblings: we all had to compete for time and attention, and lately I had become the favorite child. Alberto was spending more time with me in workouts and on crafting my training plan than he was for Adam. Adam and Alberto had been having some disagreements, including over how to best deal with a lingering ankle injury that Adam was still fighting through. Adam liked Alberto and his workouts, but was used to asking questions of his coach and having a respectful dialogue, something he and Mark had always done in Colorado. When Adam asked similar questions of Alberto, about the how or why of his training plan, Alberto would respond by asking why Adam was "doubting" him and questioning the program.

In Germany, Alberto and I searched for a good use of my time. He glanced up from his laptop with a smile. He had found a race scheduled for July 26, four days away: the 10,000 meters at the Helsinki Grand Prix. Alberto said I should do it. I'd stand a chance of logging a qualifying time for World Championships in a second distance.

"No way," I told him.

I had raced the 10,000 meters only once and absolutely hated it. The experience still hung over me like a cloud. How could he want me to try again at that distance, let alone attempt to qualify for Worlds in it? We hit a local track later that day for a workout that Alberto said would prove to me that I was fired up and ready for the 10,000. Adam and Galen would go ahead to London, while Alberto and I would head off to Finland.

I didn't feel fired up in the least after the workout. Alberto didn't care. He signed me up for the race, and the two of us boarded a plane for Helsinki.

——— ———

The 10,000 meters is the longest and most daunting race on the track for good reason. Though it's twice the distance, it's run at nearly the same pace as the 5,000. It requires patience and sustained focus, coupled with the ability to switch gears and make a big move in the end, at the point when your entire body feels like a noodle.

The meet organizers in Helsinki placed me in a hotel room with my friend Alice Schmidt, an 800 meters specialist. The hotel overlooked a pristine park with a glimmering lake, where, the day before my race, I met Alberto for a shakeout. Afterward, Alberto talked to me about the race as I did my dynamic stretching routine that involved hip rotations. When I got back to the hotel, Alice said that she had seen me out in the park and noticed the way Alberto watched me stretch. She asked, "Aren't you un comfortable being alone with him so much?"

Wow, maybe Alberto was right, I thought to myself. *Everyone outside of the Oregon Project really was jealous. They just didn't get what we were doing. They just didn't get him.*

I took to the starting line the next day, absolutely certain that I wasn't meant to be there, barely understanding what a solid 10,000 meters time for me would even be. I was nervous through the first portion of the race, but as it wore on, I realized that I felt good. My confidence built lap by lap as I hung near the leaders and still had more in the tank. I crossed the finish line in third, happily surprised, and looked up at my time: 31:17.12. *Was that good?* I wondered. *What will Alberto make of it?*

I jogged a bit to release the lactic acid that had built up in my legs. It seems counterintuitive that after pushing your legs in a race, you still have to run further, but if you sit down, you'll feel miserable, like you can't even walk.

As I shook out my legs, trotting around the warm-up track, a fellow American runner named Jen Rhines came up to me.

"You're the second-fastest woman in American history," she said.

"In what distance?" I answered, dazed.

The 10,000! Obviously!

I had just put down a time that was 27 seconds off Deena Kastor's American record, and that was faster than my childhood hero Lynn Jennings's best time in the distance. Oh, *and* I had hit the world standard.

Holy. Shit.

CHAPTER TWELVE
Rieti

To build off my success in the Helsinki Grand Prix, Alberto signed me up for the Rieti Grand Prix in late August, an annual IAAF race in central Italy about fifty miles from Rome. Instead of running the longest distance on the track, Alberto wanted me to run the shortest distance in my competition arsenal, the 1,500. It wasn't my specialty, but with things going so well he thought I had a shot at hitting a world standard time in it, making it my third event after the 5,000 and 10,000.

In Rieti on August 26, the day before my race, Alberto and I went for some strides and a short workout. We were at different hotels—there was a fancier hotel where agents and coaches stayed and a less fancy but closer-to-the-race-venue hotel for the athletes. After the workout, as evening approached, Alberto came back to my hotel with me to give me a massage. I flopped onto the bed facedown in my shorts and tank top, looking forward to having the kinks in my legs rolled out and using the downtime to visualize and strategize the upcoming race in my head.

The massage followed a typical course for a fifteen-minute flush with Alberto. My shorts were pulled up high to expose my glutes. He started on my lower legs, slowly went up my calves, then the hamstrings. I was lost in thought about the race venue, my target times, and strategy in the pack when I felt Alberto's hand making its way higher up my thigh than usual. Then, without any words, warning, or explanation, his finger went into my vagina. Several times.

There is fight. There is flight. There is also another reaction people sometimes forget: freeze.

I lay there, completely stunned.

My mind raced, but my body couldn't move. Part of me expected a joke or comment of some sort about where his hand had gone. Maybe an apology. But he just continued on with the massage as normal. He massaged my glutes, then untucked my shorts. His actions and demeanor were as if nothing out of the ordinary had occurred.

"Goodbye," he said, wrapping up the massage. "I'll see you tomorrow." Then he just walked out of the room.

I stayed motionless on the bed, for how long I do not know. *What just happened?* my mind demanded. *Did he really do that? What do I tell Adam?*

And a fucked-up concern that I had, immediately after being violated, forever seared into my memory: he didn't wash his hands before leaving; I worried if they would smell.

What it meant was that I was worried about *him.* I started to question my understanding of what had occurred, and feel guilty for even thinking that he would do something like that on purpose. *It must have been a mistake,* my anxious, confused mind decided. Since it was a mistake, it would be easier to not bring it up. In fact, to not think about it at all. To put a lid on the experience that could not be opened.

As if I had pushed some sort of internal power button, I got up.

The next day, I went to the track. I ran my 1,500 meters race in 4:05.14, a PR and a World Championship qualifying time. Alberto and I were both thrilled.

Later that night there was a party for athletes, coaches, and sponsors. I waited for Alberto to come to my hotel room so that we could go to the party together, and he was late. When he arrived, his breath smelled like alcohol.

By the time we got to the party, there was hardly any food left or open places to sit. He got us two seats off in the corner. I looked around and felt the eyes of other people on us. I had this sinking feeling that they thought there was something going on between us. I felt dirty, small, like I wanted to shrink away, disappear.

I left the party with Alberto. He walked me to the door of my hotel room and said that he would see me in the morning. He told me to get some sleep, turned around, and went back to his hotel.

Early the next morning, we were to leave Italy. I continued to keep an airtight seal on the mental compartment where I stashed my understanding of the incident, convinced that it was a mistake. Outside the hotel, athletes and coaches clustered with their luggage. They told us the vans and cars going to the airport were running out of space.

"Just get in," Alberto said to me, gesturing to a car. "You can sit on my lap."

I did as he suggested, but then a sprinter quickly said, "Oh, no, don't do that!" I jumped off and felt ashamed.

Back in Portland, I didn't tell Adam what happened. I didn't tell the police. I didn't tell anyone at USATF, which was so closely tied to Nike. And I didn't give more than a second's credence to the idea of making an internal corporate complaint.

Alberto is a terrible massage therapist, I continued to rationalize, *of course he would make that kind of mistake.* Any notion to the contrary was on me, not him. Looking back on this, I try to give myself grace. Denial is not an uncommon response to trauma.

When it came to the idea of making a complaint at Nike, anytime that the seal on my denial cracked the tiniest bit and let in the smallest puff of air, I was quick to realize that even if I wanted to tell someone, I had no idea where I would go. This made it easier to turn back around and push any such thoughts away.

I don't remember there being a hotline or email address to report violations. I knew that Nike had a human resources department, but I had never been introduced to anyone there. As athletes, we were considered contractors, not employees, so we didn't follow normal corporate onboarding processes. Even employees later alleged in a lawsuit that Nike did not have regular training focused on sexual harassment at this time, though Nike has disputed this.

Furthermore, I hadn't met a single woman at Nike in a leadership position. For a company that aggressively courted female consumers, they had few, if any, women making decisions about how their business was run. The result, in my case, was there was nobody in power I could imagine feeling safe enough with to speak to about Alberto.

As an athlete with a growing profile and cachet, one might think I could just go straight to the top, even if that meant going to a man. But Alberto had a long-standing friendship with Phil Knight (who had stepped down as CEO of the company in December 2004 but was still its chairman). He seemed to have carte blanche over how the Oregon Project was managed. When we went over budget, Alberto returned from a private lunch with Knight in the Mia Hamm building on the Nike campus to tell us that all was well. The idea of my making any sort of personal appeal to Knight, or Cap, or any other male executive with oversight on the Oregon Project, felt absurd. Alberto was chummy with them all.

As far as I was concerned, it was all the more reason to take what happened, shove it in a box, and try to forget about it completely.

By the time of the Rieti incident, Alberto was beginning to establish a sense of "us against the world" at the Oregon Project. It helped bond us as a group of athletes and coaches, but it was also isolating. Though I had made some friends on the international racing circuit, Alberto didn't like it—he made it clear that he wanted his team to stick together and not talk to other people. The occasional strange looks and comments from other runners reaffirmed and amplified the message Alberto was inculcating in me, that we were a closely bonded "family" who others didn't understand, and we should keep to ourselves.

———————

The strange looks and comments didn't only come from Alice Schmidt in Helsinki, or the sprinter in Rieti who told me not to sit in Alberto's lap. At competitions during the summer of 2006, Alberto had to be on hand to help name all of the health supplements that I was taking, many of them per his guidance, while I filled out the standard drug testing paperwork. Other athletes were often nearby, and craned their necks our way.

Doping continued to be a hot topic, with rumors swirling every which way, and some were certainly directed at Nike. Just about anyone who made it near the top of the podium was accused of cheating by chemicals, including dominant East African distance runners, and world-beating American and Jamaican sprinters. Every runner who *wasn't* winning wanted to know: *What gave the person who beat me that little bit of edge that I couldn't seem to muster?*

More times than I could count, Alberto had told us at the Oregon Project to stop obsessing about doping or speculating about other athletes. He said that we beat people by working harder than them, slogging it out. It was a message I admired and exactly what I wanted to hear. Yet, there was no question that as hard as Alberto worked us on the track day in and day out, he was always interested in wedding his punishing training methods with what he saw as the latest cutting-edge science. One of his nicknames around the Nike campus was "Dr. Salazar." He always had something to say, and some solution, for whatever ailed you. In the summer of 2006, this all became pronounced.

In the basement of the Mia Hamm building was a windowless lab where Oregon Project runners would go for blood tests a couple of times a year. The results went straight to Alberto, and we'd only get feedback when he occasionally gleaned something he thought was important and sent us an email referencing results. This was his "holistic" approach, not just obsessing over speed drills and weightlifting programs, but anything and everything involving our bodies.

Testosterone was one of Alberto's focuses when it came to medical data, especially for Adam. He wanted Adam's levels to get up a little higher. On Friday, June 2, 2006, Alberto had written Adam an email about his recent testosterone levels, saying they were "still too low." He suggested Adam start taking a supplement called Alpha Male to improve them.

A couple of hours later, Alberto emailed Adam again, this time comparing Adam's testosterone levels to Galen's as a way of showing that Adam's could be higher. He also wrote that Adam should tell me that "a recent study sponsored by Victoria's Secret proves that buying their clothes increases their husband's testosterone levels by 50%."

We were at home when Adam got both emails and read them together. We cringed at the second email, and felt uncertain about the first.

It was a doping violation to have testosterone levels above a certain threshold. Adam was nowhere near that level, but the idea of taking a supplement to increase his testosterone made us a little skittish. Alberto had ended up easing our fears by explaining that he'd even had batches of Alpha Male personally tested at a lab to ensure it was clear of any banned substances. He gave the Alpha Male to both Adam and Galen to take, emphasizing that it was full of all-natural ingredients that raised one's testosterone. He also recommended a supplement called TestoBoost, which he said was "USADA approved," which I understood to mean blessed by the U.S. Anti-Doping Agency, the official regulating body in America.

He also started to give me "USADA-approved" supplements in the summer of 2006, not for testosterone but for "fat flushing." He told me that if I dropped a few pounds, I might pick up some speed. I wish that I could say that issues with weight loss were completely behind me, but they remained something I had to confront again as I journeyed further into my professional career. I was paranoid about being fat, I followed Alberto's advice, and I gladly took the pills. However, I wasn't worried that I was violating any rules. With these and all other supplements that caught Alberto's interest over time, he repeatedly assured me, Adam, and Galen they had been tested to be clear of any anti-doping violations.

I never failed a drug test, or worried that I was in the remotest danger that it could happen, but I was embarrassed at having to declare my supplements at competitions. They included a multivitamin, amino acids, and iron. Even though they were all normal, and all my tests came back clean, I remembered how much better it felt when I did one of my first USADA tests at the 2000 Olympic Trials, the year the organization had been formed, and my paperwork was essentially blank. I also remembered seeing Regina Jacobs declaring many things on her paperwork at those Trials. Three years later, she was banned from the sport as part of the BALCO doping scandal. (Jacobs has denied that she doped.) I missed the old me who had nothing to put down.

I didn't—and still do not—believe that Alberto rigged any of my supplements. From the outside, people saw that I had transformed from an injured, inconsistent competitor to one of the top American women, but my results had picked up steadily over the course of 2006 thanks to good nutrition, good health, and altitude training. I never minded drug testing—I took it as a chance to keep proving that I had an unblemished record, that I was running and training clean. Each test was another gold star, building a long-running pattern of them.

Yet, at the same time, instead of addressing any sense I had that others were pointing fingers at me, or responding to my embarrassment over taking supplements by telling Alberto I was tossing them in the trash, I retreated into the environment of seeming safety Alberto had created. It was a space in which it was clear that others were just gossipy and jealous. They misunderstood Alberto and his advanced, multipronged training methods, and by extension, misunderstood me. I followed Alberto's rule that no one inside of the Oregon Project could talk about any medical treatment or supplements that we used, and that we couldn't post anything about our training details or times online. Unwittingly, this also deepened the isolation and laid the groundwork fueling my rationale to later deny Alberto had ever done anything wrong.

By the end of 2006, I no longer believed I was just scrappy and hanging on by a thread, but that I could pose a real threat on the track. Thanks to the extra miles Alberto had me running, I had rediscovered my kicking ability from college—a burst of speed to overtake my competitors. I was loving the versatility of competing at different distances: my hustle in the 1,500 meters added scorch to my longer races, and the mental chess I could apply in my distance events allowed me to strategize smarter in shorter events.

In 2006, I set personal records in the 1,500, 3,000, 5,000, and 10,000 meters. Adam had set PRs in the indoor mile and outdoor 2 mile.

That was great, but Adam and I didn't want PRs. We wanted titles. Going into 2007, any confusion that I had about Alberto and what he'd done in Rieti was noise I told myself to tune out. After so many years of drought for Americans atop major distance race podiums, Adam and I were wondering who might be the first to reclaim glory for the USA. If we stayed focused, and stuck to the course we were on with Alberto, we believed it could be us.

CHAPTER THIRTEEN
Heart

In early 2007, Alberto said he was inviting Dr. Darren Treasure into "the Nike family" to up our mental training. Alberto described Darren as a sports psychologist, credentials that were repeated by media outlets. I was all for it.

As great as I was feeling about my 2006 results and training program, anxiety was something I still struggled with. I had worked with a couple of psychologists off and on for years. I credited them with helping me get where I was. They'd given me techniques to calm me down when I was spinning, including journaling, thinking about the people who love me, and visualizing places that grounded me, like the forests of Duluth. They'd given me a space to talk about all sorts of feelings, from my impostor syndrome and insecurity as a runner, to the loss of my father, to explorations of ways to keep my marriage strong.

In my initial session with Darren, I told him that I felt like I had pressure to perform for the first time in years, and it was overwhelming. I started to cry. I told him about the techniques I'd learned from prior therapists to address moments like the one I was experiencing.

"That's bullshit," he responded. "You just need more confidence."

"But thinking about pine trees, the love my family feels for me regardless of my results, their encouraging smiles and words . . . *works* for me," I told him.

I was a "world-class athlete and just needed to act like it," he shot back. It became readily apparent in that session and our next few that Darren was brash. His method, if you could call it that, was to tell you things that you may not want to hear, even if it stung a bit at first. It was a kind of tough-love approach to parallel the tough work that we did every day with Alberto. His mantra was that I needed to embrace being "Kara Fucking Goucher," and say things to myself like "These bitches can't touch me" and "I'm the queen."

Not only did I not see my competitors as "bitches," I *liked* most of the women I ran against, admired them, even. Those mantras didn't land with me. I found other power phrases as a sort of compromise, things like "I am a fighter" and "I deserve to be here." *Different strokes for different folks*, I thought.

Though he wasn't exactly my speed at first, I was eager for someone to listen, and I kept seeing Darren, telling him about losing my father, my stepfather, my relationship with abandonment, and myriad other personal details of my life on and off the track. If Alberto's approach to workouts was to dig deep, I assumed that was what was being asked of me, and other Nike athletes, in working with Darren.

Then, something unsettling began happening. Alberto started repeating back to me intimate facts that I had told Darren about my marriage, family history, and personal struggles. When I told Darren that I was nervous about a big workout that loomed ahead, Alberto came to me, frustrated. "You need to trust me," Alberto said. Darren also divulged confidential details about other runners to me.

Clearly, Darren was the last person I could confide in about what transpired with Alberto in Italy, and I steered clear of that. I also began to avoid talking too much about my relationship with Adam. In addition to telling me details about other runners, Darren would bad-mouth Alberto from time to time in our sessions. In several of our sessions, Darren also repeated a gross story about a young female student he said had come into his office when he had been a teacher, leaned on his desk lustily, and said, "I'll do *anything* to get a better grade."

I felt that what Darren was doing was not acceptable in most therapeutic settings. Yet, I found a way to justify it. I believed that Darren's version of therapy was working for me, and that even if I didn't understand the mechanics of it, it was done with a master plan to make me into a better runner. I didn't love doing brutal workouts on the track or box jumps in the gym, either, but they were necessary to make me faster. It was all part of the training, and the proof was in the pudding. I was running better, with more confidence, able to dig deeper in races. My mind felt freer when I ran, I was risking more at competitions, and I started crediting not just Alberto for that, but Darren, too, pairing them together in my mind as my essential coaching team—which was reinforced as Alberto brought Darren ever more closely into his inner circle and Darren started coming with us to competitions. On a more purely rational level, therapy is also costly, and here I was at the Oregon Project getting Darren's guidance for free.

We also had a new teammate in 2007 who I was thrilled to have join: Amy Begley.

Amy, a longtime friendly rival on the track, had called me in late 2006. She was my age and we both had been on the same Midwest Foot Locker team as high school kids in 1993 and 1994. She had been a four-time high school state champion in Indiana (winning one title in cross country and three in track), and then ran at the University of Arkansas. She saw how Adam and I had both turned our results around since joining Alberto's group and wanted to know about our experiences.

In the past, when I'd mentioned to Alberto the idea of having another female runner join us, he'd told me that he didn't want to. He said that women could be "a lot of work" and didn't want to unbalance "the chemistry of the team."

But as I talked to Amy, I thought about how lonely it was being the only woman in the group and how everyone could benefit from her joining. I told her that Nike and Alberto weren't perfect, but the times that Adam and I were running made it clear that the program was working.

I spoke to Alberto about it, telling him that I'd really like to have another woman on the team, while Amy talked to Cap. Cap then spoke to Alberto, saying he liked Amy, he thought she was tough, and Alberto conceded. Amy moved to Portland over the holidays in December 2006 and began working with our group at the beginning of 2007.

The big focus for me, Adam, and Galen in the summer of 2007 was the USATF Outdoor Championships, which would be held in Indianapolis in late June for the second straight year. Alberto and I decided that I would focus exclusively on the 10,000 meters there, as that had become my best distance. It would be too much of a risk to try to run the extremely taxing double—the 5,000 and 10,000—instead of putting all my effort into one event. Adam would run the 5,000 meters and Galen the 10,000. Finishing in the top three would secure us spots in the upcoming World Championships in Osaka, Japan, in August.

When we got to Indianapolis, Alberto took Galen, Adam, and me to the track to do one of our last workouts before the competition started, and Alberto called for a "weigh-in." He had me step on a scale in front of Adam and Galen and a couple of other people who were milling around the track. The number landed in the mid-120s, and I was praised. I was much healthier than I'd been at Colorado, but it was still close to the lowest that I had ever weighed in my adult life. Adam and Galen were weighed, too; their numbers were deemed acceptable.

This weigh-in was nothing new for any of us: Alberto was obsessed by the weight of his male and female runners alike, and used these public performances as a tactic to shame and encourage us to get and stay light. He was convinced that weight and speed were directly related.

I fell deeply into the fiction. I had started recording my weight on and off in college, but when I started being coached by Alberto, I became diligent about keeping a daily weight logbook. I recorded the date, my weight, the calories I consumed, and sometimes commentary to the side of how I felt about it. My intention was to be ahead of Alberto's weigh-ins, so I wouldn't be blindsided by whatever number the scale read. My body was performing at its best level ever, yet I took on guilt about eating "too much." Next to one weigh-in number and calorie intake I wrote, "PIG!!!"

In addition to the weigh-in, there was another occurrence that added stress to my 2007 USATF Outdoor Championships. Tom Wheeler showed up in Indianapolis unannounced, a fact made apparent to me when I heard him yell at me from the stands: "Kara! Kara! It's Dad!" I tried to focus on my race, and knew that I didn't want to see him afterward for a variety of reasons, including that my mom was also there.

Another person who was in Indianapolis didn't stress me out so much as puzzle me. Dr. Jeffrey Brown, who had been brought on in an official capacity by Alberto as a consultant for the Oregon Project, offering counsel via phone calls and emails and attending some of our meets and larger competitions, flew in from Houston to watch us compete. It was the second time in a span of weeks that I'd seen him at one of our competitions, the first having been at the 2007 Prefontaine Classic a couple of weeks earlier, on June 10. Most competitions have doctors on hand, but they're not typically endocrinologists.

When the time to race came, I aimed to put it all aside and perform. I knew that Deena Kastor would be running the 10,000 with me and didn't have the standard time yet, so she would run hard to get it. Because I had already hit it, my strategy going into the race was to let her go and stay at her heels. During the race, I held on to third place, following the plan. But with three laps to go, I felt that I had more to give and closed some time on her. I finished second to Deena's hard-fought first and while I felt like I still could have run harder, I'd done enough to make the team. Adam came in third in the 5,000 meters and Galen came in second in the 10,000. All three of us would be going to the World Championships. In a non-Olympic year, this was what Alberto referred to as the professional distance running equivalent of "making it to the Super Bowl."

We went out to celebrate, elated. Alberto gave us a couple of days off to recover, both from the running and ensuing celebrations. He beamed, never having had three athletes all make the team at once. For Adam and me, it was a dream come true, precisely why we had given it all up to move to Oregon and train with Nike, to soar together.

Adam and I eased our way back to Beaverton, and on June 30, a crisp Saturday morning, we were out for an easy run together on the wood chip trail on Nike's campus, when we heard sirens approaching.

We jogged over to the Lance just as an ambulance was pulling away. Galen was there, dumbfounded, the color drained from his face.

"Alberto had a heart attack," he said.

The three of us retrieved our bags from our lockers at the Lance and drove to the hospital. On the way, we started to piece together what had happened.

As Adam and I were enjoying our Saturday jog, Alberto was on the Nike campus with Galen and Josh Rohatinsky, a runner who had just joined the Oregon Project, hot off his success on Brigham Young University's track team.

At forty-eight years old and still running regularly with no known heart conditions, Alberto didn't come off as a high cardiac event risk to any of us. Later, Adam and I learned that Alberto had experienced some exhaustion and stabs of pain in his back and neck when we were in Indianapolis, but it hadn't felt extreme enough to worry him.

As Galen, Josh, and Alberto were walking along the Nike campus discussing lunch plans, Alberto fell down to one knee, his face turned purple, and he slowly toppled over to his side. Galen dialed 911. A former NFL player turned emergency doctor, Dr. G. M. "Doug" Douglass, who happened to be on Nike's campus for a football camp that morning, rushed to Alberto. A paramedic was there, too.

The timing felt like such a cruel fate. Here he was, celebrating having put three runners on the podium at the USATF Outdoor Championships, and then boom, this happened.

By the time we were able to see Alberto that afternoon in the hospital, he was talking, but on a loop. He asked us about our workouts over and over again. Some of what he tried to say was gibberish.

Seeing him in a hospital bed, hooked to pumps and beeping machines, in a gown rather than his signature sweatsuits, was disorienting, but also a relief. He was alive.

His family arrived. He stayed in the hospital for more than a week after his collapse and Adam and I visited him a couple more times. Phil Knight did, too.

In talking to folks at the hospital, we learned that, technically, Alberto had died for several minutes, and somehow had come back to life.

When the story of his cardiac emergency spread, Alberto's profile only seemed to grow in the running world. He was not only a maverick, brilliant coach but a superhuman marvel: he literally seemed to have cheated death. We rallied to support him and his family the best that we could. We were all motivated, driven by a sense of purpose that felt larger than us or our running. A shift transpired: we could take on even more pain and discomfort ourselves, if our coach could push himself after dying and coming back to life. Alberto even joked with us about that.

Less than two weeks after the ambulance rolled onto Nike's campus, Alberto was back with the team and ready to take us to altitude training camp in Park City as planned. I was shocked, assuming that given the gravity of his medical crisis he wouldn't make the trip. I wondered if it was reckless. I was also grateful. While he was in the hospital, I struggled with meaning and purpose. I thought about the loss of my father again, feeding into that same labyrinth of anger, sadness, and helplessness. I went to the Nike campus and thought, *How are we going to practice right now? How can we pretend to be normal?* I wondered: *What was the point of my running around in circles?*

It turned my mood around when he came back. I was ready to train harder than ever before.

CHAPTER FOURTEEN
Rules

Adam, Galen, Alberto, and I headed to Park City for our altitude training before Worlds. As usual, the four of us shared one condo. There were two master bedroom suites, plus a large living area with a pull-out couch where Alberto slept.

We pushed hard in the morning sessions and we ran in the afternoon wearing plastic suits—basically glorified garbage bags—that made us sweat our pits off. Adam wrung his shorts out after into a water bottle as if he had just emerged from a dunk tank. I never got used to jogging in a bag pooled with my own sweat, but there was a rationale behind it. The weather forecast for Osaka was to be humid and hot, and this would help our bodies get accustomed to the conditions.

Alberto was napping in the living room of the condo one day, so I was trying to be quiet as I went to the kitchen to get a slice of toast and a handful of chips, when something on the island caught my eye. A tube of AndroGel, a topically applied testosterone medication, sat out in the open next to Alberto's toiletries bag.

Because Alberto was a USATF-certified coach and athlete support person, he was not allowed to possess testosterone without "acceptable justification," according to USADA rules. Alberto told Adam and me that the AndroGel was for his heart. The tube had a prescription label and considering that he was coming off a heart-related hospital stint, we believed it. However, even if he did have a personal prescription for his own use, it was dangerous to bring it to training camp with his athletes. Like all other USADA code-bound runners, we had to file "whereabouts" information letting USADA know where we were at all times, and representatives could show up at any time and see it sitting there just as easily as I had.

Not long after we talked about the AndroGel, Alberto told me I should "not be alarmed" if I saw syringes in the refrigerator. They were for Galen's allergies, he said. Sure enough, the next time I went to the fridge, I saw a cluster of syringes with liquid in them, resting under the clear flap of the butter tray.

It was easier to believe the explanation than consider the alternative. In fact, it was the forward momentum of what I'd already been doing for years. I hadn't thought about it much since, but back in June 2005, we'd had our first encounter of this sort. A coach named Vern Gambetta, who had been consulting for the Oregon Project and had worked on some light training with me while I was dealing with my compartment syndrome, left the program, saying it was because he had seen an injectable form of the steroid prednisone in Galen's room, which was illegal for runners. Alberto dismissed the incident, saying that Vern had "gone crazy" and showing us a note he said was from Galen's doctor, indicating Galen had to be on pred- nisone (in oral form). We relied on Alberto's version, and now in Park City we again trusted Alberto and then put it out of mind.

One more thing happened in 2007 that rankled me, and especially Adam, but we'd also chosen to put it out of mind.

We had heard at some point in the year from someone who worked in Nike marketing that the NCAA was investigating Galen's amateur sta- tus. This came as no big surprise to Adam and me: we felt that Galen was treated by Nike like a professional, the same as Adam and I were, with tens of thousands of dollars of free gear, his travel paid for, and his coaching from Alberto covered. We even saw Alberto directly purchase groceries and meals for Galen, and Alberto told me on more than one occasion that upon graduation from Oregon, Galen would be "well compensated."

So, every day that he trained alongside us, we were witness to what we saw as a clear violation of the rules. We didn't necessarily think they were *good* rules—there was unquestionably something exploitative about the fact that NCAA athletes didn't get a cut of the millions of dollars that their athletic departments brought in, especially in the case of college football and basketball programs. But the rules were the rules. Galen was a high school phenom and could have decided to skip college, like LeBron James or Kobe Bryant had, or followed in the path of sprinter Allyson Felix, who went pro after high school but still earned a degree from the University of Southern California. I thought he may have been trying to have it both ways, choosing to be an NCAA athlete while getting professional-level support.

Alberto held a different opinion. He loathed the NCAA's amateurism bylaws, and to him, the fact that they were rules did not mean they should be followed. Given how many millions Nike had already sunk into Alberto's training program and its star, Galen, and how protective they were over their investment, it didn't surprise me.

Alberto explicitly told Adam and me that if anyone from the NCAA asked us anything about Galen or his "arrangement," we were not to respond. If they asked us whether we'd seen anyone purchase groceries for Galen, we were to lie outright.

I didn't want to get wrapped up in any of this. I really liked Galen. He was still like a sweet little brother to me and Adam, and he was running brilliantly. I saw how hard he trained and that he had a true love for the sport. His discipline and work ethic transcended that of people twice his age. And the pressure placed upon him, to restore an entire collegiate program to glory, was enormous.

Still, I had no interest in doing what Alberto had asked. To me, it was one thing if he and Galen chose to skirt the rules and lie, but I hated that he asked Adam and me to be dishonest on their behalf. Even thinking about it made my stomach lurch—Papa and my mother had instilled a hatred of lying in me from a young age.

For weeks through the spring of 2007, Adam and I drove onto Nike's campus and wondered if it was the day when NCAA reps in suits would be there, wanting to ask us a few questions. The day never came. As far as I could tell, the NCAA investigation into Galen and Alberto went nowhere. Adam and I never heard anything more about it, and the NCAA does not have anything about Galen or Alberto listed in their infraction notices. There are no public records indicating that he, Oregon, or Nike paid any fines, that Galen faced any suspension from competing or training, or Alberto from coaching him.

Galen continued to train as a professional while competing at Oregon afterward with one exception: he now used his own credit card to pay for groceries. But on multiple occasions, I saw Galen swipe his card only to have Alberto hand him cash on the spot. They laughed about it. It seemed to me they may have beaten the system, in plain sight.

Whatever did or didn't happen with the investigation, it hadn't seemed to affect Galen's running that year. His feet had been on fire through the winter and spring. On April 29, he'd won the 10,000 at the Payton Jordan Cardinal Invitational at Stanford, setting an American-born NCAA collegiate record for the event and running the seventh-fastest time in U.S. history at 27:33.48. Two weeks after that, he'd won the 5,000 and 10,000 at the Pac-12 Conference meet to help Oregon take the team title.

Now, he was going to the World Championships. He trained hard with us in Park City in July, and was primed and ready for Osaka.

CHAPTER FIFTEEN
Flip the Switch

We landed in Osaka on August 15, 2007. The World Championships would run from August 25 to September 2, with my 10,000 meter race scheduled for the 25th. Adam had been to an Olympics and multiple World Championships, but this was something much grander in scale than anything that I'd ever been a part of. When Adam and I received our credentials with our names and photos, I looked at him with an "Oh my God, this is *real*" face. I said hello to American national team athletes like Adam Nelson, Wallace Spearmon, Lauryn Williams, and Sanya Richards, trying not to make it obvious that I was in awe. They treated me as an equal, which helped to ease the butterflies dancing around in my chest.

Adam, Galen, and I did a four-mile tempo run on a nearby track and I hit 4:40 my last mile. *I think I'm in the best shape of my life*, I thought to myself, astounded.

The smooth sailing didn't last. While we were doing an easy run, Adam twisted his left ankle, the same one that he'd had issues with before. Then, I got a sore throat, and also had "acupuncture from hell," as I dutifully noted in my logbook.

We tried not to stress, knowing that each of us had competed through far worse. Alberto and Darren Treasure were with us in Osaka, and in a change of their usual hardcore tone, they told me to take it easy. I spent a day or two in bed on a diet of bad TV via a portable DVD player. When I felt better, I did a shakeout run, going over some of Osaka's famous bridges.

Galen had a medical moment, of sorts, of his own in Osaka. He kept wearing his garbage bag–like sweatsuit that we'd used in Park City. Alberto asked me to keep reminding Galen to stay hydrated and full of electrolytes, but he never seemed to want to drink water. On the day before my race, which was three days before Galen's 10,000 meters final, Galen wasn't feeling well and went with Alberto and Bob Adams, the team doctor for

USA Track & Field, to a local hospital where he received an IV infusion of saline. Alberto told me this when they got back from the hospital. It's unclear whether saline on its own is a performance enhancer—Alberto told me that after getting his drip, Galen "sprang out of bed and had so much life"—but WADA restricts saline IV infusions because they can help mask the use of banned drugs. Exceptions are made with a doctor's approval if you're sick. (Galen has denied that he broke the rules.)

My understanding, as Alberto explained it, was that Galen was severely dehydrated, Dr. Adams thought this was an emergency situation that called for such a measure, and wasn't suspicious of any foul play. I didn't doubt it.

The day of my 10,000 meters, I was physically healthy, but mentally panicking. Little things that shouldn't have been a problem were bothering me. I usually raced with my hair in a bun, and I had tied it the same way hundreds, if not thousands, of times before, but on that day I just couldn't get it to stay up. I had to settle for a ponytail that I was certain would cause me problems that night on the track as it flopped around in the humid air.

Before we got onto the bus to go from the hotel to the stadium, Adam told me to bring my medal stand outfit, the white-and-blue tracksuit with an American flag provided by Team USA's sponsor—Nike, of course—to wear if I finished in the top three. I rolled my eyes at him, certain he was pulling my chain, and told him "I don't have room for it in my bag." He threw it in his backpack.

Alberto and Darren tried to get my mind right on the bus ride. I had only competed in the 10,000 meters three times total, and was ranked in the mid-20s. They told me that I had "nothing to lose." They said I should stay on the asses of the top-ranked runners, not to give them an inch, and look for an opportunity to make a late move. "This is the time to take risks," they said.

Though the race was at night, it was sweltering as we got off the bus, the temperature even hotter than I had imagined. During warm-ups, I wore an ice vest and kept the intensity level lower than usual to try to stay cool. The other runners and I were summoned into a call room and then led into the stadium. I was overwhelmed by its size. Even though the crowd wasn't that huge, they were loud.

I looked at Alberto and had a moment of disbelief. Just a few weeks earlier, he had been technically dead and now, here he was, coaching me at a World Championships in a pre-Olympic year. It was easy to put any doubts, concerns, and unpleasant memories that I had about him aside. I felt grateful to be in Osaka, encouraged by such a legend before a championship race.

The starting pistol went off and the pace started off relatively slow, which meant I—and nearly all of the other runners—remained tightly packed in one big cluster. Seven minutes in, I was still in the middle of the main pack, but we were less than a quarter of the way through the race. The fans in the stands maintained a steady roar as the laps ticked by. Then about halfway through, Tirunesh Dibaba, the Ethiopian defending champion, one of the toughest competitors in the world and the favorite to win, began to grab her stomach. She fell back, got some water, then somehow surged forward and rejoined us.

I had been staying close to the inside rail, and as we got into the final quarter of the race, I realized that I was getting boxed in. With five laps to go, I found space to get to the outside of the pack, a position that would allow me more room to make a move.

Then Mestawet Tufa from Ethiopia collapsed to the side of the track. Elvan Abeylegesse of Turkey was in first, with Dibaba just behind her. I was in third, with four laps to go. Jo Pavey from Great Britain and Kim Smith from New Zealand were just a couple of strides behind me.

Then Abeylegesse made a huge surge, with only Dibaba going with her, breaking open the race.

I couldn't keep up with them, but stayed racing in third a little distance back. Smith fell off behind me, then Pavey edged ahead of me into third place.

I was tired. I was hot. I felt like I was going to die. But I hadn't left it all out there yet. I thought of the women in the race, and how one of our lives was going to change forever by making that podium. I thought about all of the training that I had done. I thought of Papa. I thought of Alberto dying and coming back to life.

In the final lap, I tried to calculate when I should make a move on Pavey, mixing math with gut feeling. *Did I have enough of a kick left to pass her with 350 meters to go?* No, was my feeling. I could do 200 meters. When I hit that mark, I went for it, and pushed past Pavey. She didn't fight me at all. I couldn't believe it. If she had, I think I might have pulled back.

Dibaba had sprinted by Abeylegesse on the last lap and opened a comfortable margin. They finished one-two. Giving it everything I had, I crossed the finish line in third and went bananas—screaming, crying, in a sort of delirium.

I could have coasted into fourth and it still would have been a huge result for me. Instead, I had called bullshit on myself midrace and proved that I had another gear. My senior year of high school, I had won the 1,600 meters championship with a monster kick like that, so I always knew that I had the ability, but it had seemingly gone dormant for a long time. Now, I knew that I had a switch I could flip, if only I was brave enough to dig deep and do it—and take the discomfort that comes along with doing it.

It was a huge win on more than just a personal level. I had ended the American distance running drought, becoming the first woman to medal in a distance track event on the world stage since Lynn Jennings won bronze at the Barcelona Olympics in 1992. And I had done it as part of the Oregon Project, marking its first big international podium finish. The gap between my achievements and those of my idols was shrinking. (In 2015, *Sports Illustrated* called my race "the first step toward the renaissance of U.S. distance and middle-distance running that is ongoing today.")

Adam had a smile that stretched from ear to ear. He jumped down onto the track and hugged me tight. As it turned out, the medal ceremony wasn't until the next day, so I didn't need my medal stand outfit that night after all, but it was his belief in me that mattered. (Never having been in such a position before, Adam and I didn't know how it worked: we assumed you ran the race, then stood on the podium right after, but for those late-night races, they do the ceremonies the day after at a saner time for fans to watch.)

Alberto was ecstatic. He guided me through the ensuing media and drug testing, and waited with me as I filled out the anti-doping paperwork that top five finishers were asked to do, and provided blood and urine samples. Alberto looked over at Abeylegesse, the silver medalist, and said to me, "She's dirty."

I shrugged. "Maybe," I said. I hadn't seen her run at all in 2007 and knew it was possible, but I had just won a medal. I didn't care.

"You're going to get silver," he told me.

By the time we left the stadium it was well after 11 p.m., and the only spot open for food was a little pizza place near the hotel. From there, I called my mom in Duluth. It was one of the happiest moments of my life, hearing her dancing around in her kitchen. She told me she had been watching on TV but didn't recognize me at first because of my unwanted hairstyle change.

When we finally got to the hotel, I was surprised to find USATF staff had stayed up waiting for me. They clapped and hugged me in the lobby.

Adam still had his race to think about and went to sleep, but I was wired. I kept opening my computer and staring at my photo on the IAAF's website. I couldn't believe that it was me.

The next day, I waited in the wings of the stadium for the medal ceremony with fellow Americans Reese Hoffa and Adam Nelson, who won gold and silver in the shot put, respectively. All of our drug tests had come back clean, including Abeylegesse's and Dibaba's.

Reese and Adam congratulated me as we waited for our names to be called and the podium music to start.

"You've never had a moment this big before?" Adam asked.

"Correct," I told him.

"Not even a national title?"

I nodded.

"Your life is about to change," he said.

Adam Nelson was right. In the early fall of 2007, life felt pretty surreal. After Osaka, people in Portland started to recognize me in the grocery store and offer up friendly waves as I ran the roads. Nike executives used images of me from the World Championships in advertisements. Though I had about a year left on the $35,000-per-year contract extension I had signed in 2005, other offers began to come in from companies that were willing to buy out the remainder of my contract from Nike. Cap and Alberto agreed to begin negotiations with me and my agent for a new deal to keep me on the team.

Alberto's profile as a coach was rising in tandem with mine as an athlete. In September 2007, Lance Armstrong came to the Nike campus to train with Alberto. Lance had announced his retirement from cycling in 2005 and now had his eye on triathlons and marathons. Alberto had helped pace Armstrong when he ran the New York City Marathon in 2006 and Armstrong wanted to take on the course again in November 2007 to raise money for his foundation, which later became Livestrong. Alberto and Lance—both of them famously brash and competitive—found a quick kinship. I had read Armstrong's 2000 memoir, *It's Not About the Bike*, and it was uncanny to know he was training under the same coach I had.

On September 17, Adam and I flew to England via Chicago for the Great North Run, the largest half marathon in the world at the time, with tens of thousands of finishers each year. This was a money event, not for medals or prestige, and as this was the first half marathon I'd ever run in my life and I wasn't expected to place very high, Alberto stayed behind. With my newfound fame, though, the meet director had offered me $13,000 to run the race, a number that made my eyes pop. I'd never expected to make that kind of money in a day. My agent had then made a deal on a cocktail napkin with the meet director that said if I won, I would receive $30,000— not far off from the annual salary I had lived on for years.

While sitting on the plane, I reflected on all of the incredible things that were happening in my life. I felt so overwhelmed, so appreciative, so in awe that my dreams were coming true, that I couldn't hold it in.

I pulled out paper and a pen and wrote a letter to Alberto.

Alberto,

Adam and I are well on our way to Chicago and I just wanted to take the time to write to you and thank you for all you have done in our lives. The past month and a half has been amazing for me. For years I have dreamed of accomplishing big things in running but my body or people around me were always telling me that it wasn't possible. After running the times I did last year I wondered if I would ever get better than that. After all, I set PRs in the 1500m,

3000m, 5,000m, and 10,000m. But I also achieved world standards so my old dreamer self started to dream big again. You have made me feel like it's not foolish to want to achieve high success in running. You don't tell me all the reasons why I can't do it. You tell me what it takes, lots and lots of hard work, but that anything is possible and anything can happen. I used to have such big dreams and goals and they were lost along the way. I was always hurt, competing against drug users, I was never going to get what I dreamed of. But you have enabled me to scrape away that negative thought and opened my eyes. I know that I need to train even harder, but you believe in the reality of my dreams. I don't know how I could ever possibly thank you for changing my life in such a positive way. I look up to you and your remarkable optimism so much. You are like my friend, father, and role model all in one. I feel so blessed to have you in my life. So blessed that you are OK after your accident. Your family is so lucky to have you in their lives, and Adam and I truly feel that way. I know that we will be family forever, but it's important to me that you know how much I appreciate you and all that you have done for Adam and I. You are the one that made me believe again, and it has changed my life forever. Thank you so much Alberto! I love you so much!

Love, Kara

CHAPTER SIXTEEN
Unstoppable

I was both intimidated and in awe of Paula Radcliffe, the woman I was set to square off against in the Great North Run, the annual half marathon in England.

The British athlete was unquestionably the best and toughest marathoner in the world. She had won the London Marathon in 2002, 2003, and in 2005 when she set the world record with a scorching time of 2:15:25. She'd also won the Chicago Marathon in 2002, the New York City Marathon in 2004, and the marathon at the 2005 World Championships in Helsinki. Paula always led, pushing the pace, so if you ran against her, you knew that it was going to hurt. When Paula raced on the track, the entire field would typically PR because she dragged everyone with her.

Paula had neuroma surgery in April 2006 and then became pregnant with her daughter. She'd started back training, but got a stress fracture in her lower back, so she hadn't been in Osaka. The Great North Run would be her first race in nearly two years.

My entire strategy was to run with Paula for as long as I could. The hilly course, which went point to point from Newcastle upon Tyne to South Shields, would be grueling, and lined with spectators screaming in support of their national superstar. I just hoped I could hang in there and give them a good show.

On September 29, the night before the race, event organizers hosted a dinner where I met Paula. I was too nervous to ask for a photo even though I desperately wanted one. The next morning, I shook out my legs at the starting line. Former England National Team and Newcastle United manager Sir Bobby Robson fired the starting pistol, and Paula took off with her trademark combination of power and ease. I put aside my insecurities, reminded myself that I had proven what I was made of over the last two years, and stayed with her. Around the seventh mile, I felt superb, and began to run ahead of Paula. Then I slowed down, telling myself I was insane for trying to best the marathon world record holder. My competitive instinct reared up, quieted those fears, and I decided to push again. I could hear Paula breathing heavily behind me. I didn't really know how fast I was running. I was shocked to be running in front of Paula at all, breaking *her* in a half marathon. That feeling only deepened as I crossed the finish line first.

My time was 1:06:57. It was the fastest half marathon in the world that year and fastest ever run by an American woman. It was also the fastest debut half marathon by any woman, ever. It capped off my dreamlike 2007 season.

I called Alberto back in Portland to tell him how I had performed and when he picked up, he said that he was out running with Lance Armstrong. He handed his cell phone over to Lance, who congratulated me personally.

I went to spend two weeks in Duluth after the race. Kelly said something to me that perfectly summed up how I felt after the Great North Run.

"You're not a flower," she told me. "You're a cactus."

Five weeks later, on November 4, Adam and I were in New York City watching the marathon. Thanks to Mary Wittenberg, CEO of the New York Road Runners, the organization that stages the New York City Marathon, we had the best seats in the house: spots in two separate open-topped press cars that drive the course with the runners, one that followed the men, and another that followed the women. Part of Mary's job is to lure elite runners to the starting line, and she figured that by letting us in the cars, we'd get a handle on the course, as well as the atmosphere on race day. It was an offer with no strings attached; if either of us liked what we saw, we could sign up to run the following year. If not, no harm, it would be a fun way to spend the morning and cheer for those taking on the course that day, including Paula.

Alberto had joked with me about someday becoming a marathoner, telling me that I would love it and he would coach me, but I rebuffed the idea. I had never been so sore in my life as the day after the Great North Run. I could barely walk up the stairs to get on the plane back to the States. I couldn't see myself ever being interested in racing twice the distance.

I was a track rat. The track is all about being sharp and tactical, knowing when to kick and accelerate and decelerate, and that's what I liked. I loved how it was like a human version of auto racing, with dozens of runners packed into a small space, trying to find an opening—and not get in a crash. I thrived in that claustrophobic environment, in the drama of duking it out in a stadium. The world outside completely dissolved when I was locked into the intensity of a track race.

The marathon is almost entirely the opposite. The moves between runners take much more time and even if someone makes a break, you can still win the race by sticking to your own plan. With the longer distance, you also have more time to be in your head. You have the space of the open roads, but also the loneliness.

The day before the New York City Marathon was the men's Olympic Trials for the marathon, and Adam and I watched Dathan Ritzenhein—a fellow University of Colorado runner who wasn't part of the Oregon Project but sometimes trained out of Portland—Ryan Hall, and Brian Sell land their spots for Beijing. Standing around afterward in Central Park, I saw someone approaching me and gasped.

It was Lynn Jennings.

I couldn't speak. She had exited the broadcast booth where she was helping call the men's Trials to come talk to me.

She introduced herself and made a joke about wearing too much TV makeup. She congratulated me on ending the American distance running drought that had started with her medal victory fifteen years before mine. I've had the good fortune to meet star athletes, heads of state, and many big personalities, but this was by far the most stunned I've ever been. I fumbled for words. Adam snuck a picture of me with her. I could have floated out of Central Park that day.

The next morning, I took my perch in the press car as it wound through the five boroughs. Watching the best runners in the world charging at me, as more than a million New Yorkers cheered and waved signs, gave me a totally different perspective on the race. I finally saw just how completely infectious and unique the New York City Marathon was—a race to match its host city, big, busy, audacious, inspiring, grand.

Paula proved herself once again that day, crossing the finish line in Central Park first in the women's field to capture her second New York City

Marathon title. I had never seen a runner work that hard, push so much, for so long.

Then, it hit me.

I beat her.

I beat her five weeks ago.

After the race, Mark Parker, who had been CEO of Nike since 2006, invited Adam and me to fly back to Oregon with him on one of the company's private jets. He had a quiet confidence and was clearly a track nerd. By the nature of his job, I knew he mingled with the biggest of the big, but he never bragged about it or dropped names.

"What a race out of Paula!" he said. "When will we see you run the marathon?"

"Next year," I told him, with stars in my eyes.

———————

In December, Adam and I were fostering a dog that we literally had found out in the wild and had named Bella. I was taking her on a run when she pulled me unexpectedly and I made a funny step that turned out to have torn my meniscus and cartilage in my knee. Doctors told me I would need knee surgery the week before Christmas. I had the operation on December 17—whatever my USATF insurance didn't cover, Nike would pay the rest. Alberto also gave me money to fly Papa and Grandma to Oregon. He wanted me to stay and recover, and knew it would be easier for me if my grandparents were there. My mom and Kelly came, too, and we celebrated Christmas together in Portland.

I ran my first post-surgery mile on December 29 and spent most of January healing and rehabbing on a bike and the AlterG, trying to get ready in time for the Millrose Games on February 1, 2008. The Millrose Games are an annual indoor meet that had taken place at Madison Square Garden since 1914. I was signed up for the mile and wanted this race to reassert that I had returned, healthy and fast, at the start of the Olympic year.

My rehab went well and Adam and I flew to New York at the end of January. After landing at LaGuardia, we grabbed a cab and were driving to the hotel when I looked out the window and was gobsmacked.

Along the road was a giant billboard with my picture on it. I remembered the picture having been taken in California, but it had been photoshopped to look like I was in a snowstorm. You could even see my (fake) breath. The billboard flickered by us, punctuating what had become a surreal, *Truman Show*–like era of my career.

An image of me from Osaka crying and holding the American flag was also appearing in Nike ads and seemed ubiquitous. My friends posed for photos with the ads and I laughed when they sent them to me, but I never totally got used to it. It was on the sides of buses, atop subway entrances, and on banners outside of stadiums. It was in the Nike employee store in Beaverton, and at the Mall of America. I liked seeing myself as a representative for female athletes getting more mainstream exposure, but with many of the promotional images that Nike produced of me, I felt like I was looking at someone else. The gloss was typically dialed up, the pictures were heavily photoshopped, and I was usually shown with a calm and peaceful expression—not how I ever looked or felt as I pushed to the finish line of a race. Whereas male runners typically looked tough and gritty in promotional images, I looked like Miss America in a crop top.

I won the mile at the Millrose Games while setting a new indoor PR of 4:36.03, brushing off the knee injury and proving that I was back in form for 2008.

There was more to celebrate, too. Contract negotiations with Nike were underway while I was at the Millrose Games and I soon signed my new deal, which would pay me $325,000 a year for four years, with Nike having the option to extend the contract by a year after that. It was more than nine times the amount that I had been earning for the past seven years. Adam was still making $90,000 at the time. My agent told me that it was one of the biggest deals he had ever worked on for a female athlete. It made me proud.

A month after the Millrose Games, something more important than running required our attention. Adam's father had stage 4 esophageal cancer, and his prognosis didn't look good. We canceled the rest of our indoor races for the winter and went on March 1 to stay with him in Arkansas, where he was living. Inspired by having been with Lance Armstrong in Beaverton in the fall, we wore our canary-yellow Livestrong bracelets, which supported Lance's cancer-fighting foundation.

Alberto put his faith in religion and sent Adam's father a special rosary. The gesture moved us. But then he asked us to return the rosary, telling us he had another ailing friend who needed it. Adam's father passed away at his home on March 8. Adam went out for a run and didn't come back for hours. While grieving, we discussed how odd Alberto's request had been, to send a rosary back while a loved one was on their deathbed.

Coach's orders, no matter what.

CHAPTER SEVENTEEN
Great Expectations

My new $325,000-a-year Nike contract had all sorts of stipulations and clauses in it that my previous ones hadn't. There were performance bonuses, ranging from $10,000 for smaller victories to $500,000 for an Olympic gold medal. There were also performance requirements. I needed to be ranked in the top 3 in the U.S. or the top 10 in the world every year, and make either the World Championship or Olympic team, depending on what year it was. If I didn't, Nike had the right to reduce my pay by a quarter for the remainder of my contract term. I was required to run ten USATF-sanctioned events a year—if I ran fewer than six, they could reduce my pay by 50 percent; if I ran six or seven, they could reduce by 35 percent; if I ran eight or nine, they could reduce by 25 percent. If I didn't compete for 120 days—whether due to injury or any other reason—they could "suspend," meaning withhold, my base salary completely. In all cases, it was completely up to them to decide whether or not to lower or suspend the pay: they had the option, but it wasn't automatic. Finally, there was a promotional piece: I had to make ten Nike-approved public appearances a year, which could be anything from a photo shoot for a magazine, to going to a race-related event, to attending a Nike store opening, though there was no specific pay cut stipulated in the contract for failing to meet this term.

I kind of liked the great expectations that were placed on me. Now that I had been on that championship podium, I knew precisely how electrifying that feeling was, and wanted to get back. The performance bonuses were a very nice, though secondary, incentive. But I also knew how incredibly hard it was to meet such high standards, and I worried about being required to perform.

Perhaps it's a bitter irony that in an endurance sport, those on the business side of things don't seem to pay much mind to a runner's long-term career. To have health and longevity in a running career, you need enough time to recover after races, but many runners have deals like the one I signed, forcing them to not only compete at a set minimum number of races a year, but stay at the top of the results table or risk being dropped. This new deal cemented my status as an elite athlete, but also opened my eyes to the way runners can be made to feel they must win by any means necessary: in short, to financially incentivize doping, especially if you think that the people that you're competing against are using banned substances and just haven't been caught yet.

Another eye-opener: Nike wasn't exactly doing me a favor by renegotiating my deal a year early. My new contract would run from 2008 to 2012, and would end just after the London Olympic Games. This was apparently typical. It would mean that if I made it to the 2012 Olympics and performed well, when I went to renegotiate another contract, in a strange and cynical sort of reverse logic, I'd have significantly less leverage, and chances would be good that my pay would be lowered. The thinking was that, having put so much into preparing for and competing in the Olympics, my prime would then be behind me, and I'd be *less* valuable to the brand. (I personally know of at least two Olympic medalists who had this happen to them after coming home with their hardware. You got paid on potential, not rewarded for what you'd accomplished.)

More disturbing yet was what felt like the racist message that came through during contract negotiations. The Nike executives openly discussed that I was not only the first "American" but the first "white person" to have won a distance running medal at a major international competition in years. I was told that I was more "relatable." It became hard not to see the amplification of my own image on Nike billboards and a certain version of my story as a "fighter" as a way to try and protect whiteness in the sport.

Part of me thought I earned that big contract after Osaka. I felt proud for helping break the mold for women's deals, setting a precedent that would help all women get higher pay in the future. But I also knew that I wasn't the most talented woman out there, and the reasons for the size of my contract had to do with more than just my times. The criteria for who won and who lost on the track were pretty straightforward. The criteria for who won on the dotted line of contracts were another thing altogether.

I knew it was wrong, and I should have spoken out about it at the time. I often heard announcers and meet organizers joking about not being able to pronounce the names of Kenyan and Ethiopian runners, while journalists often used phrases like "the Africans" to lump runners from a continent of 1.3 billion people together. Female runners from Kenya and Ethiopia won title after title but didn't get the attention they deserved from American sponsors, or from the American, largely white and male, press. Those who did somehow break through often had to be twice as good, and even then, their talents were routinely dismissed or ignored.

There were so many women of color who had the combination of searing talent and incredible character that draws fans into sports. Consider Ethiopia's Tirunesh Dibaba, who beat me in Osaka. Dibaba holds three Olympic gold medals and five World Championship medals, and is a women's rights advocate. Or, Derartu Tulu, who won an Olympic gold medal at the 1992 Barcelona Olympics in the 10,000 meters. She gave birth to a daughter, then won another gold medal in the event at the 2000 Sydney Games. She won London and Tokyo Marathon titles and when she was in the lead pack at the New York City Marathon in 2009, she dropped back with four miles to go to help out an ailing Paula Radcliffe, then somehow managed to catch back up and win the race.

I wish I had done more to support them at the time. As the years went on, I saw some women, disproportionately women of color, disappear from the sport altogether. They didn't keep running, nor was their deep expertise funneled into coaching, race organizing, agenting, or sports marketing. White male runners often seemed all but guaranteed plush collegiate coaching gigs, well-paid opportunities at major shoe companies, or additional chances to compete. The male executives who controlled the purse strings too often thought of reasons to say no or push back against giving women chances to build a lasting career, failing to see the female talent that was right in front of them.

CHAPTER EIGHTEEN
Trials

After Adam's father's funeral, we returned to Oregon and tried to channel our sense of loss into preparing for the Olympic Trials, coming up in late June 2008 on Nike's home turf in Eugene. Alberto had crafted an ambitious training plan for me to vie for berths in both the 5,000 and 10,000 meters.

The June 2008 issue of *Runner's World* featured me and Adam on the cover, me in a yellow sports bra with a face caked in makeup, Adam shirtless, both of us in Nike shorts and smiling on the Ronaldo field in Beaverton. The magazine's editors had photoshopped Adam's rose tattoo off his chest. The story was by the writer John Brant—who had written a 2006 book called *Duel in the Sun* about Alberto's mythic Boston Marathon win—and was headlined "Love on the Run." It was framed around the question of whether there was competition between us. One of the subtitles was "The Trials of a Running Marriage."

"Over the last year, the world has grown aware of Kara Goucher's beauty as well as her speed," read the article, accompanied by idyllic images of Adam and me jogging in Portland under pink cherry blossom trees, playfully cutting up veggies and chicken for dinner, and brushing our teeth together in sweatpants. "The photograph of Kara crossing the finish line in Osaka, her arms jubilantly lifted and sweat glistening on her long limbs, has been magnetized onto the refrigerator doors of young runners across America," it continued, adding, "Most glance at the picture for inspiration: some, perhaps, for other reasons."

This was a cover story in the biggest running magazine in the country making masturbation jokes about my athletic accomplishment. I was offended, feeling sexualized and subjected to a double standard. I had a hard time believing that Adam or any of the male runners I knew would have their hard work minimized in that way.

But there were bigger issues to focus on, one of which was that privately,

Adam and Alberto's clashing over injuries and training plans had gone from a simmer to a boil. Alberto responded by focusing even more on me and Galen, with Adam left a bit in the dust by his coach.

On Nike's campus, I continued to sit down for regular sessions in Darren Treasure's office, wondering aloud, "If my husband and coach are fighting, where does that put me?"

I often felt puzzled when I left therapy. Darren told me not to "become emotional" about what was happening, that I was "a big girl" and not to "feel sorry for myself." Darren seemingly not taking my concerns seriously only compounded my guilt and anxiety about feeling wedged between my coach and my husband.

Eight days before the Olympic Trials, Adam, Galen, Amy, Alberto, and I were in Park City for a final pre-meet altitude camp. Amy had qualified for the Trials and would be competing with me in both the 5,000 and 10,000 meters; Galen and Adam were signed up to run the same distances on the men's side.

Alberto, still preoccupied with weight loss, staged a weigh-in at the condo, this time asking Amy to step on a scale in front of the rest of us.

Though Amy and I had been doing virtually identical workouts at similar paces, Alberto had been making constant remarks comparing the two of us physically. One of his favorite refrains was to say that my butt looked "tight and firm" and Amy's did not. This was nothing new. I had gotten used to overhearing him commenting on my butt to other runners and Nike employees with the casualness of talking about the weather. He also made jokes about my having "no boobs." (He even said this to my mother once.) I laughed it all off, pushing it aside as I'd become so accustomed to doing with Alberto, acting like it didn't offend me. *I'm just being "one of the guys,"* I thought.

At the weigh-in, Alberto looked at the scale, then sized Amy up.

"You're fat," he told Amy. "You're not going to make the Olympic team."

Amy began to cry, and left the room. It was shattering.

Adam, Galen, and I stood there, silent.

I was a horrible friend in that moment. I let it happen. For the rest of the evening, and to this day, I wished I had told Alberto off, comforted Amy, or both. But I didn't. There's no excuse for that.

The next day, I tried to console Amy and tell her that Alberto was wrong. I said that he didn't know what he was talking about. She looked great and she was running strong. On top of feeling guilty about not having stood up to Alberto, I felt shitty about being on a team with a dynamic that allowed him to use his power as a coach to do something like that in the first place. I felt choked, deafened by my own silence. I had long justified some of Alberto's quirks and methods as being in service of the goal of making us better, but I couldn't see any coaching value in what he did to Amy whatsoever.

As I considered what had stopped me from speaking out, I realized how much energy I put into trying to stay in Alberto's good graces. I believed in the need to lift women up and be lifted up by them. It was that sort of unity and peer support that had made my middle and high school running experiences so positive, and that was part of why I was still in touch with many of my running friends from back then, including Amy Hill. We had each other's backs. I felt like a hypocrite to my running faith and my belief in the kind of sisterhood, literal and otherwise, that had propelled me so far in my own life. My silence was driven by fear. I believe that was the case for everyone who objected to Alberto's behavior but kept mum. Alberto was the power broker of all Oregon Project staffers' and runners' careers. He got testy when called out for having a third drink; I could only guess how he would react to being called out about sexual harassment.

I had been brainwashed by Alberto for so long, and become so inured to the status quo of male domination at Nike, that I couldn't recognize my privilege, my platform, my power. I could have said something. I didn't. This is how abusive dynamics often work: they cause you to lose sight of your own agency. This isn't an excuse, but it may explain why I felt as crappy as I did about not speaking up after what Alberto said to Amy. Deep down, I knew something fundamental was wrong. I'd submerged it out of sight for years, but it was beginning to bubble back up to the surface.

Before we left Portland for the Olympic Trials, Alberto had us turn off our cell phones and leave them behind, along with our computers. He gave us burner phones that only he and a couple of Oregon Project insiders had the numbers for. The rationale given was that we needed to focus, but the effect was to make me feel shut off from the outside world. Family and friends were distractions to Alberto. To me, they were a lifeline. Speaking to my family before races gave me courage and a sense of self-assurance, reminding me that I was loved by people regardless of how well I performed on the track. This helped keep my ego from swelling, calmed my nerves, and allowed me to run better. But of course, whatever Alberto said went, and I didn't protest.

Shortly after checking into our hotel in Eugene, I received a text on my burner phone from a Portland area code. The message said he was the reporter Ken Goe at *The Oregonian*, and that he wanted to speak to me. I responded that I was sorry, but I wasn't talking to any press until after my races.

I received a text back: "CONGRATS!"

It was Alberto. He told me that I had passed the test.

For me and Adam, Friday, June 27, was the culmination of eight years of work. The Olympic Trials were underway at Hayward Field, and the stadium was sold out.

At 8:40 p.m., Adam ran his heat of the men's 5,000 meters and finished fifth, good enough to move him into the final. As he headed off the track, I went on. We exchanged a quick hug and then I had to focus. At 9:20 p.m., I'd be running in the final of the women's 10,000 meters, the evening's headline event. We had moved more than 1,000 miles and changed our lives for this moment, to try and make this Olympic team, together. The amount of excitement and anxiety was bewildering.

The gun went off, and the spikes of the women's 10,000 meter racers thudded on the track. From the stands: a cacophony of cheering, feet stomping, endlessly rolling applause. I hadn't seen them before the race, per Alberto's rules, but I knew that my mom and sisters were seated somewhere along the first bend. I spotted John Capriotti in his signature spot, Cap's Corner, at the top of the backstretch of the track.

My race strategy from Alberto was to float along with the pack and with 1,200 meters to go, surge so that I could take the race. But something unexpected and awesome happened. About halfway into the race, Amy, who had qualified for Trials but had yet to run the Olympic-standard time, realized that the pace of the pack wasn't fast enough to hit the mark, which would mean that regardless of how high she finished, she wouldn't make the team. Sometimes, USATF offers a two-week grace period for someone to chase the standard, but in 2008, you had to hit it before or during the Olympic Trials meet. So off she went, charging ahead to take the lead about halfway into the race, and single-handedly upping the pace of the entire field. She pushed like hell.

With three laps to go, I overtook Amy and went out in front. Then, at the bell that signals the start of the final lap, a runner named Shalane Flanagan, who had made the 2004 Olympic team in the 5,000 meters, charged past me.

Shalane was precisely the kind of competitor I needed to run with and against if I was going to realize my Olympic dreams. I had first heard of her when I ran my fifth year at Colorado and she was a freshman at the University of North Carolina. She was already being talked about as a star at that time. I had beaten her in a couple of college races, but she was young, fiery, and clearly a force. Shalane had running in her blood; her mother once held the marathon world record and both of her parents were U.S. Cross Country champions. We didn't overlap much until she turned pro in 2004 and also signed with Nike, but she wasn't part of the Oregon Project, so we didn't know each other well.

There are different ways to win middle- and long-distance events. There are runners like Mary Cain, who can kick like hell. If you haven't dropped her by the end, she's likely to smoke past you. Then, there are runners like Shalane, who, instead of waiting to flip a switch at the very end, typically move earlier, or simply go flat out the whole time. Shalane was willing to hurt for as long as it took.

Adam and I are generally in-betweeners, though Adam leans a bit more toward the Shalane tactic of risking it all and pushing early into the hurt, while I'm more likely to ride the line for a long time, hang in races without necessarily shaping them, and look to make a kick in the end.

When Shalane passed me at the Trials, I didn't fight her because I knew that I was home, and I needed to conserve some energy for my 5,000 meters race in a couple of days. She cruised into first and I was right behind her in second place. I had secured it, my first Olympic team spot. And right behind me in third place was Amy Begley, who pulled off a sprint fit for Hollywood in the last 800 meters to come in under the Olympic standard she needed to make the team. She had bested her previous PR by more than 22 seconds. The three of us were going to Beijing.

When I think of the grit and magic that Olympic Trials can bring out, I think of Amy's performance. Unbeknownst to the fans watching that night in person or on TV, Amy making that team was a powerful rejection of Alberto's doctrines. The writer Anaïs Nin had it right when she noted that "shame is the lie someone told you about yourself." Amy made her own destiny that wasn't part of the coach's plan. Alberto and others tried to take credit for the outcome, but all the glory of that race belongs to Amy alone.

She did it in spite of negative coaching. Not because of it. Moments like these were why even when this sport broke my heart, I couldn't turn away.

June 30 was a mirror image of June 27: my heat in the 5,000 meters was at 8:50 p.m., and Adam's final in the 5,000 was at 9:40 p.m. I won my race and secured my place in the final, which would be four days later. As I came off the track, Adam came on.

Alberto and Adam had discussed his strategy going into the race. Because he had battled injuries, Adam hadn't yet hit the Olympic standard for the 5,000. That's part of why Alberto advised Adam that if by the final three laps, he wasn't under Olympic standard pace, he should drop out and let someone else take it so that Adam could focus on making the team in the 10,000 meters.

With two laps to go, Adam was in fifth place and not on pace to hit the standard. Alberto yelled at Adam to stop. Adam heard him, stepped off the track, and did not finish. I saw the logic in Alberto's coaching decision and thought that his intentions were good. But it gnawed at Adam as a competitor. Dropping out in an event he had competed at in the 2000 Olympics didn't sit well with him.

For my 5,000 meters final on July 4, I wanted to win and do it by going "fully nuts fast," as I would describe it, in the last 200 meters. Put another way, all my competitors would see at the end of the race would be "elbows and assholes," as my friend's dad used to say.

I did precisely as planned and won the race in a sprint finish. Kelly later said that she damaged her vocal cords because she was screaming so loudly from the stands. I'd officially done it, qualifying for the Olympics in not one, but two events.

I could barely catch my breath before Adam went on the track for the men's 10,000 meters final. Alberto told Adam not to go with Galen, who he wanted to be in the lead pack, but sit back and wait for people to fall apart. Early in the race, Galen, three-time U.S. champion Abdi Abdirahman, and Jorge Torres made a break. Alberto yelled at Adam not to go with them.

That ended up being a big mistake. Those three kept getting further ahead, while Adam was stuck in a distant fourth. The adrenaline from my win went *poof* in the instant that it became clear the race was slipping away from Adam. He ended up finishing seventh. Our dream had been to go to the Olympics together and that clearly wasn't going to happen. In a few minutes, I would have to face a press eager to ask me about my big win in the 5,000 meters when all I could feel was my heart breaking for Adam, for both of us.

Rubbing salt in the wound was that Galen, still in college, finished second. Alberto was elated, celebrating me and Galen securing our spots to Beijing, while Adam fought back tears. He wondered what would have happened if he had gone for it. He felt like he was never given the shot.

Eight years earlier, Adam had won the 5,000 meters at the Olympic Trials and I was the one crying in the shower because I didn't want him to see me. We had been through injuries that nixed our chances in 2004, then fought so hard to rebuild for the last four years. Now everything was reversed, I was triumphant, and Adam was gutted with loss. The mixture was intense.

Galen and I were heading to drug testing, which was in a building near the track, when we saw Adam angrily confront Alberto just outside. He told Alberto that he felt like Alberto didn't care about coaching him anymore, that he had set him up to fail. He had given him a losing strategy.

Alberto was cold; he didn't even say he was sorry that it hadn't worked out. I didn't understand why he wouldn't at least mourn a bit with Adam, or encourage him to focus on Worlds, the London Olympics in 2012, or shifting to marathoning. Even though Adam had lost his composure, it was obvious there was some truth in what he was saying.

Eventually, Adam apologized, both in person to Alberto and by writing him a letter. They hugged it out and agreed to let it all go. I thought it was over after that, but Alberto continued to bring up that outburst as an example of how Adam didn't care about the team.

My birthday was just a couple of days later. Adam and I gathered with our families and close friends in Portland, who I finally got the chance to see after the ten days of the Trials were over and Alberto allowed it. I wanted to party my ass off. I also wanted to cry with Adam.

At the end of July, Amy, Galen, Alberto, and I went to Houston to train in the heat for a week. Adam came to visit a few days after we got there. The expectation was that Beijing would be humid like Osaka, which would make for a slower race. We worked on building strength and having a good kick for the end to give us power in the final laps.

On August 5, Amy, Galen, and I flew to San Francisco for processing, where the United States Olympic Committee (USOC) gives you your gear for hanging out in the village and the opening and closing ceremonies, some final pep talks, and a briefing that kind of has a freshman college orientation mood to it.

From there, we flew across the Pacific to China. My Olympic dreams were coming true.

CHAPTER NINETEEN
Beijing

Going to the Opening Ceremony and seeing the torch lit in person had always been near the top of my Olympic fantasies, and it didn't disappoint. The Beijing Olympics were the most expensive Games put on to date. The ceremony was at the glistening new Bird's Nest stadium and involved 15,000 performers and a dazzling array of fireworks. Jason Kidd, LeBron James, and Kobe Bryant were there. President George W. Bush, his father, President George H. W. Bush, and First Lady Laura Bush, all runners themselves, walked over to me and asked if I was competing in track. It didn't matter how I voted; having a sitting president of the United States making small talk with me was a thrill-inducing experience. We had been instructed by USOC officials not to stop to take individual photographs, but the Bush family offered! I couldn't help myself.

The Parade of Nations, when the athletes from each country strut through the stadium, involved several hours of waiting for our turn in a gymnasium-like room, while wearing thick polyester-blend blazers. It took so long that some athletes had pee bags, as in, bags they urinated in and discarded somewhere clearly not far enough away, if the odor was any indicator. Others just peed right out in the open. Still, nothing could knock my Opening Ceremony experience. I got emotional watching the Olympic gymnast Li Ning float through air before igniting the torch in a swirl of fire as the music swelled and the audience screamed. I'd really made it.

At first, the Olympic Village brought to mind the dormitories at the University of Colorado in a good way. There was a massive dining hall in the center with just about every food that you could imagine and vending machines with unlimited Gatorade. I saw Venus and Serena Williams and Michael Phelps walking around (and freaked out). It was like a model United Nations for sports nerds, the biggest names from around the world, draped in flag-themed sweatsuits, a symphony of languages, everyone positively giddy just to be there.

But as the Opening Ceremony faded and the competition began, nerves and anxiety began to replace the awe, and the Village started to feel isolating. Alberto and Darren had discouraged me from requesting Amy as a roommate, telling me that she would be distracting and that I didn't need a friend—I needed to be focused. Adam came to Beijing, but he wasn't allowed in the Olympic Village at all. Although I did end up meeting a few people, I'm pretty shy. I would have liked to have people I was close to around for support. As the days rolled by, I felt increasingly overwhelmed.

The mountain of self-esteem that I had been working to construct over the previous two years felt like it was eroding as my first race grew nearer. *What am I doing here?* I wondered. I looked around at the other athletes and asked myself if I was worthy of being among them.

I arrived at the sold-out Bird's Nest stadium on August 15 for the 10,000 meters final with these thoughts plaguing my mind. (Mercifully, there were no heats in the 10,000.) There were 80,000 screaming fans in the stadium, by far the largest audience of my entire career.

Alberto arrived late, compounding my anxiety as I tried to kill time in the call room by the track. It was humid, as we had expected, though not as bad as Osaka. I cried as I warmed up. This was my lifelong dream, and all I could think about was how out of place I felt.

Adam came by the warm-up track on his way to his seat in the stadium. It was comforting to see his face, but he was on the other side of a big fence, so we couldn't hug or touch. Once I entered the stadium, I couldn't locate Alberto, Adam, or my mom. I couldn't get recentered. I could hear my heart palpitating, even in the din of the Bird's Nest. It was my Olympic debut, but I felt like I was back in Duluth trying to control a panic attack before a high school race.

We lined up at the starting line. With the pop of a pistol, we were off.

Holy shit, I thought, not just because of the spectacle of being in an Olympic final—the flash of cameras, the roar of fans, the blare of the announcer calling my name in front of the world—but because the pace of the first lap was breakneck. Alberto, Darren, and I had thought it would be a "sit and kick" race. I was already grabbing the bumper of a car going highway speed, holding on for dear life. All I could think was that I had been studying for the wrong test.

Lornah Kiplagat from the Netherlands took the race out hard. About halfway through, Tirunesh Dibaba and Elvan Abeylegesse, the women who had finished one-two ahead of me in Osaka, pulled to the front. Shalane Flanagan positioned herself in third, behind Dibaba and Abeylegesse.

I saw their backs getting further and further away from me. I felt my fight slipping away, too.

I looked up to the jumbotron and saw Shalane win the bronze. There was an American distance runner living out her Olympic dream. But it wasn't me.

I finished 10th.

The numbers told the story. In the end, it was the second-fastest women's 10,000 meters ever run. Dibaba and Abeylegesse finished first and second, just as they had in Osaka, with Dibaba setting a new Olympic record of 29:54.66. The fastest time I'd ever run before the Olympics was 31:17, in Helsinki. I had won a bronze medal in Osaka by running 32:02. I made the Olympic team in Eugene by running 31:37. In Beijing, I ran 30:55, my new PR, but I still finished 10th. Shalane took the bronze by running 30:22, which was nearly *a minute* faster than any 10,000 meters time that I had ever logged before the Olympics. Amy finished 26th.

So, though I'd run the fastest that I ever had in my life, I still felt like a total loser.

I made my way from the track to the back of the stadium, spent. My limbs felt like Jell-O. On my face, it was hard to tell where the sweat ended and the tears began.

Alberto was waiting for me at the warm-up area.

"You're not a track athlete," he told me. "You're not fast enough. You need to start training for the marathon."

My 5,000 meters heat was four days away. That wasn't what I needed to hear. I was the current American champion in the distance, and he had already written me off. As I worked to catch my breath, he went on to say that he was doubting my abilities; he wasn't even confident that I was doing the best that I could. Darren was there, too, and took it a step further, saying "You quit."

My heart was completely broken and it felt like Alberto and Darren were stomping on the pieces. I asked Alberto if I should even run the 5,000 meters, the Olympic race I had worked my whole life to qualify for.

"Yeah, yeah," Alberto said dismissively.

The next day, I packed my bags and left the Olympic Village. I called Adam and told him I was coming to stay in his hotel. "I can't do this," I said. I got in a cab and I gave the driver the hotel's address, but we got lost. I spoke zero Mandarin and had no handle on Beijing's geography.

I got out and looked around the streets, unable to read anything, then called Adam sobbing and told him that I was lost. Somehow, he found me and we headed to the hotel, together.

Once we got to our room, Adam pumped me up. "You *can* do this," he said. His belief in me was a saving grace. He helped me shut down the negative self-chatter fueled by what Alberto and Darren had told me.

For the 5,000 meters heat the evening of August 19, I was emotionally drained and still feeling the fatigue in my legs from the 10,000. But I ran 15:00.98 and earned my spot in the final.

In the meantime, on August 17, Galen had run in his 10,000 meters final. He finished 13th but set his personal best time for the season in the process, 27:36.99. Alberto had hoped for a better finish, but wasn't disappointed in him like he was in me: Galen was so young, and this was "just the beginning" for him, Alberto said. Kenenisa Bekele took gold in Galen's race and set a new Olympic record, just like his Ethiopian compatriot Tirunesh Dibaba had done in my race.

My 5,000 meters final on August 22 turned out to be one of the strangest races I'd ever run. The pace was so slow that the audience started booing at us. With five laps to go, I moved into second and then the real race began. I told myself *Just hang in there*, that I knew how to close, but I didn't totally believe that I could hold on.

Don't quit, don't quit, don't quit, don't quit, I kept repeating.

But I got outkicked. Dibaba won again, her second gold medal, completing the grueling 10,000-5,000 double. Even after running one of the fastest final 800 meters of my life, I finished 9th. Shalane was right on my tail and finished 10th.

At least this time, I didn't feel like I was in someone else's race. Adam was proud of me and noted how fast I'd closed out those last 800 meters. There was nothing more that I could have done and I had rebounded from low morale to give it my all.

Mark Parker invited Adam and me to join him and his wife and son on a private tour of the Great Wall of China. Then, he would fly us all back to Portland on a Nike jet, along with Dr. Brown, who had come to the Olympics in his role as a consultant working with Alberto, and who was friendly with Mark because he treated a member of Mark's family. This was a bigger jet than the one he'd flown us on after the New York City Marathon. (I'd heard rumors that it had a gold toilet, and got the chance to confirm its existence.) Mark knew that I was bummed about my performance, and these gestures to try to make my experience end on a high note were kind.

I left China believing that my failure to medal mattered more than the satisfaction of making my dream of competing at the Olympics come true. By definition, most people who compete at the Olympics leave empty-handed. Still, there was a funk hanging in the air for me afterward.

There wasn't much time to stew in the feelings of coming up short, because in just eight weeks, I was slated to make my marathon debut in New York City.

Whether it was something to look forward to or to fear, I wasn't sure.

I had never run a marathon in my life.

CHAPTER TWENTY
"Queens Girl"

Before the wheels of the Nike corporate jet touched down in Portland, Alberto had completed his training plan for my marathon debut. As he'd won the New York City Marathon three times in a row, it was an event close to his heart. I was the first woman from the Oregon Project he would coach in the event, and the first he saw as having a shot at winning.

After a week off to recover from the Olympics, our training began. He increased my weekly mileage from 85 to 100 miles for five weeks, which was a new high-water mark for the most that I'd ever run. It brought me confidence; when I doubted whether I could run the marathon, I was able to remind myself that I already was running about four of them a week.

The site of our workouts shifted from the track to the roads, with Alberto biking alongside me with his stopwatch in hand on runs of 18 miles or longer. Marathon training is all about being on your feet as long as possible. The long run is the focal point, which for me would eventually be up to a 23-miler with hills. On the long run you kind of float along for 20 miles then bring the heat, trying to close out fast, seeing what your body is capable of when pushed to an extreme. As much as I had loved the track, pounding out the miles on the Beaverton roads and up the northeast hills to Alberto's house reminded me of how I started: jogging in the fresh air of Duluth through residential, woodsy neighborhoods. Now, I just had Alberto barking out splits next to me.

Prior to marathon training, I always listened to music during my long runs. But since headphones are prohibited in races, I had to get more comfortable with being in my own head for hours at a time. By pushing through the long runs without music, I could feel my tenacity increase. It marked a mental shift for me, knowing that I could stay calm and focused without an aid.

The very first time we ran to Alberto's house, around the 16-mile mark, he pulled a weighted vest out of his backpack.

"Put it on," he told me.

I wore it for three miles, uphill.

Then, I threw it off on Alberto's yard and ran three more miles as hard as I could on a flat asphalt loop nearby.

After getting over the shock of the weighted vest, I ended up enjoying the workout. I liked the challenge of the extra pounds, then the rush of freedom with releasing it and trying to see what kind of rocket boosters I had left. I was seeking that edge, that feeling I had first discovered running with Papa as a six-year-old testing out the extreme end of my body's capabilities. After the run, I jumped in Alberto's pool and aqua jogged to help cool down and flush out the lactic acid. He then got me a sandwich, which I ate during my massage.

This time it was Al Kupczak doing the body work. Al had worked with the Oregon Project in the past and recently moved back to Portland to become a more regular member of the team in 2008. He would come to big competitions and help with massages after bigger workouts like the one I'd just done. I welcomed the expertise. But Alberto still massaged athletes, too. Once, he gave me one on the bed in his primary bedroom and his wife walked in. I felt incredibly awkward.

Yet, mostly what I felt during these weeks of training was that the marathon was a fresh event in which I had no prior history, a chance at reinventing myself inside and out as a runner.

I also got my introductory course in the behind-the-scenes pay negotiations tied to road races. Large races, especially marathons, pay appearance fees to draw elite runners, as well as prizes for those who finish up top. I received $175,000 to start at my first New York City Marathon in 2008 from the New York Road Runners, plus other bonuses from sponsors. Nike had bonuses for time and podium finishes. One good marathon and I could easily walk away with more than my yearly contract salary. (Allegedly, men often received more money, which would be no big surprise; I heard that a male runner who was talented but had not medaled on the track at Worlds received $200,000 for his debut.)

As athletes, Adam and I felt a consciousness around age, how relatively small the window we had for doing the job that we loved really was. We looked at this $175,000, and the rest of the money we earned, not as annual income, but as a lump to throw in our coffers that we would try and make last as long as humanly possible. We knew that we would never make this kind of money again, so we saved, saved, saved, planning to put it toward paying for a house and potential child care costs in the future.

In 2008, I was outearning Adam by a significant clip, a reversal from when we first got married and indicator of our changing fortunes. There I was competing in two Olympic events in China while he was mourning the loss of his dream. And then, instead of returning to our shared training schedule and routine when we got back home, I was off doing my own thing on the open roads. A crack in our relationship seemed to expand, precisely when we needed our connection the most. With his injuries, it was unclear what his path would be. Adam began to see a therapist, with whom he discussed issues from his childhood, the Olympics, and the loss of his father.

Alberto, Adam, and I flew to New York on Wednesday, October 29, to get settled and participate in some prerace events, with the marathon to be held on Sunday.

Alberto checked me into the race hotel, the New York Hilton Midtown on Sixth Avenue, under the alias "Rachel Montgomery" (his reasons for choosing that name unknown), lest running fans or competitors try to track me down and disturb my sleep with a call in the middle of the night. Adam and I thought this was silly, especially in a place like New York City. Maybe it was part of Alberto's mental preparation before the race: he believed I could and should win the marathon, and by acting like I was a celebrity, perhaps he thought I'd live up to the billing.

It didn't work. Despite painting my fingernails black in an attempt to create a visual reminder that I was tough, I was extremely nervous about the race, and felt burdened by the weight of his expectations. There was a lot of talk about whether I would break Deena Kastor's American course record, which would also mean breaking the American debut marathon record. Alberto tried to assure me that my preparation had gone perfectly. He told me to believe in him and the decisions that he had made. The strategy was not to give Paula Radcliffe an inch, to follow her because she knew what she was doing and would set the pace and tone for the race.

In the dark of early morning on marathon Sunday, I bundled up in layers and got onto the bus that shuttled the elite racers from the Hilton to the windy, chilly starting line in Staten Island. It was a funny scene, really, a gaggle of professional athletes being well-wished by their coaches, kind of like parents putting their kids on a school bus. Alberto had gone to a store the night before and bought me a comforter that I could wrap around myself in the athlete tent. He had also left a note in my bag that said I should have faith. That I was ready. Adam, becoming the Abigail Adams of my life, said that he would see me at the finish line, and left written words of encouragement tucked into my shoes.

On the bus my nerves felt so frayed that my eyes started to well up. Paula—who I'd become friendly with over the course of the year—noticed and came to sit by me, chatting with me the whole way to help me calm down. She gave me tips about the perfect time to leave the tent and begin warming up.

I followed her advice. At the starting line, I jogged in place and stretched in my white tank, black compression sleeves, and black running shorts, as the TV cameras rolled by. I thought about how I hadn't really had the proper amount of time to train for this. I still wasn't even sure if I could run the entire distance. But I reminded myself what Papa had told me on a phone call a few days before: "You can do this, kid." Those were the words I needed to channel.

As soon as the air horn went off and Mary Wittenberg's voice blared through the speakers, I charged ahead with the other elite women. Paula took the lead right away, and stayed there.

The first mile of the course is uphill crossing the Verrazzano-Narrows Bridge, and we went through it in 6:30, slower than I had anticipated. I remember thinking, *The pressure's off. There's no way that I can break Deena's records now.*

Because the elites start early, before the other 38,000 runners, the cheering squads were still assembling during those first few miles and the roads felt open, quiet, even a bit isolated. This was still New York, though, so the noise was never far off: choppers hovered overhead and police accompanied us on their motorcycles with the blips of their sirens clearing the way.

I cruised with Paula through the 12 or so miles in Brooklyn, running north through the neighborhoods of Sunset Park, Park Slope, Fort Greene, Clinton Hill, Williamsburg, and Greenpoint, the last in Brooklyn. Then we entered Queens.

Paula led a surge, and I stuck with her. We were running fast now, and I could already feel the lactic acid building up in my legs. Alberto had told me that I wouldn't feel anything like that until 20 miles in, so this sensation coming earlier made me nervous.

God, I'm so tired, I thought.

I was running so close to Paula that she scolded me. She was right; I was on her tail to the point that when she tossed a discarded nutrient gel packet, it hit me. There were more mishaps at the rehydration stations: when I went to grab a water bottle it slipped out of my hands, and I dropped an F-bomb. There were cameras nearby and I wondered if it would be on national television.

I dropped back to fifth or sixth place, feeling completely in over my head. There's a saying about marathons that they really begin at mile 20, but I was many miles from that, with bridges, hills, and strong headwinds remaining in my way. One of the worst thoughts came to me, the complete antithesis of the Nike motto.

I can't do it.

Then, my father came to mind.

At a prerace event, journalists had asked me how I expected it to feel to run on the streets on which my father had lived and died. I didn't know how to answer. I had no clue, and deflected. But now, running through Queens, the place of my birth, where my mom and dad had their first home together, I heard a voice telling me that it was okay. That I could do it. I had never heard this voice while running before. I had never thought about my father in this way while running. I began to calm down. I got back into the race, moved past a few women, and focused on staying in the top three.

So much of the art of running is the ability to calm oneself at a moment of extreme pressure. The more you relax, the better you run. When your muscles—not just your legs and arms but your mouth and shoulders—aren't tense, your stride improves. It's true for marathoners, but if you really want to see it, look at still photographs of ace sprinters. You'll see their jaws slacking as they bolt toward the finish line.

I was in such a moment right then. I could hear the fans yelling "Queens girl!" Their support meant more to me than they could have realized—I wanted to stop and hug them. My father may have been long gone, but as I churned through those difficult miles of Queens concrete, it felt like he was with me. I tapped into something I didn't know had been there all along, the strength of being his daughter.

My pace and breath stayed even as I ran into Manhattan. When I hit 23 miles, I realized that it was the furthest distance that I had ever run. Everything from here on out was truly new.

For the last few miles, the calm disappeared. My body began to feel like it was shutting down. It started in my calves, then my hamstrings, then my back. Everything hurt with a sort of throbbing exhaustion. I felt my stomach churning. I looked around for a place to drop out and step off, but the crowds were too deep. I barfed on the course.

I'm really sorry to the fans that I puked in front of, but they also kept me going with their cheering. And thank God, because I only had a mile left.

I fought through the final stretch in Central Park and finished in third place, behind Paula in first and Lyudmila Petrova of Russia in second. To my utter shock, I had beaten Deena's records after all. It was a debut record time for an American woman, 2:25:53, and the fastest any American woman had ever run the New York course. I was the first American woman on the podium in fourteen years.

I caught sight of Adam. He was wearing a gray T-shirt that said MR. KARA GOUCHER in big white letters.

My eyes welled up, but this time I didn't need consolation. There are rare moments in life when you know that a turning point is taking place while you're in it. It felt like Adam was saying that he was along for the ride, that he was my person, that he wanted to put the work in to continue to strengthen our partnership. So did I.

When I found out that my moment of contact and connection with my father had taken place so close to where he had died, I got goose bumps. I really don't know whether there's any truth to the idea that the people we've loved and lost are angels or friendly ghosts, but I can say that I had an experience during that marathon that I can't totally explain. I'm not sure that I even want to. I'm just grateful that it happened.

CHAPTER TWENTY-ONE
Trapped

The emotional high of finishing my first New York City Marathon was short-lived.

As we sat on a bench near the finish line, Alberto told me that I had made mistakes, that I had run like I was intimidated, that I had let the other runners, namely Paula, go. He said that he planned to bypass the celebrations and fly back to Oregon early. "You still have a lot to learn," he told me. It stung.

That evening at the party hosted by sponsors, I went in with my shoulders slumped. But as I spoke with people, I was blown away by how kind and congratulatory they were, giving me hugs and high fives for having bested Deena's record in my first marathon.

That night, Adam and I talked about starting a family. It was something we'd been discussing lately, not only with one another, but with Alberto. I knew I wanted to be a mother; the timing was the question. Alberto said that after the marathon could be a good time, but now that it was here, I wasn't sure I was ready. I'd discovered a new event in which I had a promising future, and wondered if there was more that I needed to accomplish first. I told Adam that I would think about it.

"They're always going to want something from you," he said. I knew he was right. The conditions would never be ideal. But I was struggling to visualize being a professional runner and a parent at the same time.

The next morning, my body let me know how hard I'd pushed it the day before. I couldn't walk up or down stairs. As I hobbled around the hotel, I got a message from Alberto making the case that I should wait to get pregnant until the spring, after the Boston Marathon.

I thought about it, and then agreed. I would run Boston, then try to have a baby.

After reaching the podium in New York, I became obsessed with becoming the first American woman to win the Boston Marathon in twenty-four years. Alberto and I considered the race an even bigger deal than the Olympics or the New York City Marathon. I decided that with Alberto as my coach, who had won there in such a famous fashion, it was my destiny.

I inhaled a copy of Tom Derderian's book *Boston Marathon: The First Century of the World's Premier Running Event*, dreaming of seeing my own name inked in a revised edition. I wanted to be part of the lineage of iconic winners Bobbi Gibb, Miki Gorman, Joan Benoit, and Kathrine Switzer, who did what they did so I could do what I do. It was unhealthy, how much winning Boston came to fill my every thought.

The struggle for most of my running career had been a lack of confidence, but with voices both in and around me bestowing an almost religious sense of purpose on this mission, I swung toward narcissism. There was certainly a danger in this, but it did help create a potent fuel for training, and I finished some workouts that made me feel like I was in the best shape of my life.

On our way to the Lisbon Half Marathon in Portugal in March, which Alberto and I decided I'd run as preparation, we stopped in Boston to practice on the roads that formed the course. I had been there once, the month before, and was eager for another chance to put my feet down on the historic streets that I had been obsessively studying and visualizing. A big added bonus was getting to see Kelly, who was now working as the sports information director for the University of Minnesota Duluth's women's hockey team. The team was playing in the NCAA Frozen Four tournament in Boston, and it was great getting to watch her in her element, succeeding in the sports world. As for my practice on the Boston roads, it only heightened my excitement and sense of purpose for the race. There was something about the lush, leafy course and neighborhood feel that brought me closer in mind to Duluth, and got into my core.

Before my and Alberto's flight to Europe, Kelly was hanging out with us in the lobby of our hotel in Boston. She pulled me aside and asked if it was "weird" having to spend so much time with Alberto on the road, with a clear implication that he could be romantically interested in me. "No," I told her, haughtily. "He's like a father to me." I was mad at her for even suggesting something like that.

At Logan Airport, I walked through the metal detector and waited for Alberto on the other side. He'd had a defibrillator implanted in his chest after his cardiac event—similar to a pacemaker—so he had to get patted down. The top of the electrical device stuck out, and he joked that he wished he could get one with a swoosh logo.

I stood by the conveyor belt and grabbed Alberto's backpack for him. When he completed his security check, he took the backpack back from me and told me to never do that again. The bag had testosterone in it, he said—just his own prescription for his own legitimate use—and if I was caught holding it, it could look really bad.

I believed him, as usual, and got on the plane.

Soon after we ascended, Alberto took an Ambien and ordered a red wine from the flight attendant. Out of nowhere, he then launched into graphic sexual stories and probing questions. I was no stranger to Alberto's locker-room talk in front of teammates and staffers, but this was the first time he talked about sex with me alone. If his comments during practice were PG-13, these were rated X. He talked in detail about his sex life with his wife, and asked me about mine. "Do you and Adam have sex with the lights on?" he asked. "Because Molly won't do that." When I tried to change the subject, he started talking about his younger days, saying "I sowed my oats" and offering up unwanted and unsolicited details about what that meant. His speech slurred as he got increasingly intoxicated. He asked me if I knew what "jungle fever" was, which I was aware was offensive slang for interracial relationships. I was shocked by all of it. As he continued to talk, he leaned closer and closer toward me, while I kept looking away, and tilting my body further from him.

I felt the shame of having dismissed Kelly, repulsed by his behavior, and trapped in the confines of the plane. If he had been a stranger, I would have pushed the call button and asked to be seated somewhere else. But with Alberto, once again, I wasn't willing to find out what provoking his anger would entail.

Eventually, he fell asleep. Relieved, I did, too. When we landed in Lisbon, he got up and walked off the plane as if nothing had happened.

I went for a shakeout run in Lisbon, then Alberto said that I needed a massage. I lay down on the bed in my hotel room, as he instructed. He had given me a couple of massages in Boston, and all of them were normal, quick flushes.

This one was different. It was Italy all over again.

His hand moved up my leg. Then one of his fingers went into my vagina. Repeatedly.

I had told myself after the Rieti incident that it had to have been some sort of accident. My coach and father figure could not possibly be violating me before a race.

Here it was, happening again. And here I was, again, trying desperately to believe it was another mistake. I had to stay focused on my race. I kept repeating to myself that it was an accident, tamping down the part of me that felt sick and reminded me that it had happened before.

Once again, I remained frozen on the bed, a deer in the proverbial headlights. And, once again, Alberto left the room as if nothing unusual had taken place.

A terrible mix of feelings washed over me, which included guilt and embarrassment. I worried that I was the deviant for even *thinking* that he had done it on purpose, going through hoops to try and avoid placing any blame on Alberto. At the same time, I *knew* that it was wrong. And I felt stupid for having been alone with him.

Two days later, I went out and ran the first 10 or so miles of the Lisbon Half Marathon at a world record pace, just as Alberto had been telling reporters I would do. The last few miles were grueling. I dug deep to push through, and ended up winning the race with a time of 68 minutes 30 seconds, which was short of the world record by 2 minutes and 46 seconds. (Later, I found out that the course was long by 400–600 meters, but I still would not have beaten the record.) Objectively it was a major victory, but as in New York, because of Alberto's expectations, I felt that I had failed.

Back home in Portland, I didn't tell Adam about what had happened with Alberto. I remained stuck, stunned, confused. I did finally do something concrete to protect myself, though. I told Adam that I wanted him to accompany me on trips. I said that I didn't want to run big times without having him there. He happily agreed, without question.

CHAPTER TWENTY-TWO
Heartbreak Hill

My focus on the Boston Marathon was so singular, the stakes that I had built up were so high, that I was able to lock the thoughts about what had happened in Lisbon away. I had goals, shit to do. I felt like a radio dial that I could just keep turned to a particular station, one that didn't replay negative things.

New York training had been a novel experiment; Boston was my obsession. I did more miles, at a faster pace. I lifted weights in the Lance as if I were in a *Rocky* montage. I visualized myself crushing the daunting stretch of the course known as Heartbreak Hill.

In his book about marathoning, *What I Talk About When I Talk About Running*, Haruki Murakami wrote, "No matter how mundane some action might appear, keep at it long enough and it becomes a contemplative, even meditative act." That's what I came to experience training for Boston: a liberation of sorts, an embrace of the mystical and masochistic appeal of marathoning. I was less focused on the times, and more in the moment. I wasn't even worried about throwing up while running anymore: though it happened twice during my training for Boston. I'd puked in front of millions of people in New York, and the idea of doing it again didn't frighten me. Odd, the things one can get used to.

My training was going so well that I did something I had never done before. I publicly stated my intention to win. Nike developed a campaign centered around my Boston expectations. They took out full-page ads in *USA Today*. The big bold text read: "26.2 miles? Kara Goucher is taking on 24 years." And below that: "Since 1985, no American has won here. Kara Goucher, Bring Boston Home." They had T-shirts and posters printed out, too.

The final part of prerace training, in which I tapered off my mileage and eliminated the afternoon run from my schedule, was ironically the hardest part for me. Running was my Zen, and tapering, while necessary to prepare for racing, took that away from me. Time off made me feel like I was losing fitness, even though I knew deep down I had to trust the process and rest.

It was widely known that Boston didn't pay as well as the other majors. The race organizers initially offered me $80,000 to start, less than half of what New York had paid me five months prior, but they almost never paid that much, I was told. They were making an exception for me, doing me a favor. Given the event's prestige and history as the jewel of the spring marathon season, I was okay with it, honored to take part, but I did want to know that I was being paid equally to the men who were at a comparable point in their careers.

When I learned from the agent handling my pay negotiations that a well-known American runner in the men's competition received an offer of $85,000, we asked for more. The organizers came up with $5,000 to match his pay.

I give this as an example of the prevalence of pay inequality in sports, and also to do my small part in breaking open the taboo of not talking publicly about pay. I know how hard it is for most runners to make a living, and I believe that more transparency, more shared knowledge, will mean more ability for runners—especially women—to ask to be paid what they're worth.

In the weeks before the race, I was blindsided by something Alberto said to the press. He told a reporter with *Track & Field News* that Boston would be my last marathon for a while because I was planning to have a baby. I was deeply annoyed, as Alberto hadn't asked if it was okay to share this private information and I didn't feel like it was his story to tell. Now the world was clued in to my family planning decisions.

I tried to shake it off, but Alberto continued to create uncomfortable situations for me in the lead-up to the race that made refocusing difficult.

I told Alberto that I was thinking of dyeing my hair black. I felt like it was time for a change. He said no, it was a bad idea because my appeal was as "the girl next door" and "you don't want to ruin that."

In Boston, he had me stay at a different hotel than the official event one for most of the prerace week, as he thought it would be too distracting for me to be around anyone outside the Oregon Project. My actual family had all flown in, but I was told I could only see them for thirty minutes the day before the race—a tiny concession that he and Darren granted after I begged.

Alberto also made a big deal about my equipment, which I soon realized was symbolic of deeper problems. My mom, always the thoughtful crafter, had decorated pink water bottles to match my specially made pink racing uniform, and had customized them with skulls and crossbones so that I could easily spot and grab them at the water stations. They were perfect—I had developed an affinity for skulls beyond the Halloween season, pink was my favorite color, and the bottles made me feel like I was ready to run hard, take no prisoners. (The skull would later become the Oregon Project logo, which I'm fairly certain started with me and my mom.)

But two days before the race, Alberto and Darren told me that the reason I'd thrown up in New York was because my water bottles got too cold. They examined the bottles my mom had decorated, used a thermometer to take the temperature of the water, and determined that they were problematic and needed to be replaced.

I was annoyed and unconvinced that water temperature had anything to do with puking. I realized that it was silly to get worked up about water bottles, but like many conflicts, this was actually about something bigger. I was finally seeing the pattern: I'd go through months of steady preparation for big competitions, then Alberto would find something at the last minute that would throw me off-balance. I told them that I wanted the bottles my mother had made, which would provide a mental boost along the course, a reminder of my family's unconditional love and support.

Alberto won the argument. I used different bottles. My mom was not pleased—she tried to peel off the pink skulls and crossbones that she had carefully cut and taped on the original bottles and transfer them to the new bottles, but they ripped and weren't salvageable.

Alberto and Darren tweaked other equipment, too. Paula had some cool stretchy gloves that helped her grip her water bottles, but she couldn't remember where she got them, so Alberto bought me a pair of Nike football gloves. The idea of avoiding a repeat of my F-bomb in New York was a good one, but when I tried the gloves on, I was surprised by how tight they were. Alberto attempted to stretch them out for me but ended up ripping the seam of one, which he repaired using his hotel sewing kit.

Finally, the night before the race, something happened that pushed me over the edge. Alberto and Darren asked me and Adam to join them for dinner at 6:30 at a restaurant near the official race hotel, where Adam and I had finally gotten Alberto's blessing to move. That was fine, I would eat a quick dinner, then lie in bed and watch bad TV until my geriatric prerace bedtime. I would be off my feet, relaxed, and ready to race. That was my routine.

Alberto strolled into the restaurant an hour late, coming from a speech of some kind that he had given. As a Boston-area local and the star of the famed "Duel in the Sun" race, he still enjoyed legendary status at the marathon.

He ordered a glass of wine, and asked if I wanted one. I figured it must be a joke—I never drank alcohol in the last weeks of training leading up to a big race, and certainly not this close to it—but I honestly couldn't tell. I politely declined, reminding him that I'd be making my debut on the course at 9:30 the next morning.

Alberto proceeded to order another glass of wine. The occasional passerby recognized me and wished me well. I feebly smiled back and said thank you, but felt ashamed to be so visibly out the night before the race. I hated even the idea of giving the impression that I didn't take this race I had come to revere with gravitas. Alberto ordered another glass of wine, then another. Around 8:30, he asked me again if I wanted one.

"I'm not drinking," I said, firmly this time. I told Alberto that I needed to leave. He said I should relax, insisting that I stay at the table, that he would be done soon. "You don't have to be so perfect all of the time," he added. Darren chimed in to tell me I was a "big girl," and that if I couldn't handle having my schedule thrown off a bit, then how would I handle competing against the best runners in the world? I felt myself seething as the clock hit 8:45.

Finally, around 9 p.m., we left the restaurant. Standing in the hotel lobby with Alberto, Darren, and Adam, I saw Pat Lynch, the coordinator for the elite division of the race.

I was horrified. All of the other athletes had eaten at 5 p.m. *How could he think I was taking this seriously?* I worried. I apologized to Pat for being up so late. Alberto made a joke about it.

In spite of all of Alberto's prerace shenanigans, the next morning I felt good. We loaded onto the buses, coaches and support staff included, as they were allowed to join athletes at the starting line in Boston. Darren said that I was "5k ready," a nod to my sprint victory at the Olympic Trials the year prior where I wasn't just out to make the team but to kill. I felt that was true. I would charge into history.

Off we went. The pack went more slowly than I had expected, and was crowded as a result. I kept waiting for someone to make a move to the front, but no one did. The plan had been to let other runners break the windy Boston air out front for the majority of the course and burn out, while I waited to sprint and surge to the front near the end, as I'd trained to do with weighted vest workouts. I kept wanting to go to the front, but I kept hearing Alberto's voice in my head, "Don't go till Boylston."

For about four miles, my logical side said "Stick to Alberto's plan." My gut said, "Now is the time to take the lead." Maybe I was rethinking what had happened to Adam in the 10,000 meters at the Trials, the tension between a coach offering a plan and the choice that the athlete has to make in the moment of competition.

Finally, by about mile 20, I felt like I couldn't take it anymore. I was uncomfortable in the pack and my form was off. I decided to go for it. I pushed to the front and the move splintered the pack from about twelve runners to eight, and then to only three. I looked around and it seemed like everyone else was hurting while I felt great. My stride was open. *This course is mine*, I said to myself.

Then a running photographer who was on the back of a motorcycle right alongside us broke protocol by yelling "Kara! Be careful! You're running at a five-minute pace!" Doubt crept in. I slowed down. The two other

women closest behind me, Salina Kosgei of Kenya and Dire Tune of Ethiopia, caught up.

I don't have many regrets in life, but I regret this. I should have known
better than to listen to a bystander.

With a mile to go, Kosgei and Tune passed me. I remember looking
down at my legs and thinking, *What are you doing? It's TIME TO GO.* I
needed to change something, anything, and wake my body up. I tore off the
football gloves Alberto had given me.

Kosgei and Tune were running straight down the middle of the street
ahead of me. Because the crowd was so loud, I wondered if I could sneak
past them on the outside without them hearing me coming.

That didn't happen. They just got further and further ahead. I pushed
with all that I had to try and catch them, to no avail.

I finished in third place, with a time of 2:32:25.

Adam met me at the finish line. I was crying uncontrollably, in a way I
never had before, in a way I didn't even know I was capable of. Alberto and
Darren came over and told me to "shut it down" and "get it together." Their
anger and frustration only made me cry harder. Alberto hated the pictures
of him collapsing after races, even if they had become part of his lore, and
reviled my displays of exhaustion and emotion after races.

I'm sure that to some I looked like a spoiled brat, but I was completely
gutted. As an athlete, you're signed up to have some of the most emotional
moments of your life take place out in the open, then take interview questions while in that state. I didn't have much success keeping my composure
at the press conference.

Back at the hotel, a nice family came up to me and said, "You did so
good!" I tried to squeeze out a "Thank you."

Adam and I went to Darren and Alberto's hotel room, where I lay on
the carpet. Adam was next to me, Alberto and Darren were on the bed. My
body was completely shot; tears were still running down my cheeks.

"Why did you go?" Alberto asked.

I tried to explain that my stride felt confined, that I was restless, that I
thought I could make an early break and still pull off the sprint at the end. I
could tell that Alberto was so deeply mad at me, which further twisted the
dagger of my own disappointment.

Nike had several "Boston Kara" victory ads drafted. The John Hancock building by the finish line was slated to beam my initials out into the sky-line that night. I had been booked to fly to New York the next day to be a guest on the *Today* show. All of that evaporated. Third place wasn't good enough, Alberto and Darren told me in so many words.

"You screwed yourself," Alberto said.

Outside that hotel room, all my family could talk about with each other, as they later told me, was how proud they were of me for finishing on the podium in my first two marathons. The fans along the course were still clapping and cheering the thousands of runners making their way to the end of the race. But in that hotel room, I lived in a different reality. All I wanted was redemption.

I thought about the London Marathon taking place in six days, not even close to the amount of time anyone would need to recover. Nor was it the type of hilly course that I had trained for.

"I'll win London," I said. "Let me fix this."

Alberto and Darren said that we would have a conference call with Mark Parker and John Capriotti to talk about it.

There can be a positive type of humility when one fails. Especially when one fails in public. This was not that. I was the first American woman on the podium in sixteen years, but I treated it like a funeral.

The next morning, I took my brittle body for my ritual post-race, easy recovery run. Pat Lynch saw me and was clearly taken aback. He asked me why I was running. He asked why I was crying. Both were reasonable questions.

"I needed to," I said. I told him that I felt bad about how the race had gone down. That I had disappointed the fans who cheered for me every dang mile.

"You ran your heart out," he responded. "You need to forgive yourself."

I heard the words, but I didn't take them in.

I went back to my hotel room to take a quick shower before checking out. In the hallway on my way to the lobby, I saw something sticking out of the trash bin on a housekeeping cart.

It was one of the laurel wreaths given to the first-place finishers. I'd recognize it anywhere: I had walked by Alberto's Boston laurel wreath count-less times, enshrined in the building bearing his name on the Nike campus.

I lost it all over again.

A crown of victory and someone had just thrown it away. Adam tried to console me. He even offered to fish it out of the trash.

I told him not to. I didn't win it. I didn't earn it.

Adam and I flew to New York for some meetings, and got on a conference call from there about the London Marathon. Mark Parker told me he had a Nike jet fired up and ready to go to send me off to the starting line.

This was crazy on many levels; typically it takes several weeks to recover after a marathon, but the idea had a badass, hardcore Nike verve to it that clearly resonated.

Alberto pointed out the difference in terrain, that I wasn't coached for London's flat and fast streets. He proposed an alternative, that I would run at the World Championships in four months. I'd postpone having a child and that would be my shot at atonement. We ended the call. It was decided.

For two weeks, I didn't sleep, replaying the race, step by step. It still keeps me up at night from time to time, wondering what would have happened if I hadn't slowed down when I heard how fast I was running, if I had trusted myself completely.

I talked to Papa about it. "Kara," he said to me, "what do you think would have happened if you won? Would it have changed the world? You have got to move on."

It was the perspective that I needed, but I'm still working on following his advice. It's been fourteen years since that Boston Marathon. I still have a hard time talking about it. I've never watched any of the race footage.

It was the first time that I had gone against Alberto. The result did not encourage me to do it again anytime soon.

CHAPTER TWENTY-THREE
Multiple Attempts

From late July to mid-August, Adam and I spent two and a half restorative weeks training in St. Moritz, Switzerland, a luxury Alpine resort town at 6,000 feet. Dathan Ritzenhein—who had just joined the Oregon Project—Amy, and Galen were there, as were Alberto, back to treating me like the star pupil after the Boston disappointment, and Al, our massage therapist. My goal was to win the marathon at the 2009 World Championships in Berlin, which would be held August 15–23. Adam and I ran together by day, with him getting back into shape from his injuries, and every night we bought a chocolate bar, drank red wine, and watched TV. (Since joining the Oregon Project, Adam and I had shifted from being teetotalers to having a glass together on occasion.) Those weeks provided the routine and relaxation that I needed, and an opportunity to further strengthen my bond with Adam.

From St. Moritz, Adam and I went straight to Berlin. A few days before the race, I was getting a massage treatment from a professional at the hospitality center Nike had set up. Alberto and Darren were with me, while Adam was back at the hotel. Out of nowhere, Darren started questioning my marriage. Alberto then chimed in, supporting Darren's assertions, and telling me that Adam was holding me back.

"It's not that we don't think he's working on becoming a better husband," Darren said. "It's can he get there fast enough."

What is he talking about? I wondered, blindsided. He was going back to more than a year earlier when things with Adam had felt rocky, when he'd been crushed by missing out on Beijing. Darren was dredging up old news and acting like nothing was different, when everything had already been fixed. *The Mr. Kara Goucher shirt! Adam's therapy work! The apology letter he'd written to Alberto!* I told Darren and Alberto that Adam and I were doing great, that I felt like we were in an amazing place where he was supportive in the way I needed him to be. "I thought we had moved on from this," I said. It was the same pattern I'd recognized in Boston again: just before the World Championships, Darren and Alberto were throwing everything into chaos.

Come marathon time, I made a rookie mistake: I swapped out my usual American flavor of Powerade for its European counterpart, not realizing that the ingredients were different. I thought I had mastered the art of throwing up while running, but this was something else. My stomach lurched as it tried to handle the unfamiliar Powerade formula and I puked my guts out, using the wet sponges provided along the course—meant to help runners cool down—to wipe the vomit off my face. (There is no nice way to say that.)

I finished 10th. It was the highest individual finish for an American woman since 1995, and I'd led the U.S. to a fifth-place finish in the World Marathon Cup team competition, which was our best placing ever.

Once again, it didn't feel that way. At drug testing, I was physically depleted and mentally defeated. I had run my first three marathons in the span of nine months. My intended reclamation from Boston after a rest and recharge had failed. I sensed a gray kind of mood settling in.

I sat with Darren, Alberto, and Adam at the hotel bar, listening to Alberto and Darren debate whether I was "actually good" at running. Alberto said that I was, I just needed to train harder. *Train harder?* I wondered. I had done everything he'd asked, completed every workout in his plan. *What was I not giving? What would it take to satisfy his expectations? Did I need to win five more medals? Ten? Twenty? Would it ever be enough?*

Nothing would ever convince them that I was "actually good," I decided.

I went back to my room and racked my brain while taking a hot shower. I saw my birth control pills in my bag. I knew that (counterintuitively, perhaps) taking one would kick off a fertility cycle. I popped one out and tossed it down with some water.

Shortly after World Championships were over, Alberto named Darren the Oregon Project's "performance director," in addition to sports psychologist. I told Darren that I had concerns that this posed a conflict of interest, as I didn't understand how the guy who was listening to everyone pour out their secrets in supposedly private sessions could also be tasked with deciding who would get to be on the team and who would get to compete. My concerns were brushed aside.

There was nothing left to wait for: in the early fall of 2009, I was ready to try and get pregnant. Alberto talked to Cap to get confirmation that I wouldn't suffer any penalties or reduced pay in my contract as a result. He reported back to me and Adam that Cap said that as long as I stayed "relevant," there would be nothing to worry about.

Adam and I were seeking out the guidance of experts at a local reproductive clinic in Portland because I had been diagnosed with polycystic ovary syndrome in college—a relatively common hormonal disorder that that causes eggs to become cysts instead of reaching their full growth. When the fertility experts saw the hypothyroidism medication Levoxyl that Dr. Brown had prescribed and I was still taking on my list of prescriptions, they also mentioned that the high levels of the hormone prolactin that are associated with hypothyroidism can negatively impact fertility. The doctor recommended that I start taking Clomid, a hormone-stimulating pill that encourages eggs to grow. Once the eggs were fully grown, we'd do a "trigger shot" to make them fall. The day after the trigger shot, I would be inseminated.

Women respond to Clomid in different ways, but for me I felt bloated, moody, and achy—like I was on my period—all the time. It looked like it was working, though, the fertility experts deemed my eggs to be the proper size, so Adam took his sperm to the clinic, and then I rushed in for the insemination procedure.

A nerve-racking week passed. When I went in for the blood test to find out if I was pregnant, I found out it hadn't worked.

The next step was a round of ovulation-stimulating shots called Follistim—which Adam had to give me each night—then the trigger shot, then insemination. Adam practiced his needle skills on an orange, then jabbed me at night after we'd finished our running workouts for the day, often while I paced around nervously with a small glass of wine to try and calm my nerves. Again, the insemination didn't take. I was still training hard and felt like I was straddling two worlds: one in which I was a powerful athlete in total control of my body, and another in which I felt my body was at war with me.

We did another round of Follistim treatment, and still, no dice. People told us to "relax" and "not think about it too much"—common, well-meaning sentiments often heard by couples undergoing fertility treatments—but it was hard to think about anything else. I'd see women out with their babies and spiral, wondering why they seemed to have magic fertility powers and I did not. Kendall, who had given birth the year prior, had seemed to blink and become pregnant. I was completely lost in a dated narrative, thinking that as a woman I wasn't doing my job to reproduce.

By November, we were on our fourth pregnancy attempt. During the vaginal ultrasound, the doctor said that I had three good eggs. I reacted with delirium—*I was one of three kids! I always wanted that many!*—but the doctor told us it was actually a risk and potentially dangerous if I ended up pregnant with triplets. Adam and I didn't care; we were desperate.

The doctor presented us with a form to acknowledge that we understood the potential dangers of moving forward. We signed the dotted line.

A week passed. None of the eggs took.

I called Adam on his cell phone. When he picked up, he was with Alberto lifting weights. I remember feeling guilty about asking him to leave his workout early. In hindsight, fifteen minutes chopped off the end of a weight session felt so minuscule compared to what we were going through.

I was inconsolable when Adam got home. He made our couch into a bed, ordered sushi, and turned on *Sex and the City*, a show I knew that he couldn't stand but which always calms me. "I feel like a failure as a woman," I told him. "For all the things my body can do, I can't seem to get pregnant."

We regrouped with our fertility specialists and talked about moving forward with in vitro fertilization, a more involved and costly series of shots. I was ready to order the $20,000 or so in drugs, but the doctor said we might as well give another round a go first of Clomid, a trigger shot, and insemination.

We were glad we did, because the fifth time was the charm.

In January 2010, Adam and I found out that we were having a baby.

CHAPTER TWENTY-FOUR
Nine Months

The adage "listen to your body" took on a whole new meaning for me during pregnancy. Running was my life and something I wanted to keep doing at a high level, but I set an intention to always choose myself and the baby first. On days when I was exhausted, I would nap or walk, not force myself to run. But unlike the era when my mother was pregnant and literal bed rest was often advised, even for active women, I had a doctor who had run while pregnant herself, and let me know it was okay to do so. During my first trimester, I lifted weights and ran 40 to 50 miles per week—with Alberto coaching me—though often slower than my normal pace. Meanwhile, my doctor monitored my amniotic sac every month to make sure the baby was properly hydrated.

Then in March, twelve weeks in, Adam and I received alarming news. Although I was healthy, a concerning measurement in our baby's nuchal fold was found during genetic testing. A sac had not fused on time, which was a common sign of Down syndrome. Three weeks later, it still hadn't fused. We had worked so hard to get pregnant and now we had to process this information and its potential implications.

I canceled a press appearance at the Rock 'n' Roll Marathon in San Diego that I had scheduled. I went out for a long run that day and kept running over the next seven weeks—I needed that gift that it gave me of shutting down the voices of doubt more than ever. We learned we were having a boy. Adam and I discussed what our son's life might look like, the cost of specialized care and schools. We were in a position where we could afford that, we knew we would love our son fully and absolutely, and we were determined to have him.

Paula Radcliffe and I ran together often during those weeks. Not only did she happen to be training in Portland, and not only was she also pregnant with a boy (her second child; she had given birth to her daughter in

2007 and won the New York City Marathon just ten months later and again in 2008 when I made my debut), but we had the exact same due date.

Only Alberto, my family, and closest friends knew what was going on with the genetic testing. After one of our runs, Paula and I went to Panera for lunch. We didn't make it far into the meal before I broke down and told her what was on my mind.

"I'm going to lose this baby," I said to her.

After joining me for a cry, she calmed me down and reassured me, telling me it was going to be okay. Coming from her, it meant a lot.

When Adam and I went in at nineteen weeks to see our doctor, we were incredulous to learn that our baby did not have Down syndrome. I would be lying if I said that we weren't relieved.

While we were reconfiguring our vision of the shape of our son's life, Nike was planning a pregnancy announcement.

Public relations executives wanted to share the news of my pregnancy with *The New York Times*, and told me to keep the circle of people in the know extremely close until then. Meanwhile, Nike shot a photo of me with mud spattered on my face as part of an Oregon Project shoot. When the image was published, I was surprised to see my pregnant belly had been photoshopped out and nonpregnant abs had been substituted in, while my breasts, which had grown significantly during the pregnancy, were left as they were. The combination leaves an impression of a fake body, because it is one.

On May 9, 2010, Mother's Day weekend, my pregnancy announcement ran on the front page of the sports section of the *Times*. This was part of a carefully controlled initiative to market me and Nike to female consumers, and from that point it became useful for Nike to emphasize my pregnancy. I posed for another photo shoot, this time with the words "run baby run" painted in bold letters on my pregnant belly. I got lots of positive feedback about it as a feminist triumph. Alberto, however, cringed when he saw the picture, saying that it wasn't good for my image, that it wasn't "wholesome." I felt a ripple of shame.

As much as I tried to remind myself that the changes my body was going through were beautiful and supportive to my baby, I struggled with the weight gain. My pregnancy weight came slow and steady, all told about thirty-five pounds. I continued to maintain logs, and scribbled my old standby self-directed attack—"PIG!"—on days when my weight spiked. I would never dream of calling another woman that, pregnant or not, yet I had no problem applying the label to myself.

During my second trimester, with the permission of my doctor, who told me that the baby was attached and healthy, I ran about 80 miles per week. I felt full of energy and happy to be able to keep training. But then, toward the end of my second trimester, my sacrum got sore. The hot spot turned out to be a sacral stress reaction. I decided to keep working out but more gently, running about 30 miles a week, intending only to maintain my mental and physical fitness while letting my sacrum heal. I knew I couldn't try to push through things the way I once had done.

I took self-directed runs, free from Alberto's coaching, on the wood chip path on the Nike campus. I enjoyed my pregnant runs, found trails and trees I hadn't noticed before, houses that had been there all along, sensed the wind, didn't care about the pace. It felt like a gift to be able to slow down and love running for the sake of running again. My speed wasn't there, but I felt durable, my sturdy limbs pushing me and my baby boy forward. I was convinced that the extra load was making my legs strong. The weighted vest that had felt so heavy when I first trained for the New York City Marathon now seemed like a laughable challenge. I felt in awe of my body and its capabilities.

While I took my break from Alberto, his and Adam's mutual discontent deepened. Adam did an interview with *PodiumRunner* published in February 2010 where he was asked about how it felt to read forums on running websites where people called him "pretty old" and asked "Is Adam Goucher done?" He acknowledged that those doubts are "hard to overcome" emotionally, and credited me, Alberto, and his family for supporting him through it all. He then noted that it wasn't just "fair-weather fans" who doubted him but "also people who have been a part of my life and my running career for a long time," and said, "I really, really look forward to the day when I can throw it back in the faces of the doubters. It's going to be great—crossing the finish line and giving them a big middle finger."

Alberto and Cap wildly misinterpreted the whole thing as being directed at them and Nike, and were livid. Adam and I got on a conference call with them—Adam from Portland, me from Minnesota, where I was visiting my mom—and Alberto started listing what he hated about Adam, calling him a "downer" and saying that he had "bad energy." This from the man USATF had just named their "Coach of the Year" at the end of 2009. Adam remained calm and took it all, which only further inflamed Alberto. I spoke up and told Alberto how much this call was stressing me out.

After we hung up, I think Alberto felt a little bit guilty, that he might have pushed things too far. In a strange move, he called my mom—knowing that we were together—and apologized to her for upsetting me during my pregnancy. He told her that he loved me and would never hurt me, even though by attacking Adam, that's exactly what he'd just done.

It was clear that the rift with Adam was irreparable. He drifted away from the Oregon Project as my pregnancy progressed, and began doing more of his training on his own. He began upping the intensity of his workouts and thinking about taking a shot at the 2012 Olympic men's marathon team—a new endeavor for the tried-and-true track runner.

Little did I know that behind the scenes, machinations were underway by Nike, ones that would often make me wish that I could find a way to follow Adam's example and step out on my own.

———

Through Alberto, Cap had told me to stay "relevant" during my pregnancy, so I did. I completed dozens of interviews and photo shoots, including photos and an interview for the *New York Times* story that had announced my pregnancy; a cover story shoot for *Runner's World* magazine (which was paired with a lengthy feature); a shoot with Paula for the New York Road Runners; and a twelve-hour shoot and interview for *SELF* magazine (one I remember clearly because I had aggressive morning sickness and had to pose on the edge of a cliff), most of which was set up by Nike and done at their request.

I was also constantly on the road and in the air to make appearances. These included a trip to Chicago to open a Nike store, followed by dinner and a question-and-answer session with high school athletes; an appearance and photo shoot at the New York Mini 10K with Paula; an appearance at the Dow Live Earth Run for Water in Minneapolis (a fundraiser for a clean water initiative, where I got to fire the starting gun); as well as several local appearances in Portland, such as taking students for tours on the Nike campus and meeting with local middle school girls for Girls on the Run. It was a lot of work, but I loved it. Not only did it keep me busy, it gave me opportunities and a platform to talk about the experience of being a pregnant elite athlete, building off what Paula, Derartu Tulu, and others before me had done. I felt like I represented a new era in which women could talk openly about what it meant to juggle motherhood with a commitment to fitness and our careers.

My story clearly resonated; a staffer in Nike's public relations office told me during my pregnancy that I was the most requested female athlete at the company for interviews. Nike doesn't release specific data breaking down who buys their clothing, but I knew from my autograph sessions, meet-and-greets, and other in-person events that mothers made up a *huge* swath of their customers. My story helped sell shoes, shorts, T-shirts, and bras. More recently there's been an explosion of fitness brands targeted to women, but at the time, for a mainstream company, especially a sports brand, to put a pregnant athlete front and center was somewhat revolutionary. I felt like we were tapping into a community that the sports world had long neglected. Here these women were, literally lining up around the block. Instead of being told to buy things for their sons or husbands, they were, finally, being offered something to wear themselves.

It was all the more reason I was surprised when my financial advisor called me in mid-July to say that my Nike paycheck hadn't landed in my bank account. (My annual salary of $325,000 was distributed via direct deposit in quarterly payments of $81,250 in January, April, July, and October.) I assumed it was a mistake, and told him that I would contact Nike to figure it out. I reached out to my agent, who then reached out to Cap.

Like most soon-to-be parents, Adam and I had no shortage of expenses. We needed more space for our baby boy as well as for ourselves, including a spare bedroom where we could have an AlterG treadmill and some weights, so with Cap's assurance that my pay wouldn't be affected, we had dumped much of our savings into building a sprawling new house on eleven acres off Skyline Boulevard in the hills of Northwest Portland. We saw this as our forever home, and loaded it up with the usual baby gear—a crib, stroller, car seat, toys, and onesies.

Cap ended up responding to my agent about my paycheck inquiry, and what he said floored me. It turned out that Nike hadn't made a mistake. The company had suspended my pay intentionally. I couldn't believe it. I had been working hard, and there had been no indication or warning at all that this was coming, as my contract indicated would happen ahead of any suspension. The murky reasons given by Cap, through my agent, as I recalled, were my "absence" from competition, and my "medical condition." Meaning, pregnancy.

It said in my contract that if I didn't compete for 120 days, my pay could be suspended. But my last competition had been the marathon at the World Championships in Berlin in August 2009. My 120th day without competing had come and gone on December 21, 2009—seven months ago. Not a word had been said about me being in breach of contract, and since I'd been making frequent appearances, doing what Cap asked, and had kept getting paid, I hadn't worried in the least.

Adam and I got back in touch with Cap in a state of mild panic. Adam's contract would be finished at the end of 2010, but mine went another two years, until December 31, 2012, and Nike had a one-year option to keep me on the team beyond that. It was important to stay on good terms, and not rock the boat too much. We gently reminded him that he'd told Alberto that if I stayed relevant there would be nothing to worry about. (A month or so after I found out I was pregnant, Cap had even taken me, Kendall, and Paula Radcliffe, who had been in town, out to dinner to celebrate.) Cap responded that he had faint memories of that conversation with Alberto, but pointed out that nothing was in writing.

As concerned as we were, Adam and I were confident that the decision to suspend my pay would be reversed. I had been a productive Nike athlete for nine years. We appealed to a bigwig named John Slusher and fully believed that it would be taken care of. As the executive vice president of global marketing at Nike, Slusher outranked both Alberto and Cap. In the meantime, my due date was coming up.

On Friday, September 24, nine months pregnant, I went for a fifty-minute run on a trail near my home, and lifted weights.

That night, I went into labor.

As an endurance athlete I managed pain for a living. I had run an Olympic double in the 5,000 and 10,000 meters and won major marathon and World Championship medals.

Labor was so much harder than any of that.

When I run a race, I know for about how long I'll be pushing through the suffering. A 5,000 meters race lasted 14 to 16 minutes, a 10,000 meters was generally 30 to 32 minutes; a marathon was long, but even then it was less than three hours. I learned how to frame expectations of time and pain in my head.

When delivering a baby, there is no clear timeline. The baby could come out in four minutes or four hours. Or, he could be a real stinker and take a day or two. There's no control, no knowable end point.

Adam and I checked into the hospital around midnight and were assigned a room. I had fluids coming out of both ends and felt like I could barely walk, but tried to move around anyway in a slow, guided waddle. I felt like I was going to die and repeatedly let Adam know that. *With my Exorcist-style behavior,* I thought, *he's never going to find me attractive again.* But Adam was in coaching mode, saying nothing but positive, encouraging things.

I puked right next to his face.

He told me I was doing a great job.

My contractions became so violent that my whole body revolted. My cervix wouldn't dilate. The doctors gave me an epidural so that I could sleep for a few hours, but it wore off at a point when it was too late to have another one.

My doctor broke my water. The next morning, Kendall arrived and waited outside the hospital room in what would end up being the final hour of my pushing. She later noted that she "couldn't believe the noises" I was making—grunting, screaming. The word "primal" comes to mind.

I pushed for one hour, then two, and when I hit and then passed the two-and-a-half-hour mark, I realized that I could have run a marathon in that span, with enough time for a beer and a burger at the finish line.

My doctor told us that our baby was resting sunny-side up and his shoulders were stuck. They told us that they may have to consider suction or a C-section.

We opted for suction. The doctor came at me with what looked like a toilet plunger. Two contractions later, at last, our little conehead made his way into my arms.

On September 25, at 11:10 a.m., PST, Colton Mirko Goucher arrived.

CHAPTER TWENTY-FIVE
Survival Mode

In our first days at home with Colt, I bundled him in his stroller for walks. The fresh air soothed us both. My mother had flown in from Minnesota to help and when Colt was exactly a week old, I told her that I was going out for a walk on my own. Once I was out of sight of the house, I picked up my pace for a light jog.

My first run after giving birth wasn't glorious. It felt like things were going to fall out. I also didn't like being away from Colt. I stepped it back to a walk after about seven minutes. I had flashes of memory of being at the hospital, bleeding. I had shredded my pelvic wall during the lengthy delivery. *This is going to be way more difficult than I thought it would be*, I realized. But pushing through discomfort and doubt was in my DNA at this point. The next day, I went on a twenty-five-minute jog.

Adam and I had received a huge number of congratulatory messages from friends and strangers alike—the news of Colt's birth had been well publicized by Nike—but for a week and a half, we heard nothing from Alberto. He didn't come to visit us at the hospital or at home. He didn't write, or call. We had been at Alberto's bedside to see him after his heart surgery three years prior. This was a major milestone for us, and as a father of three we thought that he would understand, but we got the sense that when it came to his athletes, parenthood was an inconvenience.

When Alberto did resurface, it was to call to ask me if I could get back to workouts.

Eleven days after giving birth, I went to the Nike campus, and started to train.

I could only sit down on a donut and even that hurt as I drove to the Nike campus on that first day back, October 7. I wore two sports bras and a diaper under my running tights while completing a timed mile on the track. I tried not to show the excruciating pain that I was in. On the 13th, I wrote in my logbook, "bum really sore." (Minnesota-speak for my ass was bleeding.) On the 18th, I did a hard mile on the track followed by a weight session. "All my pregnancy parts hurt," my logbook read.

No one checked in on how I was doing—not Alberto, Darren, assistant coaches, or physical therapists. There was no talk of creating a plan for me that put my health and safety first. Nike was making money by tailoring its marketing to motherhood and femininity (or dare we call it "faux-minism"?), while up close, the story was very different. It was dangerous, and looking back, it makes my heart sick.

Don't let the slogans or glossy advertisements, including those I appeared in, fool you—we are woefully behind in America when it comes to supporting mothers. Of the world's wealthiest countries, the U.S. is the only one that still doesn't require paid parental leave. We need that, plus affordable child care, and maternal and pediatric health care that is safe and accessible. We also need to address the startling fact that Black women are three times as likely as white women to die from a pregnancy-related cause, according to the Centers for Disease Control and Prevention.

Figuring out child care with our schedules was exhausting. The internet was calling me heroic, but as I juggled training and looking after Colt while recovering from a difficult pregnancy and breastfeeding, I felt like the furthest thing from a superwoman. After bringing Colt with me to the Nike campus proved to be too much, Adam and I used some of our savings to hire a nanny to watch him in the mornings. Adam and I would both be home in the afternoons to take care of Colt and do our second runs, and by some miracle the three of us got on a similar napping schedule.

As with my July payment, the quarterly salary payment I should have received in October didn't arrive. That month, Cap made an offer to "advance" me the suspended $81,250 payment from July. He treated it as an olive branch. But it was unclear what an advance meant exactly. How much longer would my pay be suspended for? Would I need to work for free, forgoing future salary payments, in order to pay the money "back"? (In practice, as I understood it, this was how suspended salary payments were often handled at Nike.) I didn't want to give in, but with our mortgage and baby, things were getting tight. Alberto encouraged me to accept it, saying that it was better to get money up front, even if I ended up owing it back. Given that the details of my suspension were still so murky and unaddressed, it also really seemed there was a chance that it would all get worked out and I wouldn't be on the hook for the payment. I took the money.

I felt like I was in survival mode, trying to keep Colt and my career afloat. When I left practice, Alberto and Darren chided me for not "hanging out" more. "You used to be fun!" they told me. I reached out to Paula to ask if the overwhelm I was feeling was normal. After trading jokes about how I "beat" her when it came to delivering our sons (hers was born a few days after Colt), which she took in good stride, she told me that things would get better, the anxiety of trying to be a mother and working athlete would soften.

But then Colt got colic. He was crying and punching the air. And my breasts were extremely sore from breastfeeding. None of the home remedies we read about online helped, including a weird one that involved cabbage. We visited our pediatrician, who recommended gripe water for the colic, an over-the-counter mix of herbs and sodium bicarbonate, which worked. When I went to see my obstetrician for help with my own discomfort, I had dark crescents beneath my eyes. I told her about the breastfeeding pain, the fatigue, my workouts, Colt's gassiness.

She looked at me, concerned. She assured me that Colt was going to be okay, great, even. She said that I didn't need to produce so much milk, that I didn't have to be perfect. "Something's got to give," she said. I felt a pressure valve release in me.

I came home from the OB, put Colt in his baby chair, and pounded out miles on the AlterG that we had set up in our home. Adam walked in and as I told him through huffs and puffs about what the OB had said, he started to gently turn down the pace of the machine. "Slow down," he cautioned. He could sense that I was stressed in a new and disturbing way.

I realized that I had to ask more from him when it came to child care. It was scary, doing so—in large part because it meant relinquishing some control. Psychologist Brené Brown talks about "overfunctioning," meaning responding to stress by doing more than is necessary, which can numb the pain. "For overfunctioners," says Brown, "it's easier to do than to feel." I'm one of those people.

Adam responded by saying the words every new mother should hear: "You're not getting up at four a.m. anymore." He immediately said that he would help step up even more than he was doing already, taking on more feedings and helping balance breastfeeding and formula. We bought an extra freezer to store more milk as we weaned Colt.

I was slowly realizing that it was okay not to do it all alone. But when it came to my career, I didn't believe I had the option to ask for help. I didn't feel I could ever say no to competing, and never once did Alberto or anyone at Nike acknowledge my bleary eyes, and the burden I was under. The message was clear: my decision to have a baby was not to get in the way of my athletic pursuits. The stress I was under was to be kept out of sight and out of mind at practice, all while photos of me, beaming in my Nike-swoosh gear with my big belly, continued to proliferate online.

Perhaps it shouldn't have been surprising to me, then, that being a mother wouldn't mean the end of Alberto's harassment. Alberto told me that I looked "so good" with larger breasts that I should "consider implants." He shared that thought with Adam, too. He also said that he missed timing my splits during a track workout because he "couldn't stop staring" at my breasts.

He wouldn't let it drop, bringing it up around other athletes and coaches, including our new assistant coach and science advisor, Steve Magness, who had been hired in 2011. Steve had short brown hair and wore thin, wire-framed glasses. He had a background in exercise physiology. A 4:01-miler in high school, he understood grit in training. I had figured from our very first workout, done in blistering hail and rain, that Steve and I would become friends. When Alberto asked Steve if he thought my breasts had grown during a workout, saying, "Look, they've gotten bigger! Don't you think?" Steve looked deeply uncomfortable, and didn't play into Alberto's game. His not joining in Alberto's locker-room talk further endeared him to me.

I drove home, still on the donut, my chest aching in profound pain, thinking about Alberto's annoying and degrading comments, wanting respect, and wanting to be with my son. His behavior felt even more jarring as I adjusted to my role as a mother and contemplated what it meant to raise a boy.

Before the end of the year, Cap offered to advance me the October quarterly payment that had been missed. Once again, Alberto encouraged me to accept it. The messaging from him was: take the money, and get back to competition. Perform, and all will be well.

When Colt was three months old, Adam and I spotted an unusual lump on his chubby little neck. We took him to the doctor and ultimately were sent to the pediatricians at Legacy Emanuel Medical Center. We nervously watched our little chunk get knocked out with anesthesia for a CT scan. When he came out, the doctor told us he needed emergency surgery.

It turned out to be a staph infection in Colt's lymph node, which the doctor told us would have likely killed him if it had burst. We had two sleepless nights at Emanuel by his tiny bed, while he had a gauze cocoon around his neck, protecting the port the surgeon had inserted to drain fluids.

Adam and I relayed what was going on to Alberto and Darren at Nike. Alberto had signed me up for the P. F. Chang's Rock 'n' Roll Arizona Half Marathon in Phoenix—meant to be my first competition back—scheduled for later that week after Colt's surgery, January 16, 2011. I didn't want to do anything with my time and energy but take care of Colt, yet it had been 511 days since my last race, and with no clarity gained or end in sight on the contract disputes, and with my family's finances under threat, the pressure to compete was huge.

The Rock 'n' Roll Half was meant to stamp my return, and be the start of the months of tune-up leading into the 2011 Boston Marathon on April 18th. I was still unbeaten in the half marathon distance and the fastest American woman in the full marathon. A press release went out announcing my name on the Rock 'n' Roll Half roster with much fanfare.

On the morning of January 12, I left the hospital and did a seven-and-a-half mile run as part of my training for Phoenix, while Adam stayed with Colt. That evening, I drove from the hospital through light snow to Nike's campus for a 7 p.m. workout. Oregon has a way of looking very David Lynchian in the winter, gothic, austere, unrelenting, and that night it was particularly so, the sky low with dark, gray clouds.

Because of the snow, the bulk of the workout was done in the hallways of the Mia Hamm building, which were about 200 meters long when all of the doors were propped open. My body was there but my heart and mind were with Colt. I couldn't decide if I was a shitty mother who had abandoned her child at the hospital or a good one who was going to work to ensure that he was provided for. I hated feeling trapped in a no-win decision.

Alberto made the workout of fast strides through the hallways sound essential, but after I was finished Steve told me he thought that it was "crazy" and not necessary. He knew what was going on with Colt, and was sad not to have the power to tell me to go be with him at the hospital. I should have done it myself—told everyone that I wasn't going to practice, that I wasn't going to race that weekend. But I operated as if I had no choice because that's how I felt.

I left the Nike campus and went home to get some sleep. Adam stayed at the hospital, doing the things that a parent should do.

I lay in bed thinking: *This is not who I want to be.*

———————

After discussing with our doctors, Adam and I decided that we would fly together, with Colt, to the Rock 'n' Roll Half Marathon in Phoenix. I packed Colt's antibiotics, diapers, bottles, onesies, and other essentials, but forgot my own drink mix and warm-up clothes. I was a nervous wreck on the plane—the doctors had initially suggested flying this soon after Colt's surgery wasn't a good idea, before working with us to outline a safe plan to do it—but Colt was fine. He slept peacefully on his very first flight.

There were moments during the race where it felt great to be out there, suffering, pushing, as I knew I would need to be ready to do if I was serious about running the Boston Marathon. But the week leading up to it had been one of the most hectic of my life—a maze of sleepless nights, last-minute travel plans, and training, all while worrying about my ailing son. New challenges appeared: my boobs leaked as I made my way through the course, a race day problem that I hadn't considered. And when I crossed the finish line in second, behind Madaí Pérez of Mexico, I was left with the feeling that I had phoned in the performance—something that I felt was disrespectful, and I vowed never to do again. Darren was there, and after the race he told me that Alberto would "never accept" my and Adam's decision to have a child. He said Alberto wanted "the old Kara" back. I didn't.

In a private session, Darren noticed a necklace that I had with a pendant of Colt's thumbprint, a new favorite totem that reminded me of him even when I was at practice. It motivated me and made me feel stronger, knowing that little guy was depending on me. Darren rolled his eyes at it.

He told me that he was afraid I was not cut out to be a professional runner. I had written a few blog posts for *Competitor* about what motherhood meant to me, and he said that he had read them. He asked "What's this fluffy bullshit?" And "Where has Kara Goucher gone? Kara Fucking Goucher?" He told me that "we need to get you back to being a killer."

Colt's surgery left a small scar, but he otherwise rebounded to a full recovery. Yet with one crisis waning, others arose. Because we were independent contractors, we didn't get Nike employee benefits. This, as Cap told us, meant that Colt would not be able to go to the Nike daycare center on campus when he turned six months old. It was the same reason that we were never eligible for a Nike health insurance plan. For a long time, we'd had insurance through USATF. Now, we learned that our coverage would be dropped because my marathon ranking had fallen due to my pregnancy. The plan had been a lifeline over the past year and a half and Adam and I couldn't fathom losing it. We appealed the decision and while we were waiting, worried about scenarios that could lead to significant out-of-pocket medical expenses. USATF didn't come through, but the U.S. Olympic Committee ultimately did the right thing by getting our coverage reinstated.

I had to search for another sponsor—any sponsor—to help keep our budget balanced. Due to exclusivity requirements in my contract, other shoe and apparel companies were off-limits. My agent called and said that he found a company, Amway, that would ink a deal for six out-of-town appearances and some advertisements using my image.

He described how the company's brand, Nutrilite, worked. They made nutritional supplements, vitamins, and other health products that were sold by individual people, not at stores. These people also tried to get others to start selling the products.

"Could that possibly be a pyramid scheme?" I asked him.

He didn't address that. All I had to do was talk about my own nutrition habits, he told me. I wouldn't be responsible for selling any products or convincing anyone else to do so.

We had bills to pay. I reluctantly agreed.

CHAPTER TWENTY-SIX
Muzzled

In the weeks after I returned to racing in the Rock 'n' Roll Half, my agent continued to discuss my pay suspension with Nike. After some back-and-forth, I finally got word that the length of my suspension would be twelve months. I would be on the hook for a total of $325,000. This was construed by Alberto as a favor, with Nike stopping it there instead of suspending me for the full, approximately sixteen months that elapsed between the 2009 World Championships in Berlin and the Phoenix Rock 'n' Roll Half. I still didn't think this was okay, not even close. I had worked my butt off for the entirety of my pregnancy while they marketed me as a mother-athlete to consumers, yet they were effectively telling me that none of that work had any value. If I had known Nike wasn't going to pay me for all that time, I would have rested, gone to Duluth, and spent time with my family, instead of working out daily, doing endless photo shoots and interviews, and traveling for public appearances.

Now, Alberto pressured me to agree to the twelve-month suspension. He told me that it was a waste of my energy to worry about it, that Adam and I were money-hungry. He told me to focus on the New York City Half Marathon coming up in March, and most of all on the 2011 Boston Marathon in April. He explicitly said that if I won in Boston and upgraded my 2009 third-place finish to a 2011 first-place win, all of the issues with my contract suspension dispute would retroactively disappear. I wouldn't owe any money back at all. It put a ton of pressure on me, something I was feeling plenty of already.

Cap and Alberto also offered to advance me my January quarterly payment. This seemed to underscore Alberto's message—take the money, win, and all will be well. Again, I accepted.

I trained hard, and built up to running 120 miles per week. In early March, I had a breakthrough workout, a 10-mile tempo run at marathon pace where I averaged 5:22, the same pace I had hit when I did the same workout before the 2009 Boston Marathon and was feeling in top shape. When I finished, I felt so happy that I ran another seven miles. It was an important milestone for me and a huge boost to my confidence.

When it came to the contract, Adam and I decided that we needed to try to speak to Slusher again, as he had more power than Alberto or Cap, and see if we could come to a resolution. We met him on Nike's campus in early March. We sat with him over salads at the Boston Deli, named for the marathon and with a wood-paneled decor inspired by *Cheers*. There, Slusher made it clear that we weren't on the same page at all. He cited the history of male athletes whose salaries had been reduced in the past, failing to mention that all had been due to doping scandals or injuries, not pregnancy and maternity leave.

On March 15, a few days after the meeting, Slusher wrote me an email, copying Alberto, about my suspension. He said that he had been thinking about me as he watched his daughter's first track practice, that his daughter had been "amazed, after running two 1500s, to hear me tell her how much you run/train," but I was quickly proven wrong for imagining that it was a preamble to a change of heart. He said he had decided definitively that the one-year suspension of my contract was "the appropriate course for Nike. I hope you realize that I am trying to do my best to be fair—to both you and our company—in this business decision." The hypocrisy of this male executive thinking of me as a role model to his daughter while also determining that a hardworking female athlete didn't deserve to be paid during her pregnancy astounded me.

Alberto replied that I should put this matter to rest and concentrate on my running now. Sometimes "one door closes," he wrote, "but then another opens." He told me that my running was going great, and it was possible for me to accomplish my dream of winning Boston if I could just focus on the good things in my life. He asked if I'd trade any of those blessings—the health of my family, the love of my true friends—for one year of my Nike pay. He acknowledged that losing the money would "sting," but explained that he lost "a ton of money in bad investments," stewed in anger and stress about it for years, and then after his heart attack, stopped all that. "Don't waste any more energy on this money," he pleaded. He advised that I thank God for my blessings and send a message to Mark Parker to bring closure to the issue before we departed for the New York City Half Marathon the next morning.

"Do this now for yourself and move forward," he ended the message.

It felt like a cannonball hit my gut. If Alberto had ever truly been my advocate, it was clear that he wasn't anymore.

Adam, Colt, and I flew to New York the next day, March 16, ahead of the New York City Half Marathon on March 20. It was to be my first really big race after having Colt—in Alberto's plan, meant to mark my comeback ahead of Boston. During the whole flight and first night in the hotel, I couldn't stop thinking about the dispute. At 6:42 the next morning, March 17, I sent an email to Mark Parker, Nike's CEO, on Adam's iPad. I told him about John Slusher's decision, explained that I understood it was contractually legal, and said: "I am asking if that is the fair thing to do."

I told him that though I hadn't been able to compete as a distance runner while pregnant—noting that if I had miscarried as a result of high-strain exercise, it would have been a nightmare not only for me, but for Nike—and laid out my feelings about how much value I'd provided for the brand even when I wasn't racing.

> Nike promoted my pregnancy and used it as a story for them to promote the brand. Nike chose when to announce my very personal news of my pregnancy to the general public. I worked hard during my pregnancy doing appearances and photo shoots to promote Nike and my relationship with Nike, only to find out after the fact that Nike would be suspending me for my pregnancy . . . I don't understand Nike's policy on pregnancy as it seems that there is no set standard for how female athletes are treated during and after their pregnancy.

I told Mark that I was dreading the upcoming questions at the New York City Half from the press about whether Nike supported me. "I am finding it more and more difficult to lie," I said. I told Mark that I hated being put in a position where I had to hide the truth. "I appreciate our relationship and feel as if I have nowhere else to go."

I clicked send. I powered off the iPad, fake-smiled my way through the day's press conference, and turned my focus to the New York City Half.

The race started in Central Park at the time (now it ends there) and I set off with the pack. It was bright and very cold at first, and I found it hard to get in a rhythm, but I felt better as the miles ticked by. About 10 miles in, I was running strong, when Caroline Rotich and Edna Kiplagat (no relation to Lornah), two Kenyan superstars, charged in front of me. I finished in a close third, but it was a very fast race, and I ended up with a time of 1:09:03, the fastest for an American woman in the distance that year. All three of us broke the existing course record. I was happy—I'd proven that I was still quick and competitive in a major event. Galen, now nearly twenty-five, had a very good day as well, finishing third in the men's race in his half marathon debut. Mo Farah, a megastar from Britain who was three days away from his twenty-eighth birthday, won the race in his own debut at the distance.

At the beginning of 2011, Mo had come to Oregon and started working out with Alberto on the Nike campus. It was an odd thing: not only was he leaving his sponsor, Adidas, after completing one of the best seasons of his life, but a member of Team Great Britain was joining a group whose stated purpose was to bring glory back to American distance running. I hadn't been consulted about him joining—which was customary when new runners came to the Oregon Project—and no reason was officially given for bringing Mo to the group, beyond murmurs that it would help Galen.

The *Oregonian*'s report on the New York City Half read, "Alberto Salazar's training group, the Oregon Project, enjoyed one of its most productive race days Sunday in New York City. Kara Goucher, nearing tip-top shape again after giving birth in September, finished a strong third in the women's New York Half Marathon—an important litmus test on her way to next month's Boston Marathon. Meanwhile, Galen Rupp and his new training partner, Mo Farah, made splashy debuts at the half-marathon distance."

"I felt great," I said at the finish line, as photographers snapped pictures of me, Colt, and Adam. The truth was, I felt muzzled.

I cooled down, ate, showered, and was packing up ahead of our night flight back to Oregon when I saw a message in my inbox from Mark Parker.

He congratulated me on my race, but in response to my questions about the pay suspension simply wrote, "I will check back with John Slusher to review the final outcome."

It was clear to me that this was lip service. I took it to mean, correctly, that he would stand by the suspension. The brand I had revered as a child didn't mean what I thought it had.

I did two things that pushed the bounds of the confidentiality clause in my contract that had kept me from speaking to more people about my pay suspension. The first was that Adam and I called around Portland searching for a lawyer to give us advice. At least three times, we were turned down by firms that told us that Nike had them on retainer, thus creating a conflict in taking me on as a client. We finally found someone who advised that even though I was a contracted worker, not an employee, I might have a case worth putting forward. She asked me to gather up a list of all the work that I had done for Nike while pregnant.

The second was that I quietly reached out to women I trusted in the running world. At the New York City Half, I had opened up about the situation with my old high school friend Carrie Tollefson, as well as Mary Wittenberg of the New York Road Runners, and Joan Benoit, among others. They had assumed that I was being paid during my pregnancy and thought it was wrong that I wasn't. They encouraged me to fight. However, I also learned the depressing news that this kind of pay suspension during pregnancy was commonplace for runners sponsored by other shoe companies as well. It seemed like no matter where you went as a female runner, you were in a man's world, subject to contracts written by men, for men.

For the first time, I wondered if I should retire.

CHAPTER TWENTY-SEVEN
From the Sidelines

After the New York City Half there was just a month before the Boston Marathon, which meant a lot of time on the roads training with Alberto, just me and him, meeting up near his house in the Portland hills for afternoon runs. As soon as 5 p.m. hit, he would start drinking, often while watching me do my strides. Finally seeing things differently, more clearly, I started to wonder if the reason our morning practices at Nike typically started around 10:30 a.m.—much later than I'd heard happened on other teams—had more to do with accommodating the USATF Coach of the Year's hangovers than doing what was best for our performance. I remembered how often he arrived to practice looking fatigued, his eyes pink, skin clammy.

Alberto told me that while he was happy with my performance at the New York City Half, I needed to lose weight before Boston, often saying I was still slow because I was "still too heavy." He said that I needed to take Cytomel, a prescription hypothyroidism drug that can cause weight loss as a side effect.

This was the first time that Alberto had asked me to take something for which I did not have a prescription, and it scared me. I was still taking Levoxyl, as prescribed to me by Dr. Brown, and had no intention of adding another thyroid medication. Nonetheless, Alberto was obsessed with the idea that additional thyroid medication could boost metabolism and lead to weight loss. Galen was taking Cytomel, prescribed by Dr. Brown, and Alberto instructed me to ask Galen to give me some of his pills.

At practice a few days later, realizing I hadn't asked Galen for the pills, Alberto handed me a bottle that had a label torn off and "Cytomel" clumsily written in Sharpie on the side. I took the pills home and hid them away for good. The next day at practice, I lied to Alberto about having taken them. It was a quiet protest, but after treating his wish as my command for so long, an important change.

Nike scheduled photo shoots for me ahead of Boston and Alberto accompanied me to them, telling me that I looked "too sexual" in one where I was wearing a sweater and a long skirt with my running shoes on and asked to pose sitting on a desk. Alberto said that they had dressed me as a teacher "because people fantasize about their teachers." I was tired of his overbearing criticisms and inappropriate comments. During one of our Boston practices he told me that my "butt looked like a Russian butt," a bizarre comment I think he intended to be a compliment about my muscularity. *What was going on? Was he possessive over my body? Jealous?*

Another unsettling realization hit me in the weeks before Boston. The Oregon Project had recently installed a CryoSauna on campus—a small vertical cabin that serves a similar function to an ice bath, cooling the body to aid in recovery. (It was so cold that it once froze my breast milk when I went in before pumping.) Alberto loved the CryoSauna right away, and after hard workouts, at least twice a week, he oversaw the Oregon Project athletes' use of it. He told all of us, men and women alike, that we should keep our shorts on in the CryoSauna but take our tops off, explaining that it helped the treatment get to "the core." I had bought the rationale and been fine with it because the sauna was mostly enclosed, with just my head sticking out, so it seemed like I had complete privacy. But one day in early April 2011, I was helping Adam use the sauna. (He no longer had a Nike contract and wasn't getting paid, but they allowed him to keep using the training facilities.) I was standing where Alberto normally stood, and felt a shiver down my spine. I could look down into the machine and clearly see all of Adam's chest. *Holy shit*, I thought. *Alberto has been watching me topless, all these months.* I felt sick to my stomach.

Marathon training cycles are always pressure-filled and come with a bit of grief at the end. You work so hard, your focus directed toward one day. But this time, if I had a bad day, I came home to Colt and felt like there was more to life than running. Instead of looking to my performance as the only source of validation, I could look at the two teeth that had started to sprout through Colt's gums. Of course, I never said that to anyone at Nike because I was worried that they would think I wasn't dedicated. I felt such a high burden to prove that I was back, that women could be more than one thing.

I arrived in Boston on April 14, four days before the race. I was excited for the event but lacking the same brash confidence and gung ho spirit that I'd had two years earlier. As much pressure as there was on me to win, as much as I wanted to win, and as good of shape as I had gotten myself into, I felt I hadn't quite had enough time to train to be really competitive for a place atop the podium against the elite Boston competition.

When race day came I took off with the pack, but my hamstrings felt tight. The discomfort stayed with me through the first couple of miles. *Relax*, I told myself. *It's early. Ease into it.* But when I hit the 16-mile mark, I knew that I was out of podium contention. Desiree Linden (going by her maiden surname Davila at the time) tore by me, looking like she had a full tank of gas and a chance to make it to the front. As she passed, she gave me some encouragement, which was a classy thing to do. "Keep your eyes up," she said. I tried my best, but the pack of ladies ahead of me got smaller and smaller in the distance as the miles ticked by.

Des came achingly close to winning and finished second to Kenya's Caroline Kilel. I finished fifth in my first marathon as a mom, set a new personal best time by a minute—2:24:52—and in doing so, hit the Olympic standard. I would have preferred the laurel wreath. But I had pushed hard, taken the pain, and I recognized that this was a major accomplishment.

As usual, Alberto saw it differently.

"You're just too heavy," he told me after the race. Kelly, who was there, later told me that Alberto had said the same to her as they were making small talk waiting for me to finish media and drug testing. "What are you talking about? She is *not fat*," Kelly responded. She was a soccer coach, and while she talked about fitness and performance goals with her athletes, she would never set weight numbers for them. To hear that kind of thing from any coach, let alone the one working with her sister, "felt like acid," she said.

After the race I held on to Colt, not quite seven months old, wearing his little black Nike sneakers, and felt the relief and love of looking at his smiling face. He didn't care if I won or lost. He just cared that I was there.

———————————

After Boston, Adam and I flew with Colt to Minnesota. It was a comfort to be back in my safe place, with family members gushing over my baby while I went on runs on the wooded trails. Papa and Grandma Ola Jean—who were getting up there in age and couldn't travel much anymore—met Colt for the first time. Papa was so excited and eagerly arranged for Colt to be dedicated at his church. He still cared about my running, but he cared about my happiness and my new little family more.

Alberto called me while I was in Minnesota. I had mentioned to him that I had obtained a lawyer for my contract suspension dispute. On the phone, he said that he had informed Nike of this, and while my lawyer never actually reached out to Nike directly, it seemed they must have feared the possibility of her getting involved. Nike was improving its offer, Alberto explained, and would reduce my suspension from twelve months to six months, which he considered generous. I would forfeit my next two payments as a method of reimbursing Nike, and the suspension would be done. However, they would also extend the terms of my current contract for another year, locking me in until December 31, 2013. (The additional year was not the option year, it was a new extension on the contract, so the original option year still remained.) I would still be subject to performance requirements, and reduced pay if I didn't hit them. He told me to take the deal, that I had a healthy child and my "obsession" with money had gone too far. I told him that it wasn't an obsession, it was about being treated fairly for the work I had done.

Adam and I were driving into the parking lot of a Walgreens when the offer terms officially arrived by email. Adam told me not to agree to it, that I should keep fighting because Nike punishing me for being pregnant was wrong. I told him the truth: that I was exhausted beyond belief and my desire to continue the battle had waned. All that I wanted to do was move on with my life. We needed the money. Wearing someone down is a weapon of its own, and Nike had all the resources to keep doing that indefinitely.

I agreed to the deal. At last, it was over.

In 2011, Alberto was at work on his memoir in collaboration with the writer John Brant. It would be called *14 Minutes: A Running Legend's Life and Death and Life*, the title referring to the amount of time Alberto had apparently been dead for after his cardiac event. Brant was the same writer who had penned the *Duel in the Sun* book about Alberto's 1982 Boston Marathon win, and who had written the 2008 *Runner's World* "Love on the Run" cover story about me and Adam, focusing on my looks as much as my times.

In April, just before the Boston Marathon, Brant had been sitting with Alberto interviewing him for the book and asked Alberto about doping. Did he have "anything to confess? Was there something that would come back to haunt him?" Brant inquired.

"Absolutely not," Alberto said. "Next year at the London Olympics, people can root for Galen, they can root for Kara, they can root for any Oregon Project athlete, and feel confident that they're clean. Every day we train on the Nike campus. Phil Knight can look down from his office and watch us work. Do you think I would do anything to embarrass Phil, or betray the trust he's put in me? Do you think I would do anything to harm Galen or Kara or any other runner in the Project?"

For so long, I had believed these sorts of statements from Alberto completely. In the summer of 2011, however, after Boston, doubt finally started to creep in. I have the cyclist Tyler Hamilton to thank for that.

Adam, Colt, Colt's nanny Anna Kate, and I were in Park City on May 22. Adam had become an essential and supportive training partner for me, not to mention a primary caretaker for Colt, and though he and Alberto weren't on the best of terms, they managed to get along. We had our own condo this time—separate from the condo where Alberto, Galen, and Mo Farah were staying—and were sitting on the couch when Tyler Hamilton came on *60 Minutes*. At the time, Hamilton was a close friend and teammate of Lance Armstrong's and an Olympic gold medalist. We listened, rapt, as he not only implicated Armstrong in a doping regime, but admitted to doping himself, and in doing so broke the omertà of cycling. He explained that a lot of performance-enhancing drugs are used not to get stronger and hit more home runs like Mark

McGwire, but to help your body recover faster. He alleged that Armstrong had done exactly that, using a type of blood doping known as EPO that stimulates the production of red blood cells. Hamilton said he had witnessed this personally. He saw the vials in Armstrong's refrigerator and said that Armstrong had injected them. The details were vivid, the charges not easy to explain away. I thought Hamilton was brave. I didn't know him personally, but I also thought he looked so broken in his interview.

That night, Adam and I met Alberto for dinner, eager to his hear his take. Alberto had stayed close with the Nike-sponsored Lance, and I'd seen Lance on the Beaverton campus as recently as March 2011, when he talked to me about how his form was thrown off by running with a stroller. He made a nod to me that I knew "what that was like." I responded that I didn't, because my husband was the one who ran with the stroller.

"Of course Lance was doping," Alberto told us. Adam and I locked eyes for a minute, shocked. We'd never heard Alberto say this before. "But Tyler is going to write a book and he's just trying to sell copies," he continued, chalking up Tyler's motivations for coming forward as purely selfish ones. Lance was Alberto's friend, so it was no big surprise that he would look for a way to discredit Hamilton, no matter how flimsy. But still, Alberto accepted Lance was doping and didn't care, and that alarmed us.

Two weeks later, I was in Eugene for the Prefontaine Classic. Adam stayed in Park City with Colt, while I traveled to race the 5,000 meters, and cheer on my teammates. Galen ended up pulling out of the 10,000 meters, but Mo was racing, and I stood along the rail at Hayward Field, the sun having set, the lights on, watching him fly.

Mo had always been a force on the track, but he was known to struggle with getting outkicked at the end of races—the last 600 meters always seemed to vex him. At twenty-eight, he was past the age when runners typically are able to develop a kick. Lately, though, I'd noticed a change in Mo. There was an Oregon Project workout we did called Ks, which consisted of six reps of 1,000-meter runs with very limited rest. It's brutal, so Alberto's routine had always been to take it easy for two days after to recover. But on at least two recent occasions, I had seen Mo, as well as Galen, do the Ks, and then smash a hard track workout with only one day of rest instead of two, while I sat on the sidelines, wiped out. Other times, I'd do a hard

morning workout with them, then they'd tear it up again that same afternoon while I'd be jogging.

What Galen and Mo were doing didn't make sense to me. I had been
training with Alberto for seven years. I knew his patterns, his progressions,
and this didn't fit the mold. So I asked Alberto about it. "What am I missing here? How did they do it?" I inquired. Alberto deflected, not really
answering and telling me that I was just behind where Galen and Mo were
because I'd had a baby. Which also didn't make sense, given that I had run
the Boston Marathon faster in 2011, after having Colt, than in 2009.

At the Prefontaine Classic, I watched Mo defy gravity. He surged to
a win at the end of his 10,000 meters race as the crowd roared, setting a
new British and European record in the process. Nine runners cracked the
27-minute barrier that night, a record for a single race, and Mo was ahead
of them all.

It was like someone dropped a mirror on the ground in front of me and
it broke into a million little pieces. My mind flickered through a montage
of images: the AndroGel and vials in the refrigerator in Park City in July
2007; Dr. Brown showing up at our races; and more recently, the unmarked
prescription bottles, and the meetings between Alberto, Mo, and Galen
that I wasn't invited to. I had assumed that this was them pushing me out
after my pregnancy, after Adam and Alberto's falling-out, but now I wondered if it wasn't about me at all. *What was this sudden need for secrecy?* I
wondered. As Mo celebrated his win, it all flashed—crashed, really—into
my head. Taken in isolation, each thing didn't seem so bad, but together,
they unnerved me. I still couldn't exactly determine if they all fit together
but there were too many data points to ignore.

I stepped away from the bleachers and called Adam. "I don't understand what I'm seeing," I said, telling him about Mo's results.

"Do you think they're cheating?" he asked.

Without hesitation, I answered: "Yes."

I had believed everything that Alberto had told me and I was surprised
at what came out of my mouth. Finally, in that moment, I felt my trust in
him shatter.

CHAPTER TWENTY-EIGHT
Proof

I rejoined Adam and Colt in Park City on June 4 after the Prefontaine Classic, where I'd finished ninth in my 5,000 meters race, three spots behind Shalane Flanagan. Then, from June 23 to 26, I was back in Eugene for the USATF National Championships, competing in the 10,000 meters. As with Boston, the stakes were high. I had to make the World Championships team, or else Nike could choose to reduce my salary by 25 percent for the remaining life of my contract. In order to make that 2011 World Championships—scheduled to take place from August 27 to September 4 in Daegu, South Korea—I needed to place in the top three *and* hit the world standard time in my Nationals race in Eugene. After not competing in 2010, the only reason I had gotten a spot in Nationals at all was thanks to a rule that allowed runners who had medaled at a World Championships within the past four years an automatic bid to enter Nationals.

Mercifully, I had a strong race at Nationals. Alberto was confident that the race would be fast enough to hit the standard, so I ran behind Shalane and Jen Rhines in third, checking our splits, then outkicked Jen in the last mile or so. The finish got me under the world standard time, and Nike executives were happy. *Thank God*, I thought. They were also happy because Galen had won the men's 10,000 meters.

In July, however, after returning to Park City for training, I started having pain in my left hip. I tried to keep up with workouts, doing a hard one with Galen and Mo on July 22, and the next day saw them go out and run hard again, while I had no choice but to take an easy recovery day. To my continued questions about how they were doing it, Alberto just kept telling me that I was slow and behind because of having Colt. It was offensive, and it nagged at me. On July 24, I went for a 20-miler and felt pain radiating from my left hip throughout the lower left side of my body.

I flew back to Portland and got an MRI on July 29, leading to a diagnosis of a stress fracture in my femoral neck, the bone that links the leg and the hip. It was a relatively common overuse injury among runners, but it meant that my entire season was potentially wrecked. I talked to Alberto about whether I should skip the World Championships in Daegu to let myself heal and focus on the Olympic Trials, which he thought was a good idea. Then he talked to Cap, and changed his mind. He said that Cap said I'd already gotten off light for "the pregnancy thing," and if I didn't run at Worlds, I'd have my salary reduced by 25 percent. I remembered a Nike campaign from 2008 before the Beijing Olympics, featuring my face and bold-letter words that read: "BROKEN DREAMS HURT MORE THAN A FRACTURED FEMUR."

After the months of contract disputes over the suspension, I wasn't prepared to take any more conflict with them. So, I kept training through the injury. Anytime I tried to run outside, it felt like daggers were piercing into my hip. I tested out using an elliptical machine, but even that hurt, so I shifted to aqua jogging and used the AlterG. It was a nightmare: if I didn't run at Worlds, I'd throw a quarter of my salary down the tubes, and if I did, I'd be competing injured, which I thought was shameful. I'd be taking a spot on Team USA that I knew tons of other healthier runners would have killed for, because the ink on my contract said I had to, and the people who could decide otherwise were choosing to treat its word as gospel.

If I dropped out of Worlds, Des Davila, the ascendant runner who had passed me in Boston for a brilliant second-place finish, would get to go. I had been in that exact position before in 2006 when I'd gotten a spot at the World Cross Country Championships because Lauren Fleshman was injured, and I knew firsthand how huge of an opportunity it would be for Des. I still had a limp and was in Portland in August for the last stretch of training, aqua jogging with Alberto watching, when I asked him: "What good is it for Nike if I go?" He told me that I had earned my spot on the Worlds team fair and square, and I should compete. In private, Adam and I discussed the idea of me starting the race at Worlds and then quickly dropping out, but didn't entertain it for long. It was a crummy thing to do: if I started the race, I wasn't going to step off the track.

I went to a doctor for cortisone injections—a legal, and common, way to reduce swelling and relieve pain. "You don't have to do this," the doctor told me.

"Yes I do," I answered.

I got three shots in three days.

I didn't feel much better afterward—in addition to the hip and leg pain I just felt tired and off—and told Alberto. His solution: Cytomel. Alberto consulted with Dr. Brown, who, without examining me or even talking to me, wrote me a prescription for it, and emailed Alberto to say that I "should immediately start on the cytomel 5 micrograms twice a day. The first dose she should take with her levoxyl and the next 12 hours later and so on." Dr. Brown also told Alberto that the cortisone shots would affect my thyroid levels, and the Cytomel was needed to help balance those out. *Is that true?* I wondered. *Or are they just trying to get me to lose weight again?* I didn't trust them, but I felt I had no choice. I had decided to appease Nike, for now, and do everything possible to avoid having my salary reduced. Cytomel wasn't a banned substance. I took the pills.

As soon as I sat down with Alberto for the lengthy flight over the Pacific from Portland to Daegu via Tokyo, I realized how long it had been since we were alone together on a trip like this. Galen and Mo were already in South Korea, and Adam was staying in Portland with Colt. The attendant came by for drink orders and Alberto requested his red wine. He popped an Ambien. I was exhausted. All I wanted was a calm flight.

In no time, it was like our flight to Lisbon all over again, with him talking explicitly about sex. He told an unsettling story, involving a hot tub, about having sex with a professional female runner I knew. Then he said he was just kidding. He had wine crusted in the corner of his mouth. Then, things escalated. "We've both wanted this," Alberto said, propositioning me directly for the first time. He said that we should kiss and that "no one would find out." Before I could respond, he moved his head toward me.

I instantly recoiled. "You're drunk," I told him. I needed to get away and I didn't want to wait around to see what he would say. I charged out of my seat, and bolted to the bathroom. I closed the panel door behind me, locked the latch shut, and the harsh, dingy light flickered on.

I stood in front of the tiny metal sink, looking in the mirror in a state of disbelief. Tears came. I couldn't catch my breath in the stuffy, claustrophobic air.

I had left my child and husband to be on this plane, to compete while injured, to try and stay in Nike's good graces.

How did I get here? I asked myself.

And how do I get out?

When I returned to my seat, I found Alberto asleep. He spent the rest of the flight with his baseball cap pulled over his eyes. I remained on edge.

"Oh man, I was so drunk, I don't remember what we were talking about, do you?" he said when we landed. "No," I told him, needing space to think. I knew that this time I couldn't push it away. I wouldn't compartmentalize and pretend it didn't happen. But after seven years of doing exactly that, my initial instinct to pretend that all was fine was well honed.

When I called Adam from Daegu, I didn't tell him what had happened on the flight. The words still hadn't arrived for me: that I felt more hurt and disrespected than I could possibly explain, that I had trusted someone who had violated me. Adam was going to be coming to Daegu the day before my race—Kendall had generously offered to watch Colt for us—and I was also worried that he'd blow up at Alberto when he got there, which to my mind would only make matters worse.

Alberto and I met up with Galen and Mo just outside the city for a few final days of training. Alberto had us run indoors on treadmills with altitude masks on. I'd never done that before a competition and couldn't understand the reason, since we were about to run outside, in humidity, at the Championships. Alberto didn't bother to give me an explanation when I asked why we were doing it. Galen and Mo seemed unfazed.

At breakfast, Alberto handed me, Galen, and Mo small blue pills. He told us that it was B12, an over-the-counter vitamin, but when I had taken that before (by my own choice, not at Alberto's request), it had come as a gel tab. It looked like a prescription medication to me. This was the first time that Alberto had ever directly plopped a pill in my hand and said, "Take it."

Mo then shocked me by asking why he had to take the pill instead of "getting a jab like last time." (Mo has denied any wrongdoing, including that he ever doped.)

A jab: British-speak for a shot. I freaked out, but hid it well—it was an Oscar-worthy performance. I pretended to take my pill, then wrapped it up in my napkin under the table. I finished the meal on high alert, terrified of what would happen if Alberto saw that I hadn't taken it, holding the wadded-up pill and napkin in my hand, which I chucked into a trash can on my way out.

My 10,000 meters race was on the first day of competition, August 27. Three days before that, I was driven to the hotel in Daegu that Nike representatives had booked. In keeping with our us-versus-them culture, Oregon Project athletes had a block of rooms that were separate from the athletes' village, isolating us from the rest of Team USA. My room smelled heavily of cigarettes, and there was no restaurant in the hotel—not helpful in easing me back from my already agitated state.

The day after I moved to the hotel in Daegu, Alberto and I were in a car going from the hotel to the practice track when I overheard a phone conversation between him and Jim Estes, who worked with USATF. As I understood it, Alberto had apparently asked Jim to get Dr. Bob Adams to set up an IV with saline for Galen ahead of the competition. (Alberto has denied that he requested a saline drip for Galen in Daegu, and Galen has denied he ever broke the rules.) Jim was calling to say that Dr. Adams didn't feel comfortable doing that. Dr. Adams was the same team doctor for USATF who had gone with Alberto and Galen to a local hospital in Osaka in 2007 for a saline solution IV drip when Galen was dehydrated.

Alberto began to seethe. He told Jim that Dr. Adams had done it for him in every other competition. He said that the British team, which was handling Mo's saline infusion, would just do Galen's as well. When he hung up, Alberto called Dr. Adams "a pussy."

I remembered the infusion in Osaka and felt sick. That wasn't an isolated case, it seemed, but part of Alberto's routine. IV drips still were not allowed before competitions, as they could mask banned substances.

Just get through your race, I kept telling myself. *You'll deal with everything else after.*

Darren arrived in Daegu, and on race night he and I got in a cab to go to the stadium, where Alberto was waiting. The cab ride was long, about forty minutes, and soon after we got in, Darren handed me a drink—the first time he'd ever done that. "What is it?" I asked. "Don't worry," Darren said. "The whole British team is drinking it." I didn't like it one bit that I was being given something like this, blindly and under pressure. Yet, stuck in the cab, I couldn't fake it like I did with Alberto's blue pill. With shame washing over me, feeling like I had no choice, I tipped back the drink. It was sugary. I hoped it was Gatorade powder, but thought it was more likely to be L-carnitine, an amino acid derivative that can supposedly boost energy and lead to weight loss. L-carnitine is banned as an infusion above certain thresholds, but is legal as a drink. Alberto had been talking about L-carnitine drinks; I'd heard him say that he had them, but only enough for Mo and Galen. I had never taken it before, nor had I ever been given a special drink before a race. Given that it was allowed I wasn't worried that I was breaking the rules, but like the treadmill and "vitamin" incidents before, it was all so out of the ordinary, and it made me uneasy.

Five laps into my 10,000 meters race that night, my left leg began to throb. The pace was relatively slow, but every single step sent a shot through my body like an unwelcome lightning bolt. All I could think about was that I had taken someone's spot on the team, had taken the Cytomel pill that Alberto insisted on, had drunk the mystery solution that Darren handed me, and here I was, having the worst race of my life, barely trying to finish a World Championships event in which I had once made the podium. My anger—at myself, at others—ran deep.

With about two and a half laps to go, the lead pack lapped me. It was a final blow, just when I didn't think that I could feel any more pathetic.

I cheered on Sally Kipyego as she charged ahead of me. She won the silver medal, just behind Vivian Cheruiyot and ahead of Linet Masai. It was a Kenyan podium sweep.

I finished 13th out of 17.

After the race, I changed into sweatpants. Shalane Flanagan had finished 7th, and I could tell that she was disappointed, too. I told her that for the next two or three weeks if she wanted to find me, I'd be roaming around Portland—where Shalane now lived and trained out of with a different Nike-sponsored group—wearing my mom jeans.

At the post-race drug testing, my urine was deemed to be too diluted, so I had to wait and try and pee again. The medalists came into the drug testing area and I burst into tears, not because I was afraid of testing positive, but because I had gotten lapped by them at the World Championships, and now had to wait there even longer and prolong the embarrassment. It was midnight. I felt it was the end of everything I'd ever worked for and believed in: running, competing at the highest level, trusting Alberto.

After I finally got it together and managed to pee, I found Alberto, Darren, and Adam waiting for me outside. Adam had spent the race in the Nike spectator section. We all left together, had a quick bite, then said our goodbyes since Adam and I were leaving in just a few hours. Adam and I went back to the hotel and got on a Skype video call with Kendall, who had something big to show us.

"Look at this!" she said, first holding up Colt's tiny hands as he walked, then gently pulling her hands away as Colt took his first steps on his own.

I lost it again, the tears rolling down. I had missed it.

The part of me that logged my splits in pink pens, blasted pop music when I drove, laughed with my sisters, and always tried to see the sunny side felt so far away. Everything sucked.

When we got in a cab for the airport, Adam said that he had something to tell me. I responded that I did, too. He told me to go first.

"I can't do this anymore."

"I was just about to say, you need to leave."

He didn't know all the details of what I'd been through with Alberto, but he knew the effect that being in the Nike Oregon Project was having on me. He could see that it was time.

CHAPTER TWENTY-NINE
Confrontation

I spent a few days in Portland at the end of August, wearing my mom jeans, with all of my attention on Colt. It seemed everything was new and exciting to him as he neared his first birthday. I took him to the mall, as he looked to be doubling in size every few weeks and needed new clothes. We went to the Oregon Zoo in the city's West Hills, Colt wide-eyed at seeing in real life the elephants, tigers, tortoises, and orangutans from his books. The next day, we went to a pond and fed the ducks. I loved watching him light up. Much of the time, though, I felt heavy and downtrodden.

The Olympic Trials in the marathon were four and a half months away, on January 14, 2012, in Houston, and I still wanted to take my shot at making the team. I wasn't ready to retire. But I no longer trusted Alberto, and I was injured. I needed a plan, and I needed Adam to understand what I'd been through so that he could help me form it.

I talked to a close friend in Portland about what had happened with Alberto in Daegu. She encouraged me to tell Adam. "[Alberto and Darren] have been trying to break up your marriage for years," she told me. "You can't have secrets."

On September 2, Adam, Colt, and I drove from Portland to Seattle to see Adam's mom and her husband. They were there visiting some of her husband's family. We checked into a hotel and were sitting in our room when I began to tell Adam about the plane rides to Daegu and Lisbon. I did not tell him about the massage incidents in Lisbon or Rieti.

It was one of the most difficult conversations of my life, and I was glad that we were in a hotel; it meant I'd never again have to return to this place. Adam was shocked. He was mad at Alberto, and he was mad that I hadn't told him sooner. I explained that I had held off in Daegu because I didn't want him to get in a fight with Alberto there. He understood, but it was a lot for him to process. He called his best friend, Tim Catalano—a running teammate from the University of Colorado—to talk it through.

I was ashamed of having held back secrets from Adam, overwhelmed, and couldn't yet bring myself to tell him about the massages in Rieti and Lisbon. I wasn't yet sure how to even talk about those incidents to myself. I had all sort of fears that I couldn't articulate.

The next morning, I emailed my mom and sisters.

I've been too embarrassed to tell you all how stressful Alberto has made my life the last few months. When he gets back from Europe I am going to tell [him] I can no longer work with him. . . . Also, something happened on the flight to Korea with Alberto that I was too embarSsed [sic] to tell anyone, but I told Adam last night. I'll tell you all later. Don't pass this info on!!! I don't want this any-where!!!

When I called my mom in Duluth, I described what happened on the plane, that he had done things in the past like putting his arm around me in photos and getting a little too close, but nothing like this forced kiss attempt. I told her that he was drunk, and I mentioned a comment Alberto had made about my being "half naked" around him all the time in my sports bra and shorts, wondering if this had given him some kind of false impression that I was wearing those clothes for him, trying to invite his sexual attention. I kept telling her that I felt like it was somehow my fault for going to Daegu. I didn't tell her about Italy or Lisbon.

My mom stopped me. She told me bluntly: "What Alberto did was wrong. What happened wasn't your fault."

She said that she hated him. She reminded me that being drunk doesn't absolve you of your actions, especially if they harm others—a lesson she knew as well as anybody. She explained that what Alberto had attempted to do by citing my clothing as a reason for trying to kiss me was a classic way of putting responsibility for abuse on the victim instead of the perpetrator—the "she shouldn't have been wearing that" defense. The sports bra and shorts I wore around Alberto were issued to me by the company that we both worked for. I was wearing them to do my job.

I told her how confusing and gut-wrenching this all was for me, that for years I had worshipped Alberto as an athlete, coach, and father figure. The fantasy version I'd held up of him for so long was a projection. Alberto was, in fact, a narcissist, and I'd fallen for the enticing fallacy that if I just let things go, turned the other way, it would wane. The truth, which was so painful for me to start to see, is that when narcissists aren't challenged, they gain more power, and the more power that they get, the worse their narcissism becomes. Mo Farah had won the 5,000 meters in Daegu and placed second in the 10,000. Alberto's ego and reputation were swelling to new extremes. He acted untouchable, godlike, and for so long I'd treated him in kind.

Back in Portland, Amy Begley and I met up for lunch and I told her about the Daegu plane ride incident. Like my mom, she was understanding and was compassionate. They gave me what I—and anyone in a similar position—needed. They listened. They didn't judge me.

I set up a time with Alberto to meet in person with the intention of telling him that I was leaving the Oregon Project. I felt like I owed it to him to say it to his face, not over email. Adam offered to go with me, but I told him no, that this was between me and Alberto.

When I arrived at the Nike campus for our meeting, I was surprised to see Darren there, but proceeded anyway. I confronted Alberto and Darren about their unhealthy hatred for Adam, which took a lot of courage for me. I said that over the past year Alberto had mostly left me on my own without a coach, and Adam had picked up the slack, pacing me on runs, keeping me focused. Alberto and Darren responded with more criticism of Adam. Then they wondered aloud about who else would ever agree to coach me. "Jerry Schumacher?" they suggested, grinning. It was a joke to them.

Jerry had long been a target of Alberto's and Darren's antipathy. He was the former running coach at the University of Wisconsin, who Adam and I had visited in the summer of 2004, just before we were recruited to the Oregon Project. He was a father of four, wore socks with sandals, and had a proud Wisconsin accent. He looked a bit like Jim Carrey, and he made no secret of his great admiration for Chris Farley. In 2008, after the Beijing Olympics, Alberto hired Jerry to coach with him at the Oregon Project. They quickly had a falling-out, and Jerry began to work with his own Nike-sponsored training group on campus. The idea was still for Jerry's and Alberto's runners to train together, but again, that didn't work out. Jerry didn't trust Alberto or Darren, so they turned on him.

Jerry and his runners became a separate entity from our Oregon Project group, though we'd still see them from time to time around campus, and wave as we went about our days. Some elite runners from his Wisconsin teams had followed him out to Portland, including Chris Solinsky, Evan Jager, and Matthew Tegenkamp, who had run the 5,000 meters in Beijing. In 2009, Shalane Flanagan joined Jerry's group. Since then, other successful runners, including Lopez Lomong, had trained with Jerry. I liked Jerry and his runners because, well, they were likable.

Alberto wanted to make light of it, but the idea of me going to Jerry's team would be a stab in the back to him and Darren. What should have been nothing more than a friendly bit of inter-company competition became a bitter rivalry in Alberto's hands. Alberto would bad-mouth Jerry to the Oregon Project athletes and staffers. In an email to Adam, Alberto had referred to Jerry and his runners as "our mortal enemies." I told Alberto and Darren the truth, that if I left the Oregon Project, I had no idea who would coach me, and I hadn't talked to Jerry or anyone else.

I did not definitively tell Alberto and Darren that I was leaving before we ended our meeting. There was a lot on my mind. Darren had always told me that if I couldn't hack it with Alberto, it meant I wasn't cut out for the sport at all. During our conversation on campus, Darren also implied that I wouldn't be good without his own guidance and work with me. Sadly, these arguments gave me pause. Furthermore, Nike controlled so many of the big events, in addition to sponsoring the USATF and the IAAF, and I worried whether they might retaliate against me, such as by denying me admission to races. Thinking further into the future, Adam and I had always figured that when our running careers were done, we would transition into professional roles at Nike—perhaps in coaching, or even marketing or shoe design—and I wondered what leaving would mean for those plans.

In our personal lives, we considered ourselves adopted Oregonians. We had dumped all of our savings into what we thought was our forever home in Portland. We had built relationships with our neighbors and in our community. Kendall and Bret and their kids were close by. She had a daughter only six months apart from Colt, and we valued the time when our children played together.

Now, it seemed like everything was changing at once. Around the time of my meeting with Alberto and Darren, Adam, who had quietly kept up his training on his own but hadn't raced for more than a year and a half, decided to take his shot at qualifying for the 2012 Olympic Marathon Trials. He went to Philadelphia for the Rock 'n' Roll Half Marathon, where he'd need to break 65 minutes. (Running a fast half marathon is one path to qualifying for the Trials in the marathon.)

He ran 64 minutes and 52 seconds at the distance, securing his spot in Houston in January. I was so proud of him. But on the plane home to Portland, his knee swelled. Upon a doctor's examination, Adam was told that he would need surgery to clean up his meniscus. The Trials were off. He knew it was the end. The grief and frustration of his once-comet-like career coming to a close in a slow sputter was heartbreaking. Yet, instead of closing himself off, he channeled it into being an even greater supporter of me and my career than he'd been already. "It's time to put you first," he told me. He helped me train, took care of Colt, and bought the groceries. He also began talking to his friend Tim more seriously about making a company they had started called Run the Edge, which provided training plans for runners and hosted virtual fitness challenges, into something bigger.

I exchanged emails with Alberto after our meeting on the Nike campus, with me confiding in him about how painful I had found it, that I was stressed, and thanking him for all he'd done for me and my career.

Alberto called me. "Have you ever heard the saying 'Love conquers all'?" he asked. I told him that I had. He said he loved me. I said I loved him, too. "Let's work it out," he said.

I sat with all these feelings, turned them over, and decided that I had to face my fears. There was no turning back. It was time to go. By the last week of September, it was clear to both me and Alberto, at last, that I was on my way out. I was going to start looking for another coach to help me train for the Olympic Trials in January.

On September 27, Alberto emailed me. He wrote that he was "impressed at how sure and determined" I was to leave, whereas he had wavered for some time. After thinking it through at length, however, he had come to believe that my "instincts were right and that it is best for us to part ways at this time." He said that he would always remember me fondly and wished me happiness and success in running and in life. It was the last email that I ever received from him.

CHAPTER THIRTY
The Fight for Two Spots

Finding a new coach was a challenge. Publicly, Alberto was winning awards, writing a memoir, and leading his runners to podium finishes, but behind the scenes in the running world, rumors of the possibility that his athletes were doping had spread far and wide. One team that I reached out to and inquired about joining, Terrence Mahon's California-based group, voted not to take me on, with a person I'd thought of as a friend casting the deciding "no" vote. That stung.

"Does the entire industry hate me?" I asked Adam, as more rejections came in.

I decided that I had to get over my fears of the internal Nike chaos it could create if I reached out to Jerry Schumacher, which were reinforced by Cap initially telling Jerry that he couldn't coach me because it would kill Alberto. I trusted Jerry and contacted him confidentially, telling him that I was leaving Alberto's group, and wondering if he'd be willing to take me on.

Jerry came over to our house and talked to me and Adam. He made me feel excited about running again. He and I were only eight years apart, and were both parents of young children. He seemed to get me and the dynamics between competitive running and my family. When he left our house, Adam closed the door and said, "That's the guy."

About a week later, we met Jerry again, this time in the Lance building on Nike's campus. Jerry, through some sort of magic, said he had convinced Cap to let him coach me. However, out of respect to Shalane, I felt like I needed her blessing first.

I was nervous. It was a massive ask, runner to runner. We were just a few months out from the Olympic Marathon Trials, and I was asking Shalane to share her coach with someone who would be directly competing with her in Houston for one of the three U.S. team spots. Shalane and I were both going to be in San Francisco on October 16 for the Nike

Women's Marathon, and I decided I'd ask her there. The day before the race we made plans to go for a run together. As I shyly worked my way into what I needed to ask, it became clear that Shalane already knew what was coming. She said that she had even talked it over with her family. She had decided to let me join her and Jerry in training.

Thank God, I thought. It was great news: not only was Jerry a top coach who I felt extremely comfortable with, but because he was part of Nike, I could put off the messy process of leaving my contract. Cap's word certainly didn't feel to me as good as gold, but having his approval to switch coaches was enough for now.

The more Shalane and I talked, the more I respected her. She felt there was room enough for the both of us, that we could work together to elevate each other instead of tearing one another down. The idea of training together was refreshing. Team USA had three spots for the women's marathon. We were hell-bent on getting two of them.

––––––––

My first practice with Jerry and Shalane was October 18, just twelve weeks before the Trials, and it kicked my ass. We did a 20-mile run. Ten miles in, I died. My fitness had dropped off since returning from Daegu; I was still suffering the effects of the stress fracture in my femoral neck.

Jerry's coaching philosophy was simple: work, work, work. He didn't believe in gadgets, saw AlterG running as using "training wheels," and preferred his runners to put in tons of mileage, lots of time on feet. Shalane had a training partner named Lisa Uhl, an NCAA champion out of Iowa State, who we ran with often. Otherwise, because Shalane and I were the only marathoners, beyond lifting weights with the people on Jerry's team, we mostly trained on our own. As I got closer to Shalane and saw her routine, my respect for her shot through the roof. Having trained some with Paula Radcliffe, I'd gotten a taste of the brutal, but I became enamored with how tough Shalane was. She didn't only bring the heat in racing, she brought it every single day she put on her running shoes. She was the most disciplined runner I'd ever seen, a professional, through and through. I had catching up to do.

The pain of the alarm clock hit every morning. Jerry's athletes were early risers, and my 8:30 a.m. alarm became a 6:30 a.m. one. I felt this was probably the schedule that I should have had all along, had it not been for what I thought were Alberto's late nights of drinking, as it would better prepare my body for the early-morning start of the Marathon Trials, but it was still a rude awakening.

For weeks, I continued to lag behind Shalane. We did an interval workout in which she completed four sets and I could only do two. Six weeks later, I had only gotten up to three sets. Jerry pulled me aside and told me the truth, that I was hanging on by a thread. It was a blow to my ego, but his assessment was accurate. *If I couldn't match, let alone beat, Shalane in workouts, how was I going to make an Olympic team?*

I doubled down. I tried to ride it out, one day, one workout at a time. For fuel, I thought about how nobody cared if I was a mom at the finish line, and that my 2007 bronze medal from Osaka was getting dusty. People had written me off. To some degree, I had written myself off. I didn't want to do that anymore.

Shalane and I shared stories during our runs. She told me that she remembered running behind me during her freshman year at the University of North Carolina. Her coach had told her to follow me, and "do what Kara does." We laughed, and later I dug up photos from the race. Sure enough, there she was, shadowing me. Now here I was, shadowing her.

As a coach, Jerry was focused on the details of my training, but he treated me like an adult, and didn't try to control my life. He was more of a peer and a collaborator than a father figure. When I left practice, Jerry didn't come with me, literally or figuratively.

Old habits could still be hard to break, though, so I approached Jerry to tell him I was thinking about dyeing my hair black. I asked if he cared. Not only did he not care, he looked confused about why I would ask in the first place. Sometimes it takes being confronted with a healthy alternative to realize how unhealthy the past was. When I struggled in workouts, Shalane and Jerry sent me encouraging texts. They didn't know all of the details of what had transpired at the Oregon Project, but their encouragement—taking the place of Alberto's and Darren's recriminations—helped start a healing process for me.

Part of that was owning up to the things I regretted. Amy Begley had left the Oregon Project in July 2011—two months before me. She had frequently been injured in 2010 and 2011, so I hadn't seen her much lately, but once I left, we started getting sushi together on Tuesdays. Over these meals—away from the Nike campus, Alberto, and the male-dominated Oregon Project culture—we got to know each other in a way that we never had as teammates. Out of fear, as well as a troubling desire to remain the more popular woman in the group, I hadn't stood up for Amy or been the type of feminist that I aspired to be. I apologized for that. I also confessed to her that Darren had told me that she was talking smack about me, which I now realized wasn't true. Amy was incredibly compassionate and forgiving. Over time, I learned that Alberto had actually made Amy sign insane contracts saying that she couldn't be on the team if she gained a certain amount of weight, and that she was not allowed to befriend other athletes on the team, which is part of why she'd left.

In retrospect, I wished that we had opened up to each other about our experiences with Alberto and Darren while we were still in the Oregon Project, so we could have become allies instead of living in our own silos, suffering in silence. But I realized that a large part of what made that impossible was their actively working to undermine it. Driving a wedge between us was a way to control us.

I arrived in Houston on January 11, 2012, for the Marathon Trials, uncertain of what kind of performance I could realistically expect of myself.

Out of the 183 women set to start the race, ten of them—myself included—had already hit the Olympic standard, making it a very competitive field. I had worked my butt off training with Shalane, but still wasn't quite at her level. In addition to Shalane, there were also Des Davila, Deena Kastor, Amy Hastings, and Janet Cherobon-Bawcom, all of whom were running fast and seemed to be peaking at the perfect moment. I calculated that something around a 2:26 time would be needed to make the team.

At the same time, I was motivated to fight with everything I had. Alberto and Darren would be there. Cap would be, too, watching all of the Nike athletes, including me. Although I wasn't looking forward to the potential awkwardness of seeing them there, I was also desperate to assert myself as a runner independent from them. Having Adam, Colt, my mom, and Kelly all there supporting me—and actually being allowed to spend time with them before the race, now that Jerry was my coach—provided a huge boost to my confidence. Adam and Jerry had ElliptiGOs and were planning to cheer me on from along the perimeter of the course when possible.

While training in Portland, Jerry and I had been having realistic conversations about my being a long shot for the team. But the day before the race, he, Shalane, and I were doing strides in a plaza near our hotel, and he told me that he believed I could be top three. He said that I had made considerable progress in the last two weeks. Because he had always been so honest with me, I knew he meant it.

We'd built considerable trust, and feeling its power in that moment, I decided right there and then to tell Jerry about the final episode that had led me to leave the Oregon Project: Alberto attempting to kiss me on the plane to Daegu. Even if I wasn't ready to share the complete story of all of Alberto's abuses, I was ready to take the first step. Jerry listened, and thanked me for having the courage to speak to him about it. He felt that I should tell Mark Parker what happened, but it wasn't something I was comfortable doing. He understood that it was my choice.

The morning of January 14, race day, the skies were clear and the temperature a chilly 40 degrees. The course was flat and mimicked a criterium course like London's: it started with a 2.2-mile loop, then three repetitions of an 8-mile loop through Houston. While Houston had few turns, though, London had an extreme amount of turns and changes in footing along the way.

We took off and it quickly became clear that it would be a tactical race. About 10 miles in, Amy Hastings began throwing in surges—I lost count of how many. I hung in. The parts of the course that went through downtown Houston were packed with fans, but other parts of it were on the highway, and when those sections opened up, Adam and Jerry hovered around me on their ElliptiGOs like some sort of *Star Trek*–meets–*Arrested Development* husband-coach duo, cheering me on. It made the race feel less scary, and more like any other workout.

By around the 13-mile mark, the race really took shape, and it became clear that there were four women who were fighting it out for those top three spots: Shalane, Amy, Des, and me. Des started to pick up the pace.

I knew that it was too hot to hold for long, but with about 6 miles left, I could feel that Amy was suffering. Jerry had told me to trust my instincts, that I would be the quarterback. I made the call to go hard for a mile, even though the pace was over my head, to try and break Amy. It worked.

With 3 miles to go, Jerry yelled at me that I could catch Des Davila. "NO I CAN'T!" I yelled back. He disagreed.

As I made a turn into the last 200 meters, the crowds moved me. I wasn't going to catch Des, but I was going to make the team. I put my hand on my chest and started crying before I crossed the finish line, in a state of mild lunacy, joy, confusion, fatigue.

Shalane won and Des came in second. My time was 2:26:06—exactly what I had predicted would be needed—and the last spot on the team was mine. Shalane called it the deepest field ever to vie for the three women's marathon spots.

An American flag was draped over my shoulders. Relief and joy washed over me. Almost nobody who saw that race knew the backstory of all I'd been through, and why it meant so much.

CHAPTER THIRTY-ONE
The FBI, London, Randos

Through the rest of the winter and spring of 2012, Shalane, Jerry, and I prepared for the London Olympics.

On February 8, we flew to London and ran the marathon course over two days for practice—10 miles on one day, 8 miles the next morning, and the last 8 miles that afternoon—taking in all of its strange twists and turns. On March 18, I ran the New York City Half Marathon and finished in third place. After that I went with Jerry and Shalane to Mammoth Lakes, California, a town at 7,800 feet of altitude, and did long runs of two and three hours at a time. We did 20-by-400s, 5k repeats, milers on grass, and lots of fartleks (drills that play with speed, mixing fast runs with easier and moderately paced stretches). When it came to 5k repeats, we tried to see if we could emulate the workouts that Liliya Shobukhova of Russia—a London Marathon winner and three-time Chicago Marathon winner who we highly suspected of doping—was doing. We had read that she did four reps per workout. We tried to do three and felt destroyed.

The training was all-consuming. There were times during our workouts where my mind went completely numb, my body pushing through a punch-drunk volume of miles harder than it ever had before. We ramped up to running 130 to 135 miles per week. Shalane still dominated our workouts, but, realizing that there was no way I would have placed top three in Houston without those weeks of having my butt kicked by her in Portland, I felt less like I was falling short and more like her example was driving me forward.

For our last races before going to the Olympics, Shalane and I were given a choice between the USATF Half Marathon Championship in Duluth, or the 10,000 meters in the Olympic track Trials in Eugene. It was a no-brainer for me. I went to Duluth in mid-June and won the race, fist-pumping joyfully to the support of an incredible hometown crowd.

Then at the end of June, I went to Eugene to cheer on Shalane and our friend and teammate Lisa Uhl, who was also running the 10,000. Shalane competed as a training opportunity—she didn't intend to run the event in London—but she finished third, and Lisa also made the team. Then, Jerry told us to head back to Portland to stay out of the fray, so we watched the rest of the meet on TV.

The at-home viewing included the 5,000 meters final, where we were rooting for a friend of ours, Andrew Bumbalough, who ended up finishing fourth, while Galen won and secured his spot on his second Olympic team. It was all too real an example of why doping—which I believed Galen was doing—should be treated as a crime. Andrew had been barely staying afloat financially, and making the team would have been life-changing for him. Instead, it was likely his pay would be reduced, and future sponsorship opportunities would disappear.

I thought about Tyler Hamilton, and his bravery in whistleblowing against someone as powerful and beloved as Lance Armstrong. A heaviness pressed against my chest. Because of my silence, people like Andrew were being screwed. *Why am I still protecting people who I think are cheating?* I wondered.

On my birthday, July 9, I went for a long, hard run and came home to find two men in suits sitting at our dining room table with Adam. At first, I thought that he had decided to entertain Jehovah's Witnesses (which would have been a first), but Adam introduced them as FBI agents. Six months earlier, Adam had gotten beers with a friend of his who worked for the FBI, and had told him about some of our concerns regarding doping at Nike, that we worried it could affect the London Olympics, but neither of us were expecting this visit. I was nervous yet excited that they were there. They assured me that everything I said would be kept confidential. I sat down and explained what I believed: that with Alberto's help, Mo and Galen were at best pushing the limits, at worst doping, and had shots at winning medals in London. I told them that the progress that Mo and Galen had recently made seemed impossible to me without assistance. It felt amazing to say that out loud, to people who might have the authority to do something about it, no less. (Mo and Galen have disputed this.)

In its July 30 issue, *The New Yorker* ran a glowing profile of Alberto. It was written by Malcolm Gladwell, who in addition to being the bestselling author of *The Tipping Point* and *Blink*, was a runner and running fan. The piece valorized Alberto, calling him "the greatest distance runner in the world" for the first half of the 1980s. Gladwell's assessment was that "Salazar's greatness lay in his desire." Neither Galen, Mo, nor I were mentioned. The timing of the publication, just at the start of the London Games, with reference to Alberto's "absorbing" memoir, brought even more attention to him and further built his image as the mastermind coach of the most advanced team in American distance running.

On July 23, Jerry, Shalane, Lisa, Matt, Evan, Adam, Colt, and I all flew together to Europe. The plan was to stay in the Netherlands for about a week, getting settled in a place with a similar climate and time zone to London but away from the pre-Olympic hustle and bustle. My mom and Kelly also joined us in the Netherlands to help out with Colt and support me. I was glad that I had gone to the Opening Ceremony in Beijing because in 2012 the ceremony happened before we even got to London. The marathon would take place at the end of the Olympics, which meant that I still had training to do.

On August 1, we all arrived in London. We stayed in a hotel near the starting line of the marathon, not far from Buckingham Palace. It was the antithesis of the loneliness and isolation of my experience in Beijing.

The night before my race, August 4, Galen and Mo's 10,000 meters final was on. "Go to bed," Adam told me. "Don't watch it. Focus on your own race." It was the right advice, but I couldn't help it. I sat on the edge, eyes fixed on the TV screen, as Mo fired his new kick into gear at the end of the race. The home crowd in the sold-out stadium were on their feet in total euphoria as he closed out his last lap in 53.48 seconds and won gold, the third of the day for Team Great Britain, marking their best day in Olympic history. Galen, trailing Tariku Bekele of Ethiopia (Kenenisa's little brother) with 60 meters to go, then surged ahead to win the silver, making him the first American man to reach the Olympic podium in the event since Billy Mills won gold in 1964.

Alberto hugged Galen and Mo at the finish line, a picture-perfect ending, the culmination of ten years and millions of dollars of investment.

I clicked off the TV and lay down in bed, feeling the anger. I didn't want to let Galen or Alberto take away my focus. I had a race to run.

The next morning, Shalane and I got ready. The race would be true to British form, with intermittent showers and occasional downpours. We were glad to be so used to soggy Oregon.

Shalane and I stuck together and led for the first 13 or so miles, running against the stunning backdrop of Buckingham Palace, the Houses of Parliament, Big Ben, and the Tower of London. I kept waiting for Liliya Shobukhova to make a move, but she ended up dropping out around the halfway mark. At approximately the 15-mile mark, a pack of runners pushed forward. Shalane went with them, while I hung back. This was not unexpected and something Jerry had prepared us for: the plan was for Shalane to stay out in the lead, where she thrived, while I kept on being the "steady burn" that I was. We thought that we could both finish in the top five with this approach.

But something odd was happening. The pack that Shalane was running with was made up of women who weren't well-known as marathoners. I kept thinking, *Who the hell is this?* as another runner went by me. As I fell deeper back, I got pushed and grunted at.

Soon, Shalane was falling off the pace as well. I wanted to quit but told myself to keep going, to soak it all in. I reminded myself that Paula, who was injured, would have killed to be running that race. In the end, Shalane finished 10th, and I was right behind her in 11th. We were disappointed and a bit shell-shocked. After fumbling my way through interviews at the finish line and then drug testing, I threw my shoes in the trash. It wasn't that Shalane and I didn't make the podium, or even that we got beaten, rather that it seemed like something bizarre was going on that day with the field.

We were baffled to look at the top nine finishers and see some names of people who had barely competed on the international stage, if at all. It wasn't like losing to Simone Biles or to Michael Phelps, where you know you gave it a fair shot and came up short against one of the all-time greats. This sort of "coming out of nowhere" story just isn't how the sport of marathoning works. We suspected foul play.

The day after the marathon, my body wiped out, I went for a short run and then flew with my family to Croatia to explore my father's roots. For a few days my aunt ushered us around to see cousins and long-lost family members, who I enjoyed meeting, but I was burned-out and glad when we got home to Portland for some long-overdue rest. All of us on Jerry's team were given time off after the Olympics, but when I took Colt to the pool on the Nike campus a few days after getting back to Portland, I looked out the window and saw Shalane doing a workout on the grass fields. I understood what was driving her, and felt like I was ready to join. I was pissed about London, too. I told Shalane and Jerry that I was ready to roll for the next workout.

As it turned out, my mind was ready, but my body was not. The Olympic Marathon had dinged me up, the turns and cobblestones of the London course exacerbating a minor pain in my heel. I kept training, but could tell that I was losing a step.

In September, Tyler Hamilton's book *The Secret Race* came out. I devoured it right away. So did Jerry, and we eagerly discussed it. Among the many revelations in Tyler's book was that using artificial altitude was a favorite tactic of Lance Armstrong's and the Tour de France riders' to cover up the use of the hormone erythropoietin, or EPO. Whether that had anything to do with Alberto's fondness for altitude tents—or his sudden suggestion that we use altitude masks in training camp in Daegu—I couldn't be sure. But given the time Alberto and Lance had spent together, no theory seemed far-fetched to me, and I wondered if Alberto was using the altitude masks in Daegu to throw off Galen's and Mo's drug test results.

Adam, Colt, and I, along with Jerry and Shalane, were in Adam's hometown of Colorado Springs in January 2013 for an altitude camp when Lance Armstrong's interview with Oprah Winfrey aired. In it, Lance admitted to using performance-enhancing drugs. Other cyclists including Floyd Landis had corroborated Hamilton's story and added to it, building an ironclad case. Finally, Lance was owning up to his crimes. After the interview aired, Travis Tygart, the head of the U.S. Anti-Doping Agency (USADA), was on another channel talking about the case and his reaction to Lance's doping admission. Tygart described the incredible pressure that he'd faced to not pursue the charges against Lance, from anonymous death threats, to entreaties from powerful organizations including the governing body of cycling.

I was roused by the story. Adam and I had never heard back from the FBI after sitting down with them in our home in July. Over the past couple of months, Adam had wondered aloud if we should try again, but there were three things holding us back. One: we didn't know where else to go. Two: we were terrified—we knew that if Nike found out that we'd talked to the FBI or any other authority, they'd find a way to kill my contract, and maybe my career altogether. Three: if we came forward, we were going to be asking whoever was listening to believe that I was clean. Truth-tellers like Hamilton had been credible because they admitted that they had broken the rules themselves. Would authorities have the same confidence in me? But after watching Travis Tygart talk about the hurdles he'd barreled through to prosecute Lance, something changed. I felt a personal, emotional connection to him. And I thought that if anyone could understand the power that Nike wields, and find a way to protect us from it, it would be him.

There was one more reason I felt compelled to take the risk and try coming forward. In late 2012, a Nike employee told me that a high school running phenom named Mary Cain had started working with Alberto and the Oregon Project. The idea of a teenage female runner being under Alberto's influence unnerved me. I didn't think that Mary would be receptive to my reaching out to her directly and trying to convince her that Alberto was bad news. But I thought that if I finally did the hard thing and talked to someone like Travis Tygart, perhaps he could do something to stop Alberto.

It struck me that if I was looking around and wondering why someone hadn't done something, it might be a sign that I was the person who was supposed to do it. I thought about the example that I wanted to set for Colt, and the example that my mom and Papa had set for me in their pioneering work with MADD.

"If we can sit down with that guy," I told Adam, looking at Tygart on the TV screen, "I'll go in and talk."

Adam reached out to a friend who had a connection and got us Tygart's number. We called his cell, not knowing that he was in Europe and we were waking him up in the middle of the night. He told us that he would be back in Colorado in February, and we set up a time to meet on February 7.

I took a rare afternoon off running for the USADA meeting. Adam and I told our nanny that we should be home in an hour or two. We met Travis and two USADA lawyers in a conference room at their headquarters. Travis has a southern accent, brown hair, and came into the room sipping out of a University of North Carolina mug, a nod to his alma mater. His demeanor was respectful, but direct. They offered us coffee, and calmed my nerves (though only slightly) by assuring me that everything I said would remain confidential. I knew I needed to do this, but there was part of me that still felt like I would be betraying my old coach and teammates, some residue of obedience still clinging to me. I took a breath, then I started to talk.

I told them I didn't have a smoking gun in hand, but explained what I'd seen and why I believed Alberto and Galen and possibly Mo were breaking the rules. (Charges both of them would later deny.) Since leaving the Oregon Project, one thing in particular had been on my mind: the Andro-Gel testosterone medication that I'd seen in the Park City condo in 2007. Explaining that Alberto frequently massaged his athletes (without mentioning a word about the Rieti or Lisbon incidents), I told them that I had started wondering whether he could have used AndroGel on Galen during massages. Alberto would often massage Galen even when we were scheduled to have a professional masseur work on us, which felt off to me. Since Mo had joined after I had Colt and I'd stopped spending as much time with the team, I hadn't personally witnessed Alberto massaging Mo, so I explained I had less evidence to support my suspicion there, but believed it was likely he'd been getting the same treatments.

I said that I did not think Alberto ever used any sort of testosterone gel with me during massages, but I couldn't be totally sure and I was worried about it. I was willing to give USADA all of my medical records and lab results so that they could look at my levels over time. I admitted that there was some amount of me that was petrified that they might find something incriminating in my records that I myself hadn't been aware of, but I didn't think it was likely. Adam and I also told them about all of the supplements we'd ever taken. I said that Alberto had always told me they were fully tested and "USADA approved."

"What?" Travis said, with a laugh that stopped me in my tracks. "That isn't a thing." A shiver went down my spine, and then a rush of embarrassment. Both Alberto and one of our assistant coaches, John Cook, had told me that line on multiple occasions, and I'd bought it. I felt like a fool.

Though I did not talk at all about the massages in Rieti or Lisbon (incidents that I still had not told Adam about), I did tell them about Alberto's unsettling behavior and questions on the flight to Lisbon, and his attempt to kiss me on the flight to Daegu.

I also mentioned Dr. Jeffrey Brown, who was still currently my prescriber for hypothyroidism medication. I noted that Dr. Brown had diagnosed others in the Oregon Project with the condition, including Adam, Alberto, and Galen. Even some of Jerry's runners had been diagnosed by Dr. Brown, after Alberto had told Jerry to send his athletes there. As I was saying it, I started to realize how absurd the coincidence sounded of so many runners being diagnosed with hypothyroidism. I didn't understand what, if anything, was suspicious about it, but in that setting, in a conference room with the head of USADA and two lawyers, everything started to take on a different light.

Travis and his two colleagues then asked me and Adam very specific questions—they wanted to know what had happened at certain meets, on certain dates, and clearly had done a lot of research. I recognized what this must mean: there was already an investigation in progress.

The meeting lasted four hours. Travis and the lawyers showed us out, and said they'd be in touch.

CHAPTER THIRTY-TWO
Bombs

I was unsettled after the USADA meeting. I felt that Travis and his investigators believed that I was telling the truth, but now that I'd spoken it aloud, I couldn't shake the worry that Alberto might have rubbed testosterone gel on me at some point without my knowing, or spiked my supplements with something that would make me look like a liar, and that Dr. Brown could have been involved in some way. Late into the night, restless, I wondered: *What if I have to give back everything I've worked for, everything I've achieved? My Osaka medal. My marathon podium finishes. My titles and records. My reputation.* Alarm bells were going off left and right, and I didn't know which ones to listen to, what to trust. But the worrying was useless, and I knew it. I'd done the hard thing, and come forward. The risks were worth taking. I believed in my heart of hearts that, naive as I may have been at times, I was clean, and my records would show it.

In the meantime, I continued to fight through injuries—adding a hamstring problem to my heel pain—while training in Colorado Springs with Jerry and Shalane. Our focus was now on the Boston Marathon on April 15. The hamstring injury kept me from feeling like I was in top physical form in the final weeks of preparation, but the marathon training gave me the familiar routine and structure that helped anchor me mentally and emotionally.

A big contingent of family joined me in Boston, including my mom, Kelly, my aunt Davorka (my father's sister), two of Adam's aunts, one of his uncles, and Adam and Colt of course. They cheered me on during the race, which, given the injuries, didn't end in a bad result for me at all. I finished sixth, Shalane finished fourth, and Rita Jeptoo of Kenya won the title. I ran hard, I ran well.

After the race, I met my family near the finish line for a quick picture. Then Adam's aunts and uncle left, and I asked if my mom, sister, aunt, Adam, and Colt would do me a favor and pick up some food on the way back to the hotel, where I'd meet them after going through drug testing and media.

I found my family up in my hotel room, inhaled the sandwich they'd gotten for me, and realized that it was almost 2:50 and I had to rush out to make my three o'clock massage. I was just about to leave when something completely inexplicable and literally earthshaking happened.

BOOM. The windowpanes of the hotel room rattled. I felt a reverberation in my chest. I'd barely gotten ahold of myself and gotten out the words "What the hell was that?" when, *BOOM*, a second blast shook the room.

I grabbed Colt, freaking out. My mom went over to the open window to try to see what was going on.

"SHUT IT!" I yelled. Clearly there had been some kind of explosion—what type, I had no idea—but I could already hear the sirens wailing. We turned on the news, fearing the worst, that we'd learn people had just been killed. We worried that an attack had begun and could still be underway. Someone on the hotel staff, I assume, called the room phone and told us that the hotel was on lockdown and that we should not leave our room. I peeked out the window and could see law enforcement pulling up in SUVs that were filled with racks of guns. It alarmed me, but my mom told me that the fact they were staging themselves close to the hotel could mean we were in a safe place.

The news reports confirmed there had been a bombing at the finish line, there were indeed casualties and injuries, and those responsible were believed to still be on the loose. We called Adam's aunts and uncle and were relieved to get through to them: they had left the finish line before the bombs went off, and were safe. Our phones chirped with texts and calls from concerned friends and family across the country. Shalane's mother called me, not having been able to get through to Shalane. Shalane and I had been texting, so I knew that she was in the hotel with her dad and okay.

I couldn't pull myself away from the TV. The finish line was cordoned off by police and looked like a paramilitary area. There were officers and bomb-sniffing dogs all over the hotel. Hundreds of unclaimed bags rested in the street. It didn't feel real. Evening came and the hotel staff told us it was safe to leave our rooms. My mom tried for hours to get me downstairs to eat some food. Eventually I acquiesced, wandering down in my pajamas, in a fog. I didn't sleep that night, thinking about the people who had been

hurt and those who were safe, replaying the events of the day on loop, anx-
iously wondering if the bomber (or bombers) had been found. Nonsensical
questions kept coming up: *If I hadn't asked for that sandwich, would my
family be dead? What is the point of running if it puts lives at risk?* The sanc-
tity of this special place and day, maybe of road races everywhere, felt like it
had been permanently violated. It was hard for me to see how marathoning
would ever be the same. People had died. Colt had been in danger. Racing
felt stupid in light of it.

The next morning, we flew to Minnesota. I remained parked in front of
the TV in the sunroom at my mom's house for the next few days, entertain-
ing two-and-a-half-year-old Colt with an iPad while I obsessively followed
the story of what had happened in Boston. It wasn't healthy. I still couldn't
sleep, and every little noise—the garbage truck roaring by, Colt dropping a
toy, a door closing—startled me.

When we got back to Portland, we learned that the police had searched
our house while we had been gone, as it hadn't been immediately clear
what the bombers' motives were and there was a possibility that they could
have been targeting specific runners.

I continued to be on edge, Adam struggled, too, and we fed off each
other's unsettled energy. Colt, we noticed, wasn't himself, either. Instead
of gently petting and cuddling our cats and his stuffed animals, he started
grabbing for their necks and kicking. Rather than losing himself in playing with his toys, he never wanted to be out of my sight. We took him to
a therapist who specialized in childhood trauma. We sat with him on the
floor as he re-created the bombing with Playmobil figures and a black toy
ball, talking about "the big boom" and how "Mommy got scared" and "people got hurt." I was amazed by how much he had taken in, his precocious
insight.

After Boston, Shalane and I needed a goal, and we set our sights on
trying to qualify for the World Championships in the 10,000 meters. In
late June, we went to the USA Outdoor Track and Field Championships in
Des Moines. It was incredibly hot and humid, and I went out way too hard.
The heat got the worst of me and halfway through, I knew I wasn't going to
make it in the top three. Shalane won. I finished fifth.

A runner named Jordan Hasay finished second. I'd heard that Jordan,
who had just graduated from the University of Oregon, was thinking of

joining Alberto's team. Shalane and I had reached out to her together in the days before our race. We'd set up a time to meet at a Panera Bread in Des Moines, where we planned to share our concerns about Alberto with her. She canceled the meeting, announced on Instagram that she was running with Alberto, and wore an Oregon Project jersey in our race. I later learned that Jordan had already begun working with Darren and had done some training with Alberto before her senior season of college. The third-place finisher was Tara Erdmann, also an Oregon Project runner (she'd joined in 2012). Mary Cain, to my dismay, had joined as well. She was seventeen. She finished second in the 1,500 meters final. Galen also won the men's 10,000. It all broke my heart. I didn't know what to believe, but it was clear Alberto was having a banner day. It was frustrating, especially since we had barely heard from USADA since our meeting in February. I was starting to doubt that their investigation was going to go anywhere.

In terms of my own performance, I felt like I couldn't do anything right. I was working and fighting hard, but falling short. On June 28, I was doing a three-mile cooldown after a tempo run when my foot began to throb, and I had to stop. *Great*, I thought, *now I can't even do a cooldown*. Shalane picked me up and drove me to my car. I thought maybe I had tied my shoe too tight. When Jerry saw me, he told me to get an MRI as soon as possible. On July 5, I got the MRI and I was told it would take a while for the results to be ready, so I was walking to the parking lot when a nurse ran out and yelled at me, "You have a broken foot! You need to stay off your foot!" I had to wear a boot for eight weeks, which felt like a century. Jerry told me to work out creatively. I did my elliptical machine in the boot for 80 minutes in the morning while binging *Laguna Beach*, then again for 40 minutes in the evening. I had signed a contract with the New York Road Runners for $200,000 to compete at the New York City Marathon in November but had to back out.

In October, my foot wasn't yet fully healed, but as I knew too well, per my still-active Nike contract, if I hit 120 days without competing, Nike had the right to suspend my pay. On top of that, I still needed to run six more USATF-certified races within 2013 to hit my total of ten for the year, or Nike could reduce my salary by 50 percent for the remainder of my contract. I made a madcap plan to fulfill the terms of my contract and avoid going through the horror of contract arbitration all over again.

On October 12, 118 days since I'd last competed, I drove north from Portland with Adam and Colt on Interstate 5. Our destination: Evergreen Christian School in Olympia, Washington, specifically, their Glow Run—a USATF-certified 5k. The event website was written in Comic Sans. I arrived to find that the festivities also included glow-in-the-dark face paint, a walking event, and a kids' dash (free admission). Colt had a blast with some glow sticks, and we noshed on Chipotle afterward. My foot was sore—I was still wearing my boot around the house, and icing it at night—but I made it through (and won) the race.

At the end, I asked the organizers for my time and a polite volunteer told me that their chip system had broken. I'm sure she was confused to see the look on my face, as if my life depended on this victory, but she assured me they would publish my name on their website as the winner to verify I had completed the course.

A week later, on October 20, Shalane and I jogged the Nike Women's Half Marathon together in San Francisco. I still needed four competitions after that, so I came back to Oregon and signed up for any USATF-certified event that would have me, which turned out to be three cross-country races that I ran in October and November. That would put me at five races down, with one left to go by the end of the year.

On November 1, Adam and I flew to Denver and were driving to Boulder to cheer on CU in the Pac-12 cross country championships, when I saw an email from Cap's office. It said that they were providing me official notice that I hadn't competed for 126 days. Instead of reducing my pay by 50 percent, he said, they would do me a favor and suspend me instead for that period, meaning that to make up for it, I wouldn't get paid for that number of days going forward.

But my position was that Nike was wrong. They were considering the half marathon in San Francisco my return to competition. I *had* raced before the 120-day mark, in the Glow Run, and could prove it.

Cap also said they were not going to take the option year that was in my contract, and instead we would renegotiate a new contract after my 126-day suspension was up. What they didn't say was that by not exercising their option, I now had the choice to leave Nike once and for all, free and clear. And all thanks to the Glow Run, I could do it without having any of my pay reduced or suspended.

I loved Jerry and Shalane and was grateful to them, but after more than nine years of living in Portland, and all Adam and I had been through, we had started wondering what else might be out there for us.

I had broken it off with Alberto two years earlier. Now it felt like it was time to break things off with Nike.

"I'm free!" I told Adam.

He cheered.

On Pearl Street in Boulder, Adam and I ran into our college coach, Mark Wetmore, and his co-coach, Heather Burroughs. Heather had been a CU teammate of mine, two years ahead of me. Not long after graduating, Heather and Mark had started dating. Mark was in his mid-forties at the time and Heather in her mid-twenties, and to be frank, Adam and I had thought it was odd, but by now, they'd been committed to each other for many years, were partners in every way, and I didn't see anything wrong with it. (It's also worth noting that Mark had never made me—nor, to my knowledge, any of my teammates—feel the least bit uncomfortable as our college coach.)

Out of the blue, I asked Mark and Heather, "Have you ever wanted to coach a marathoner?"

They seemed understandably taken aback as I explained that I was thinking of leaving Nike. It's not common for a two-time Olympian to throw aside a big shoe contract and ask to go back to a college coach.

It had been more than a decade since I was at CU, but Mark still knew me and my work ethic, and I still knew Mark as the man who had brought me back from the dead as a wounded high school runner and made me into a collegiate champion. He had no ties to Alberto or Nike, which would make it clean. I also knew that Adam would love to return to his home state.

Mark told us that he was leading a group of runners the next morning to Magnolia Road, or "Mags" as the locals call it, and that we should join them. Mags is one of the steepest dirt roads in the country. Some of the miles are at a 17 percent grade, so it's more like a rock climb masquerading as a jog.

Adam and I stayed out too late that night. When Mark picked us up the next morning, I knew we were in trouble. I did an eight-mile loop and my logbook recapped the experience well: "DYING!!!"

At the same time, I loved it, and it reminded me of everything that was great about Boulder. I thought that I had a shot at making a third Olympic team in me. A trip to Rio de Janeiro, Brazil, for the 2016 games, at the age of thirty-eight, would be the crowning achievement of my career. Colt would be old enough to remember coming along and it would cement my consistency as a runner. With Mark, and a fresh start, that seemed possible.

Mark and Heather called me the next day. "We would be thrilled to coach you," they said.

I was all in.

Jerry, no surprise, was a class act. When I told him that Mark and Colorado were where my heart was, he said that he was disappointed, but also understood, and immediately said, "Let me know how I can help." He showed me that it was possible to leave a coach and keep a friend.

My last official race as a Nike athlete was a Turkey Trot in West Linn, a suburb of Portland. It was my tenth and final race in 2013, completing my nutty quest to fulfill my contract requirements and ensure that I couldn't have my pay suspended. Shalane, ever the willing training buddy, came with me. The very nice folks working and running the event seemed taken aback to see Nike athletes there, in our full neon running gear amid the sea of joggers in foam turkey hats. The winner would receive a pumpkin pie.

Off we went, the leaves crunching under our feet. I darted ahead of Shalane in the last stretch (kind of a bitch move), which we laughed about. I won the pie, and brought it to a Thanksgiving party. (It was delicious.)

After wearing the swoosh in two Olympic Games, four World Championships, four Olympic Trials, and more than 100 other races, my time with Nike was done.

CHAPTER THIRTY-THREE
Return of the Buffaloes

In January 2014, we put our house in Portland up for sale and crammed into a small two-bedroom apartment in Boulder.

Because Mark and Heather were college coaches not backed by a shoe brand, Adam and I had to start looking for a sponsor that would support me in my continued effort to make another Olympic team. We had mutually decided that Adam would now act as my agent (instead of paying 15 percent in agent fees to someone else), and we started to take meetings with sponsors together. Though my contract with Nike was up, they had a "right of first refusal" stipulation on my next deal, which meant that they could match any other offer I got. If I refused to sign, Nike could impose a 180-day freeze during which I would be unpaid, still have to wear Nike gear, and couldn't compete for anyone else. I was nervous that this would impact our negotiating with other brands and delay or even kill a new deal, but Saucony and Skechers both shrugged it off, and Saucony offered me a six-figure deal without any pay reduction or suspension clauses. I spoke with other brands, too.

While I appreciated the interest, I found myself again and again in rooms with male executives explaining women's running to me. There seemed to be more interest in how I would look on a poster than in having real conversations about how the sport could evolve. I was becoming increasingly mission-driven, wanting to do more than just run fast times. I wanted to be a change-maker. I wanted to go beyond posing for photos and having my tweets reviewed by Nike prior to publication. I had launched a blog and was putting more into it, writing about my experiences as a female athlete. The brands I was meeting with didn't seem to get it. They didn't seem to get *me*.

One company, however, seemed different. Seattle-based Oiselle (pronounced *wah-ZELL*; French for "bird"), was a women-led apparel (not shoe) brand founded by runner Sally Bergesen. They were still small, with only ten employees, but expanding. At the beginning of February, Adam, Colt, and I flew to Washington to meet Sally and her team.

We arrived on a Saturday when an indoor track meet was taking place at the University of Washington. Oiselle had a few sponsored athletes in town for the meet, including U.S. 5,000 meters champion Lauren Fleshman—the same runner whose injury in 2006 had bumped me up a spot onto my first World Championships team. Oiselle had signed Lauren *while* she was pregnant, which made an impression on me. We got to Seattle too late to watch the meet, but we attended the company's party that night. Nike's parties were famously drunken bacchanals. (I went to one after the 2008 Olympics, and heard stories from friends and Nike employees about other ones. Later, in 2018, these parties would be noted in a class action lawsuit from women in the company, who described them as forums in which they were consistently subjected to demeaning treatment, claims that Nike denied.) Everyone at Oiselle's shindig seemed to genuinely like each other without being brown-nosey. Sally's team was full of women at all levels, something I'd never seen at a sports company. They seemed enthusiastic, and hungry to make a difference.

The next morning I joined Oiselle employees for an open group run, and that evening Adam and I watched the Super Bowl with Sally and her husband, Alec, plus Bob and Sarah Lesko, who both were very involved in the brand. (Adam had a tough time since his beloved Denver Broncos lost.) Between touchdowns, we discussed what I didn't like about Nike and how I wanted a fresh start. On Monday, we visited the Oiselle office above a bar in downtown Seattle. If spending my days on the Nike campus had come to feel like living in the Death Star, visiting Oiselle felt like being in the apartment of a cool friend. The square footage of the entire office probably equaled that of John Capriotti's office alone. Sally gave me a tour and I got an even better sense of how deeply everyone at the company cared about the work that they did. Even stranger, they seemed *happy* at work.

At our sit-down, Sally asked, "What are you passionate about?" I wasn't prepared for the question, and, feeling embarrassed, said something about how I was passionate about the ways I could help the brand. That didn't land with her. She explained she wanted to figure out how Oiselle would amplify my voice. It made me recognize that I still had a lot of work to do on myself to figure out what that was.

By the end of our visit, Adam could tell I was smitten. I asked Sally what I could do to be part of Oiselle. She said she'd get back to me.

On our way out of Seattle, we got the great news that Kendall was in labor in Portland, so I went to be with her and meet her new baby. After the visit, I had landed in Denver and was in my car, starting the forty-five-minute drive home to Boulder, when my cell phone rang. It was Sally.

Here it is, I thought giddily, *the offer*.

"We can't make you an offer," she told me.

I nearly drove off the road. Sally explained that their budget for sponsoring athletes was so meager that any figure that she could throw at me would "be insulting to your talents." She added: "We'll always be fans."

The offers from other brands were generous and a long way from the zero dollars I made running in college or the $35,000 I'd started out getting from Nike. I tried to get myself excited about the Saucony offer, which would pay $1 million over five years with no reductions and plenty of bonuses. In March, at home in Boulder, I stared at the paperwork they sent over on my laptop.

"I know you want to sign with Oiselle," Adam said. "Do you want me to call Sally?"

He reached Sally at her daughter's soccer game. "Make us an offer," he told her. "*Any* offer." A couple of days later, she got back to us: $20,000 a year for four years. Plus, a 2 percent stake in the company. My heart soared.

"I'll take it!" I said.

I felt empowered. It was one-fifteenth of my previous annual Nike salary—but this time, I was the one choosing the reduction. And they gave me literal ownership in the company. I was an athlete and an investor. If they triumphed, so would I.

Before I could finalize the deal, we had to share the details with Nike and give them the opportunity to match. When Adam called Cap to give him the information and ask for my official release, Cap seemed taken aback. Of course Nike could match the $20,000-a-year offer—and might even see it as a small price to pay for keeping me quiet for another 180 days, knowing that I'd refuse it. But then, Adam told Cap the kicker: Nike would also have to give me a 2 percent stake in the company. For once, we had them beat. Nothing gave me more pleasure.

Because Oiselle only made apparel and not shoes, Adam and I were also able to strike an unconventional shoe-only sponsorship deal with Skechers.

I couldn't believe it. Twelve and a half years as a Nike runner, more than a third of my lifetime, and it was over once and for all. I opened up my closet and pulled out every single piece of clothing with a swoosh on it. Tank tops, leggings, shorts, socks, windbreakers. A giant neon mountain grew on my bed, which Colt gleefully climbed atop.

I had the thought of putting the whole pile in the trash, or even having some sort of bonfire in the backyard. But I couldn't fathom wasting that much apparel. I loaded it all into my car and donated it.

Somewhere, I'd like to think that Marie Kondo is beaming.

It sparked a lot of joy.

During the first three months of practices with Mark and Heather I struggled a bit, but once I settled in, I entered a training period that was undoubtedly the happiest of my life. I was back on the dirt roads where I had gone from a hobbled student athlete into a collegiate champion. The thin air and sweeping mountain panoramas and breathtaking skies greeted me every day. One workout at a time, I felt my fitness and strength returning.

Mark and Heather believed in me and made a point of telling me so, words that I still needed to hear. We set the goals of a strong performance at the New York City Marathon in November 2014, then making the 2016 Olympic Marathon. I found myself looking forward to doing workouts with them. They often invited me to bring Colt to practice, which was especially helpful, as Adam was at work with his friend Tim expanding their company Run the Edge. Mark and Heather set up mats for Colt to play on, took an interest in him, and treated him as an extension of the team. When I had a big workout scheduled during a snowstorm, Mark and Heather came to help shovel the first lane of the track for me. Sometimes, I ran on the track with other former CU runners who Mark and Heather were coaching—Olympians Shalaya Kipp, Emma Coburn, and Jenny Simpson—but as I was the only marathoner, when I was out on the roads, I was often on my own.

In the early months of 2014, two years after I first sat down with them,

USADA also finally reached out about getting my medical records and lab results from Dr. Brown. They sent a release form to get all of the information they would need, which I signed. When I moved to Colorado and left Nike, I'd readily dropped Dr. Brown as my physician and started seeing a different endocrinologist, Dr. Kimberly Lerner in Boulder, so I also wanted to get medical records for my new doctor to use in planning my care. However, USADA and I both soon ran into the same problem when it came to getting the documents. Again and again, I asked Dr. Brown's office in Houston, as well as the Nike labs in Portland, to transfer my records to my new doctor. I was told it would happen, but nothing was getting sent.

Then, I ended up on crutches. At first, I thought the pain in my butt was only a spasm. It turned out to be a sacral stress fracture. I wanted to punch something, but channeled my energy into going all out on the stationary bike instead, until there was a puddle of sweat on the floor. I kept cross training through the summer and was healed enough to get ready for the New York City Marathon, as planned, on November 2.

From the start of the race, though, I knew that I was in over my head. The pace was aggressive, and the women in the lead pack were tough. I stayed with them all the way through Brooklyn and Queens, but when we were crossing the Queensboro Bridge into Manhattan, they were going faster than I was fit to keep up with. Des Linden—coming off a 10th-place finish in Boston—cruised by me, then Deena, too, looking as swift as I felt haggard, and shouting encouragements my way. (Shalane wasn't racing—she had set a new Boston Marathon record time for American women of 2:22:02 in April, then run the Berlin Marathon that fall instead of New York.)

For the first time ever in my career, I completely hit the wall. This is the fear of marathoners, be they professionals or weekend warriors, when the body's glycogen gets depleted and your positive self-talk lands in the crapper with it. I felt like the harder I pushed, the slower I was running, that anvils had been added to my shoulders. My brain had turned to mush.

I felt embarrassed. I wanted permission to drop out from Mark—who says I looked right at him when I hit the final miles in Central Park, though I have no recollection of this—from God, from anyone, but I also didn't want to let people down. I ran 2:37:03, suffering and slogging to the bitter end.

I finished 14th. Colt's post-race summary was accurate: "Mommy ran, she died, she cried."

After New York, I asked Mark and Heather: "Am I done?"

I meant it honestly, but they said no. This was a setback but not an ending—I had more big races ahead. Their support and belief meant everything and pulled me out of what could have been a long, dark mental rut. We returned our focus to making the team for the 2016 Olympics in Brazil.

In the meantime, it seemed my medical records were still being withheld by Dr. Brown and the Nike labs. A former New York Police Department detective with a background in complex drug investigations named Victor Burgos, who now worked for a private intelligence and investigations company, had been brought on by the lead attorney representing USADA, Bill Bock, to help build their case. Victor became my primary contact. He was frustrated as well: "This isn't like my old job," he told me. "When the NYPD asks, people usually respond." We talked about what could be going on, and thought that Nike may have been afraid of releasing my records because of the precedent it would set. When USADA came knocking for Galen's and Mo's and other athletes' records as well, what could they say then, if they'd already released mine?

Adam and I talked about it and weren't sure what to do next. On the one hand, we were some of the only people with firsthand experience of Alberto's doping culture, and nothing was going to change unless we stopped waiting for something to happen and really put our necks out there by going public. On the other hand, I was certain that putting my claims out there in public would be career suicide. People would assume that Adam and I had been dopers since we had our best years at Nike.

Then, in November 2014, a reporter with ProPublica, David Epstein, reached out to Adam. Epstein had first come to Adam before the 2012 Olympics with some questions and suspicions about the Oregon Project and doping. Adam had talked with him at the time—I had not—but Epstein had been honest with Adam in saying that he didn't have enough people on the record to publish. Now, however, he was back, saying that he had more sources, more research under his belt, and with our help he could build a real story. He wanted to know if we would talk.

I told Adam absolutely not. I would keep speaking to USADA or law enforcement agencies that guaranteed our confidentiality and anonymity, but I was still competing, and couldn't stomach going to events where I'd have to face former Oregon Project teammates, Nike executives, and Alberto in person, after coming forward about them in public.

Adam felt very strongly that he needed to do it. I was extremely nervous about it, but respect was a cornerstone of our relationship, and it was his decision. Epstein flew out in February 2015 with a film crew from the BBC, which was partnering on the story with ProPublica, and shot an interview with Adam at a hotel. They wanted to meet me, and I sat with them, off camera, at a picnic table at a nearby park as Colt kicked around a soccer ball. They talked about the story they wanted to put together. They seemed kind and empathetic.

From the moment we waved goodbye, my silence started to gnaw at me. I wished that I'd had Adam's bravery. I prayed about what to do. And I found my answer.

I needed to come forward. At this moment, I realized, my power wasn't in my legs. It was in my voice.

CHAPTER THIRTY-FOUR
Going Public

Adam and I called David Epstein and told him that I was ready to speak on the record. He and his crew booked flights back to Boulder. They set up their camera and lights in the living room of the rental house we'd moved into, and positioned two chairs—one for me, one for Adam—facing the lens. Though confident in my conviction, I couldn't shake that feeling of guilt, that I was doing something wrong by speaking out publicly.

I didn't prepare for the interview—I just said my piece the best that I could, as completely as I could. I kept reminding myself of my purpose. I was doing this for the good of my sport. It deserved to be clean. It needed to be worth loving. I talked about what I had witnessed—the Cytomel, the concerns that I had about Galen and Mo (though they were denied and not proven), and the Oregon Project. I focused on Alberto's role, and didn't talk extensively about Dr. Brown. Nor did I talk about the sexual assault incidents, or even Alberto's lewd comments. Mark Daly with the BBC, who was working with Epstein on the story, did ask me about a rumor that he'd heard that Alberto had "hit on me," to which I replied that it wasn't what I was there to talk about.

Weeks passed after the interview with no word; then David reached out to let us know that on June 3, the written ProPublica piece would be posted online and the BBC documentary would air. We invited a few close friends over that day to watch the documentary air live, knowing we might need the support.

Steve Magness, my former assistant coach, who had left the Oregon Project right before the London Olympics in mid-2012, only a year and a half after joining, had spoken extensively to the BBC and ProPublica for the documentary and article. I was in awe of how he'd expressed himself in those interviews, and thought that he showed the most bravery of anyone. When we heard he'd left the Oregon Project, Adam had reached out to him, suspecting that doping concerns may have been part of what had spurred him to quit, but Steve wasn't ready to talk about it then. In the ProPublica article, however, Steve revealed a number of concerning things he'd witnessed that I had never known about. As a running nerd, getting a job with the Oregon Project at the beginning of 2011 seemed like a dream come true to him—like us, he'd been drawn in by Alberto's charisma and passion for the sport. Among the concerning things Steve talked about was being in Alberto's office when blood test results of Oregon Project athletes were put on his desk. On Galen's, Steve saw a medical note, dated December 2002, when Galen was sixteen. The note read "presently on prednisone and testosterone medication." "When I saw that, I kind of jumped backwards," Steve said. He'd taken a picture of it, which he showed the reporters.

Steve also said that Alberto and Dr. Brown had been experimenting with the banned testosterone medication AndroGel—the same medication that I'd seen Alberto bring a tube of to Park City—on Alberto's sons. Steve said that it was clear to him they were testing out just how much AndroGel could be used without triggering a positive doping test. My jaw dropped at this one: I remembered Amy Begley telling me, in one of our conversations after we'd both left the Oregon Project, that at some point in 2009 during a checkup in Houston, Dr. Brown gave Amy a sealed envelope to take back to Alberto, which she did. Her suspicion was that it contained testosterone. (Later, this was confirmed to be true—it was some of the AndroGel that Alberto used to experiment on his sons.) The pieces clicked into place.

I thought Adam and I had come off well in the documentary and article. We'd spoken honestly. Perhaps I shouldn't have been surprised, but some of the reactions on social media were far less kind. In fact, many were brutal. People called me a liar and said I was desperate for attention. That never made sense to me. *Who wants this type of attention?* They said that I was obviously doping, and everyone knew it. Some claimed that I'd had an affair with Alberto that went bad, and worse yet, that Colt was Alberto's child. My sisters called me, crying because they were so upset. Adam was angry and protective. In my logbook I wrote: "so tired inside."

I heard crickets from some people in the running world and received love notes from others. Josh Rohatinsky, the runner who had been with Alberto during his heart attack, came to our defense publicly, raising questions about things he saw as well. It was clarifying: who was in my corner and who was not was now apparent. There were some people tied to Nike who sent me private messages of support, but publicly kept silent, which frustrated me, but I also understood. People had families to feed and jobs to keep.

Alberto and Nike went on the defense to deny our claims and Steve's about him and Galen. Alberto penned a lengthy open, two-part letter on the Oregon Project's website to refute them. He said that the vials I had seen in Park City were standardized "weekly injections to help control [Galen's] allergies and his asthma." (Steve Magness had reported seeing similar vials on a different occasion in France.) About the tube of AndroGel that I'd seen in Park City, Alberto admitted that he did use testosterone, but said it was a valid prescription for personal use. He said he'd had a prescription from a Dr. Kristina Harp since before I had even landed at the Oregon Project, and he was later prescribed it by Dr. Brown to help correct low testosterone levels stemming from a condition called hypogonadism that he said was the result of the damage he did to his body as a runner. As for Steve's claim that Alberto and Dr. Brown had been testing out AndroGel on Alberto's sons to see if they could get around doping controls, Alberto admitted that he had asked Dr. Brown to set up an "experiment" with AndroGel on his sons, but came up with a wild excuse. He said that he wanted to learn whether it was possible for an athlete to be sabotaged by someone rubbing testosterone on them, as he was worried that something like that could happen to Galen. Steve called this explanation "ludicrous." I agreed.

In regard to the conversation I'd overheard in Daegu about Galen getting an IV drip, Alberto flat-out denied it. "As the US team doctor has confirmed, at no time did I request the US team doctor to give Galen an IV or saline drip while he was in Daegu in 2011," he said. Regarding Cytomel, Alberto published emails between me and him that were meant to suggest that he "was thrilled" with my body weight in 2011 and didn't want me to lose pounds. However, he also admitted that "there was one time when I gave Kara Cytomel. It was in August 2011 in Daegu, South Korea. I did so after being expressly directed to do so by Kara's endocrinologist, Dr. Brown." Alberto seemed to be trying to conflate the time I had an actual prescription for Cytomel with when he was trying to get me to take the pills without one, in the name of losing weight.

As for Steve's alleged proof that Nike's own internal medical records showed that Galen had been on testosterone—which was outright banned in running—Alberto said that Galen "does not recall exactly which supplement he took in 2002. It could have been TestoBoost, Alpha Male, Tribex or ZMA. All are legal supplements that make essentially the same claims." He said "I then stated that Galen, as a 16-year-old kid, must have misspoken about the supplements he was taking." He also gave a long response to the mention of the common steroid prednisone—which is prohibited by the World Anti-Doping Agency in competition because it can block pain and enhance oxygen consumption—saying that it was used by Galen for his asthma on rare occasions for short-term use when pollen counts were high, and that "Galen has never taken prednisone for a competitive advantage."

We hadn't told Travis Tygart and his colleagues at USADA ahead of time that we were doing the interview, and were worried that they would be mad about it. As it turned out, it was the opposite. Travis reached out, congratulated us on the interview, and said that his tipline was brimming with messages from people who said they had information to share. We had helped to break something open, and the truth was starting to come out.

At the end of June, I went to the 2015 U.S. Outdoor Track & Field Championships at Hayward Field to run the 5,000 meters. I felt healthier after my sacral stress fracture and the disaster that was the New York City Marathon, and Mark and Heather and I decided that I should run a shorter distance to help get my speed back, then go back to the marathon. We knew it was unlikely that I'd make a 5,000 World Championship team, as it was no longer my discipline, but in my Oiselle gear and Skechers shoes, there was no harm in giving it my all and trying.

I knew that Cap, Alberto, Darren, Galen, and other top Nike brass would be in attendance. *I belong here*, I told myself. *I'm not going to go away, I've done nothing wrong.* I had been listening to Beyoncé's album *I Am . . . Sasha Fierce* a lot, in which she takes on a powerful, swaggering alter ego, and tried to channel some part of that. I took to the track for my stretches, pretending that Alberto and the others weren't in the crowd. They didn't own me. I was there for myself.

That worked well enough during warm-ups, but when the gun went off, I wasn't so fierce anymore. I finished 18th out of 20 runners. Then, a USATF representative guided me to a tent behind the bleachers, telling me that the media members gathered there were "all waiting for you." I didn't want the focus; all I wanted was to go home. The media was so excited about me in spite of my terrible finish, while the women on the podium failed to get the attention that they deserved. I later posted a photo of them—Nicole Tully, Marielle Hall, Abbey D'Agostino—and their results on Instagram.

When asked by the media about the allegations in the ProPublica and BBC reports, I said: "I would welcome that opportunity for myself, for every former Oregon Project member, for every doctor that has been involved, to go under oath. I feel very good about [the USADA case]. I believe in the truth and I know these things take time. . . . Think of how long it took for Lance." Despite whispers going around the running world that the case had been dropped, Travis had assured Adam and me that his investigation was moving slowly yet steadily. On a final note, I said, "I want my son to be able to believe in the sport and the system, I want USADA to show they work, and I want justice for everyone involved."

I showered and packed my bags to head home to Colorado, while Cap and other Nike executives hosted a dinner in Eugene with a Mafia theme where they joked about shooting and killing their competitors, as an executive from a rival shoe company told me. Even if it was a joke, considering the angry messages I was still receiving daily on social media since coming forward, not to mention the overall concerns about safety after the Boston Marathon, this didn't sit well with me.

I also knew that a story was going around about Danny Mackey, the coach of the Brooks Beasts running team, being threatened by Cap, and I mentioned that to the media after my race. The story was that, three days before my race, on June 25, Cap had physically threatened Mackey in the athlete medical tent. There was a person who had appeared in the BBC documentary with his face shaded and voice altered; everyone knew it was Mackey, and Cap was furious. A police report that was published online later that summer gave the full details of how the encounter played out. Cap grabbed Mackey's arm and tried to pull him up out of a chair. He poked Mackey in the chest with two fingers and said, "Well then we'll go

outside motherfucker." Mackey told him to relax and that he needed to finish speaking with an athlete. "You know what you fuckin' did," Cap replied.
"I'm gonna fuckin' kill you." Cap called Mackey a "Pussy. Liar. Scumbag.
You are a shitty person. Let's go outside and fuckin' deal with this." They
yelled at each other for a while, and then Cap left.

Though I'd told the press that I felt good about the USADA case,
I knew how much the agency was up against. While Alberto kept on
coaching, Nike hired a fancy lawyer named Maurice Suh. A partner at
Gibson Dunn, Suh's clients had included Deutsche Bank, Pricewater-
houseCoopers, and Toyota. He'd served as the deputy mayor of home-
land security and public safety for the city of Los Angeles, and had also
represented various Olympic committees, the NFL Players Association,
and several other large corporate sponsors (including Nike) and professional leagues around the world. It turned out that in addition to Alberto,
he was representing Oregon Project runners, including Galen, Mo, Matt
Centrowitz, Jordan Hasay, Tara Erdmann, and Dawn Grunnagle, among
others.

From USADA's side, an investigator assigned to the case told me that
what he was seeing from Nike was "unprecedented." Nike and its lawyers
seemed to be trying to slow down an already tedious process by stone-
walling USADA, drowning them with some documents while withholding
others, and filing seemingly frivolous legal motions. A lawyer working for
USADA told me that a hearing, in which I would have to face Alberto with
my claims directly, could be where this whole thing was headed.

In mid-August, Adam took a few days off so that he could run (for fun)
the TransRockies Race, a multiday and multipoint Colorado trail run that
started about two and a half hours away from Boulder in Buena Vista, and
ended in Beaver Creek. I stayed behind with Colt. On August 14, I was on
the sofa watching bad television with a handful of peanut M&M's when I
noticed the glow of a text message. It was from Chris Chavez, a journalist
who covers track and field. He asked me how it felt to be a silver medalist.

I wondered if he had the wrong number. "A silver medalist in ... what?"
I responded.

He told me that Elvan Abeylegesse had failed a retroactive drug test from samples taken at the 2007 World Championships in Osaka. Abeylegesse was the runner who had beaten me at that championships for second place in the 10,000 meters. Her medal would be revoked, and mine would be upgraded to silver.

I wondered if I was being punk'd. *Was this real? Did I really just win a World Championship silver medal sitting on my couch in my sweatpants?* Right after our race, Alberto had told me that Abeylegesse was doping. *How did he know?* (Abeylegesse ultimately had her results from August 2007 to 2009 annulled, and the bronze medal that Shalane won at the 2008 Olympics in the 10,000 meters was upgraded to a silver.)

It seemed like a deluge of these stories were coming out at once. In August 2015, Liliya Shobukhova, the Russian marathoner who Shalane and I had always been suspicious was doping, had all of her results from 2009 on annulled due to abnormalities over time in her "biological passport" (in simple terms: her test results). She was stripped of her 2009, 2010, and 2011 Chicago Marathon wins, as well as her 2010 London Marathon win and 2011 London second-place finish. London asked for the prize money back. Shobukhova then had her ban cut short by offering "substantial assistance" to the World Anti-Doping Agency (likely information about systematic doping in Russia).

The same month, an anonymous whistleblower from within the International Association of Athletics Federations provided British and German journalists with files on 12,000 blood samples gathered from 5,000 athletes who had competed between 2001 and 2012. Scientists and anti-doping experts reviewed the information and found a marked increase in doping and blood transfusions since 2001, suggesting that over a third of the athletes who won medals in endurance events between 2001 and 2012, including athletes at the London 2012 Olympics, weren't clean. The IAAF had done nothing about it. (In a statement, the IAAF said that the reports were based on "private and confidential medical data which has been obtained without consent.") My and Shalane's suspicions that something was off in London when so many inexperienced runners beat us seemed even more on point. (The report also alleged that 80 percent of Russian medalists tested showed dubious lab results.)

Thanks to new techniques and methods that were being applied to retroactive drug samples, kooky, anticlimactic moments like the one I had were happening all over the place. My shot-putter friend Adam Nelson found out he was actually an Olympic gold medalist when a reporter called him as he was driving to the Atlanta airport. Shalane's "podium ceremony" for her 2008 Olympic upgrade consisted of a USOC representative show-ing up on her doorstep with her new silver medal.

It was great that I went from a third- to second-place World Cham-pionship finisher, but in truth, it wasn't justice. I missed out on the glory of the moment and the bonus money, which contracts don't allow to be retroactively awarded. I'd also often felt that my third-place finish in Osaka was a lucky squeak onto the podium; if I'd known earlier that I should have finished second, just strides away from being the world champion, I would have believed in myself more. As I saw it, bronze might be a fluke, but not second place. I couldn't help but wonder if things would have turned out differently had I finished with that better result. Pauline Boss, PhD, has coined the term "ambiguous loss," which may come closest to capturing the sentiment. It's a complicated sort of loss that begs unanswerable questions.

In November 2015, the news emerged that longtime IAAF president Lamine Diack, along with several other top IAAF officials, were under in-vestigation in France and would later be charged with money laundering and corruption. Among the charges was that Diack was paid off by Rus-sian athletic authorities to cover up their positive test results. In September 2020, Diack, the head of the anti-doping department at the IAAF, and oth-ers received prison sentences.

I'd scroll through the headlines and feel melancholy for the health of the sport. I'd then put my shoes on for a 22-mile workout with Mark and Heather. Even if it seemed like the whole world was cheating, I was doing this for me, my way. I wanted to take my shot at making my second Olym-pic Marathon team and going to Rio. I had a job to do.

CHAPTER THIRTY-FIVE
The Haunted Place

On November 8, 2015, I ran a half marathon in Monterey Bay, California, as a buildup toward the 2016 Olympic Marathon Trials. I won and ran faster on the course than I had expected. After the race, I found Mark Wetmore in the lobby of our hotel with a huge smile. He told me that I was exactly where I was meant to be, that he felt good about my training.

After my latest string of injuries and my awful USATF Outdoor Championships, it was validating to win a race and get that kind of feedback. I could feel the joy of running again. I doubled up workouts every day but Saturday, and went out for long runs in the cold. Heather and Mark carefully mapped out training routes like ace cartographers, loaded with twists and turns to mimic the course I'd face in Los Angeles for the Olympic Marathon Trials, which I'd be running in approximately three months, on February 13.

The ritual of training for another marathon now felt like a refuge. I loved building up my fitness as I worked toward 115-mile weeks, experiencing the slow revelation of being in better shape than I had thought, still capable of more than I expected. Whether you're an elite or a first-timer, that's the magic of marathoning, the recognition of your own potential that had been there all along. There was such satisfaction for me in hitting that first 18-mile long run, then 20-miler, and so on. Race day is fun, but training gives you moments of the extraordinary in the ordinary. I'd have these moments on training runs thinking, *Oh my God, could I really make my third Olympic team?*

Ten days out from the Marathon Trials, Mark and I looked at the weather forecast for Los Angeles. It would be hot, and the risk of heatstroke was real, especially since the start time was later than many marathons, with the women's race starting just after 10 a.m. We'd originally thought that a 2:25 finish would be needed to make the team, intimidatingly fast, but now we reasoned that a 2:30 had a shot. My plan was to run at a 2:29 pace. As much as I grimaced at the thought of L.A.'s heat, I also knew it would be a decent preparation for what the runners who made the team would face in Rio. A week before the race, a nasty flu hit me and I spent a couple of days in bed. We had to rethink our strategy. I did my last big workouts indoors, with layers on.

I was grateful that Adam, Colt, and Heather would be at the Trials with me. Mark had to accompany his CU athletes to a competition, and couldn't be with us, but my mom, Kelly, Kendall, Sally from Oiselle, and even some of my high school teammates were going to make the trip to L.A.

The night before the race, I went out to dinner with Adam, Heather, and my friend Shanna Burnette at an offbeat Italian place downtown. We were eating our carbs when Galen, Darren, and Alberto walked in. In a city of 3.9 million people, of all the gin joints, they walked into ours. We paid our check and got up and left. I felt particularly proud of Adam for holding it together when I knew that he wanted to throw a plate of spaghetti their way.

The next morning, I put on my Oiselle racing singlet and Skechers shoes. Adam and Heather took me to the starting line. For the first few miles, I kept to the front of the pack. It was blisteringly hot, but I felt like my training was there. Then Shalane and Amy Cragg (formerly Amy Hastings) took a big lead, and it looked like it would be me and Des Linden competing for third. Des opened up a gap ahead of me and Heather yelled that I had to close it, but I was worried that if I did, I might not have anything left for the end of the race. I remember thinking that I'd rather be against anyone other than Des because she's such a good marathon closer. With five miles to go, Des made her killer move and sped away.

At the end of the race, there was a hairpin turn, after which I could see Shalane up ahead. She'd been passed by Des, and I realized that she was struggling, but it was too late for me to catch her. Amy finished first with Des 34 seconds behind her and Shalane another 25 seconds after that. Shalane collapsed into Amy's arms, and had to go to the hospital for an IV drip to rehydrate. I finished fourth, 65 seconds behind Shalane, with a time of 2:30:24.

My first thought as I crossed the finish line was: *Don't cry. Don't cry. Don't cry.*

Of course, I started to cry. I roamed around the finish line aimlessly. I wanted to disappear. Alberto and Darren weren't there to critique my race, but there was no shortage of criticism from within. Fourth was my nightmare. Des came over and hugged me and offered some kind words. Amy, too. I felt so dehydrated and begged for water. The race organizers couldn't seem to find any but gave me a bag of ice chips.

What had gotten me out of bed for months, years, really, was the hope of making the 2016 Olympic team. I wanted to prove my haters wrong, but mostly I wanted to say thank you to the people who supported me. Those last two miles, knowing that wouldn't happen, may have been the hardest two miles of my life. I wanted so badly to go to Rio with Colt, to have some sort of storybook finale to my career. I now saw the truth: that wasn't going to happen. Most athletes don't get their happy ending. Adam hadn't with his career, and I wouldn't, either.

"It's a great team," I told journalists waiting at the finish line. "I just kept asking myself, 'Am I doing everything I can?' And I was. So . . . Obviously it's a really hard pill to swallow . . . but, they were better." Inevitably, I was asked about Alberto and the Oregon Project. A reporter told me that Galen came in first in the men's race. I was infuriated, and made all the more so by the fact that I was being asked about Galen instead of the race I just ran, the experience I just had, my career, or how Shalane was doing.

"Justice is coming," I said. "People ask, 'How did you come back?' Letting go of that shit is how I came back. I lost 200 pounds of fucking baggage I've been carrying around, and they can't touch me anymore. It means nothing. I don't care."

Maybe it wasn't the most eloquent statement, but it was honest. The old me worried what my coaches would think, but Mark and Heather didn't care about my uncharacteristic public swearing in the least. ("We don't give a fuck," I believe, was the specific response from Heather. "You're a grown-ass woman.") Yet, Skechers and Oiselle received letters from customers saying that they were outraged they had backed me. Negotiations I was in with Procter & Gamble for a six-figure deal came to a standstill.

Heather, bless her, tried to console me after I finally made it through the long corridor of media, but with little success. "You did everything right. There is nothing to apologize for," she said. "There's more ahead for you." I could see Adam, my mom, and Colt in tears. It was bad enough that

I was such a waterworks. When I managed my way through the crowd and got over to them, Colt hugged me tight.

Finishing 4th at the Olympic Trials is the haunted place. I wished that I had been 50th instead. Back in Boulder, I couldn't sleep, replaying the ghost story of the race again and again in my mind.

———————

On February 25, Bill Bock, the lead attorney representing USADA, called me and said that my medical records had been reviewed and experts had found something suspicious. It was about my thyroid condition that Dr. Brown had diagnosed me with, and the Levoxyl that I had been on for all of the years since. I never had the condition, the experts said. I did not need the prescription. The diagnosis was wrong, and as I understood it, made—without my knowledge—to test out whether the drug would improve my performance. Why Dr. Brown did this, I do not know. USADA did not believe I had attempted to break the rules nor did they believe I had even gained any performance benefit, a belief that I share. What was completely certain was that my trust had been abused. I felt anger and shock. In 2004, when I'd met Dr. Brown, I had felt like a nobody. I never would have thought to question a doctor.

I talked to Travis about all this. I told him the fears that had been playing in my mind over the past five years, since I'd first sat down with him in Colorado Springs, that my medical records could hold secrets. That part, I now understood, was true. The other part of my fear had been that those secrets would mean I was doping without knowing it, that my career, everything I had worked for, would be made null and void. That part was false.

"If you found something, anything, that broke the rules, you'd charge me, right?" I asked Travis.

"Yes," he responded. "You think I'd *let it go*? That's not how it works here."

I tried to wean myself off Levoxyl but three months in, I felt extremely fatigued and had to start taking it again. Because my thyroid didn't have to work for so many years due to the medication, I'm now reliant on the medicine. Doctors who I've consulted, and who I trust, said that I may be on it for the rest of my life. Adam had more success and managed to stop taking his Levoxyl around 2014. I have switched to a different hypothyroidism medication called Synthroid, but the effect is the same. Every day that I take it I have the smallest of reminders that my body was used in what I felt was some sort of experiment I still don't entirely understand, to win at all costs. The crazy thing is, Dr. Brown did this to me and Adam before he even met Alberto Salazar. When the two connected, it was a match made in heaven.

I attempted, halfheartedly, to train for the 10,000 meters at the Olympic Track Trials, which would be in July at Hayward Field. My knee started to hurt. My doctor had me get an MRI. It showed that I had torn my meniscus. I tried to train through it, aided by cortisone shots, but the pain remained excruciating. I had surgery in May. My doctor had operated on many of the CU football players, and I went under thinking he was going to clean up my meniscus. When I woke up, I saw Adam, upset. The doctor had found that I was missing cartilage, that I had "bone on bone." He said he didn't know if I would ever be able to run again.

I had been running 115 miles a week just two months ago. I was the fourth fastest female marathoner in the country. I didn't buy it; it couldn't be true. I looked into stem cell procedures and fired off anxious emails to USADA to find out if they were permissible. They were, if you followed protocols, and I had a procedure in July, but it wasn't effective enough to let me run the way that I wanted to.

I sank into one of the deepest depressions of my life. I felt aimless about my career, and isolated and ostracized for having gone public about my claims of wrongdoing at the Oregon Project. I couldn't bring myself to say the R-word ("retire"), even though it was on my mind. I felt stuck in a limbo. I jogged on my own and tended to Colt. Adam was working every day at Run the Edge. I thought about how great of a reinvention he'd created for himself. *Will I ever have something like that?* I wondered. Nothing good felt possible to me.

I watched the Rio Olympics from home on my couch. On a visit to Duluth, I borrowed a bike from my sister-in-law, put on a giant knee brace, and went riding on country roads. Then, the bike got a flat tire. I didn't have my phone with me. I walked two miles to the nearest store and asked to use their phone. I didn't know anyone's number except Adam's because, well, cell phones, but he wasn't in Duluth. I asked him to give me my mom's number and let them know that I was stranded. Kelly came to get me.

I decided I would train to make the World Championships team in 2017. Maybe *that* could be my redemption story. Rest up, and run a flat, speedy world standard qualifying time in the marathon in early 2017. Even with this half-baked plan in hand, my emotional well-being didn't improve. I'd get angry when we'd watch football games at home. At the end of the game, the players would bring their kids onto the field and everyone would "oooooh" and "ahhhh" and I'd just say to the screen, "Why isn't anyone asking where this dad has been for the last eight months?"

Then came November 2016. Even after I was released from my Nike contract with its strict confidentiality agreement and had become active on social media, I had always been afraid to say anything about politics publicly. I was worried about alienating people and wanted to focus instead on bringing them together through the deep and unifying force that is running. My own family is also very politically divided. Forget pissing off the public; I was only a tweet away from ruining Thanksgiving.

On Election Day, I proudly cast my vote for Hillary Clinton, and that night I watched the results come in with Colt and Adam, thinking how cool it would be for our young son to witness the first female president of the United States. We all know that's not how it ended. I spent a few days reading the news and trying to process what happened. Six days after the election, I pulled out my iPhone and fired off what I thought was a relatively mundane tweet.

> Not going to lie, feeling really worried that tomorrow it will still be wishful thinking to tell a girl, "you could grow up to be president".

Apparently, it wasn't mundane to some people. I received furious emails through my website, some saying that they were ashamed that their daughters had once thought of me as a role model.

There was one silver lining: I was losing my fear of saying the wrong thing, of what people thought of me. *Is this the worst that will happen?* I wondered. I could take it. I was running out of things that I felt were holding me back from speaking my mind.

It wasn't long before that notion was put to the test. A professor at CU who taught an "Ethics in Sports" class sent me an email saying that he thought a pair of shoes had cost me a spot on the Olympic team. Soon, there was a big public debate about the topic.

The Vaporfly was a brand-new shoe that Nike had developed as part of Breaking2, its initiative to crack the men's two-hour marathon barrier. Nike designers were calling the Vaporfly a "built-in secret weapon." At first, I didn't get what the fuss was all about, but as details began to spread on running blogs and Twitter in early 2017, and then Nike officially released the shoe on March 7 as the Vaporfly Elite, I started to take notice. The shoe had a carbon fiber plate embedded in its thick soles, which acted as a sort of spring. In marketing materials doled out during the shoe's release, Nike reported that lab testing done at the University of Colorado in Boulder (of all places) had proven that the shoe reduces the amount of energy required to run at a given pace by an average of 4 percent.

Both Amy and Shalane had been wearing prototypes of the shoe at the Trials in Los Angeles. They were my friends, and there was no question that they had both run masterfully that day. Yet, I couldn't help but wonder whether we were actually in the same race. Were they on Harley-Davidsons while I—and everyone else not wearing the shoe—were on Schwinns? Were they bouncing on trampolines while I was running on concrete?

Adam and I pored over the IAAF rules, which clearly stated that an athlete's shoe cannot contain any "technical aids," like say a spring. They also said that athletes can't have shoes that give them an unfair advantage over competitors, and the shoes needed to be approved and available for public purchase before being used at a race, which the Vaporflys were not during the Trials. However, there were never any findings that the Vaporflys violated any IAAF rules. Publicly, it seemed, Nike stayed rather mum.

Unlike in the past, I spoke up right away and enlisted allies. I reached out to the IAAF multiple times. Sally from Oiselle filed a formal protest on my behalf with the IAAF. Mark and Heather wrote to the IAAF about their worries that the fairness of the sport was being tarnished with this technology that had been used in secret. Other athletes did, too. On March 20, I did an interview with *Runner's World* where I stated my opinion in public.

"At the end of the day, if technology is affecting races and what times people are running, if that is found to be an unfair advantage, then that's an issue," I said.

Given that the IAAF's president had been arrested for corruption less than a year and a half earlier, I might have been skeptical that they'd take real action, but initially I really believed that they would quickly ban or somehow restrict the shoes from competition. Instead, Nike and the IAAF made moves to work around that fate. I heard that Nike altered the description of its carbon fiber plate in its patent from a "springlike" device to a "propulsion" device, in my mind, to skirt the rules. Later, Steve Magness pointed out on Twitter that he thought the IAAF had quietly helped. They changed their regulations to allow shoes that had one plate and soles 40 millimeters thick or less, the exact dimensions of the Vaporfly Elite. As one runner, Blake Russell, put it, "They made the rule to fit the shoe rather than the other way around." Nike broke the rules, then the IAAF helped them rewrite history.

There was no public announcement of these changes, and none of the formal protests that we filed with the IAAF ever got a response. As additional research was conducted over the rest of the year, the extent of the advantage the Vaporfly Elites provided became even more clear. It seemed the shoes conferred up to a 2.7 percent performance benefit in elite marathon competitions, meaning times that were that percent faster than they would have been otherwise. (In 2019, a *New York Times* analysis found that the Vaporfly "may give runners an even bigger advantage than we thought" and calculated a 4 to 5 percent faster time for a runner in Vaporflys over one wearing an average shoe.) At the 2016 Trials, I'd finished with a time of 2:30:24. A 1 percent improvement in my time would have put me in the top three; a 2 percent improvement would have meant something like a 2:27:23 or 2:27:19 finish. Amy's winning time was 2:28:20.

Getting this emotional about an ugly, neon, awkwardly soled shoe did not feel good. But the truth is, when I'd finally felt like I was starting to accept and move past the Trials, it opened up the floodgates of depression again. The way that the IAAF had seemingly swept the Vaporfly controversy under the rug didn't exactly bolster my faith in the processes of the governance agency on issues big or small. My career was still hanging in the balance. So was the USADA case.

CHAPTER THIRTY-SIX
Under Oath

In March 2017, the same month that I filed my concerns to the IAAF about the Vaporfly, Travis told me that USADA had charged Alberto with doping infractions. This information was not public and was being closely guarded. I couldn't believe it: after all this time, something was actually happening. They would need me to testify in an arbitration, but weren't yet sure when it would be scheduled because they thought that the Nike-paid lawyers representing Alberto were still making it impossible to get the documents that USADA needed.

In May 2017, the confidential report that USADA had compiled about Alberto's case was leaked. It revealed something I'd had no idea about. In November 2011, shortly after I had left the team, Alberto and Dr. Brown began to conduct a wave of L-carnitine infusions on athletes, including Galen, Mo, and even Steve Magness. (Alberto later claimed that he only gave an infusion to Steve, while everyone else's were done as injections.) Infusions were banned, while certain levels of injections were allowed, as were drinks. Infusions are not allowed because, according to WADA, they can mask blood manipulations. The report also alleged that he lied to athletes about the infusions being WADA-compliant. Finally, it claimed that several athletes had been stonewalled in getting their medical records, just as I had.

One evening in July 2017, I was home making dinner. Adam and I had finally bought, renovated, and moved into a house in Boulder in April 2016 where we could settle, with a lush front yard, close to public schools and parks. Our rescue dog, Freya, began to bark. I looked out the front window and saw two people milling about in the yard wearing jeans and polar fleeces.

Adam went out to see what they wanted. "Honey," he came back saying, "it's the FBI."

It had been almost five years on the dot since we first spoke to the FBI at our dining room table in Portland. It seemed in my life like everything was always happening at once. After so much time waiting for someone to take action, it looked like the FBI was following USADA's lead and joining the party. After a long day and a long run, though, I was exhausted. "Great," I told Adam. "Could they come back after we eat dinner?"

To their credit, the FBI agents agreed and returned after we'd eaten. I told them everything that I had explained to their colleagues in Portland in 2012, and the BBC, and USADA. They asked about John Capriotti, and if we knew anything about Eugene landing the IAAF 2021 World Championships. I didn't, beyond the fact that it had been announced in April 2015, and I was caught off guard. The implication, as I took it, was that Nike might be wielding its influence in potentially corrupt ways. Maybe this thing was getting bigger than Alberto or even the Oregon Project alone.

What I did not, still could not, mention to the FBI agents in Portland, or the USADA lawyers—or to Adam, for that matter—was anything about Alberto's massages in Italy and Portugal. I couldn't tell anyone else about them because in many ways, I had continued to block them from my own mind. Dissociating had come to feel like the only safe course for me.

As much as I wanted that to last forever, it was a proverbial house of cards. In fall 2017, Bill Bock and his team told me that it looked like an arbitration date for Alberto had finally been set that would hold. It would be in May 2018, and it was time to start preparing to testify. I'd have to tell my story while sitting in the same room as Alberto and his lawyers.

In early 2018, Bock and his team flew to Colorado from their homes in Indianapolis and New York and set up in a conference room in a law office in downtown Boulder where we met. They walked me through the process of being a witness and conducted mock interviews, asking me questions that they wanted put on the record at the arbitration, and training me on how to respond to the sorts of attacks Nike's lawyers might use in an attempt to poke holes in my story. Documents were being submitted back and forth for review between USADA's legal team and Alberto's. The process gave us a glimpse into the strategy that Maurice Suh might use at the hearing. One of the documents Suh's team submitted was the thank-you letter that I had written to Alberto after winning my medal in Osaka. It seemed he would try to paint me as a woman scorned, bitter about my career not having gone better, and fabricating claims to go after Alberto as a result.

I cracked open a bottle of wine when I got home, feeling completely spent. USADA was doing their job, and I wanted nothing more than to help, but the retraumatization was burdensome. Because all of this was understandably top secret, I also couldn't tell anyone about it, which made things harder, as I wasn't able to talk to friends and family who could provide support. We scheduled additional preparation sessions that would pick up in January 2018 and continue once a month from then until the arbitration.

In February 2018, I was getting a massage from a licensed massage therapist in Colorado when his finger slipped and grazed my anus. He stood back, aghast, apologizing profusely and offering to terminate his services instantly. The incidents with Alberto came rushing out into my consciousness from where I'd hidden them away. For a moment, I could see the truth, and I felt like I was going to throw up. *If what he'd done to me had been an accident, this would have been his reaction.*

I was aware of the tectonic shift that was occurring around how our culture treated sexual abuse, but not seeing myself as having a role in it. In August 2016, *The Indianapolis Star* had published an investigation of USA Gymnastics team doctor Larry Nassar that cracked open an abuse scandal that went back decades, and led to Nassar's indictment. Survivors gave impact statements that were heard around the world. Dozens, then *hundreds*, of women and girls were coming forward saying that they had been abused by him. Yet, after the moment of clarity during the massage, I quickly returned to dissociation. The house of cards was still standing, but the roof had been knocked off.

Then, during a prep session for the arbitration, on April 9, 2018, it came up that I had told USADA investigators about Alberto's attempt to kiss me on the flight to Daegu and his gross and unsettling questions and stories on the earlier flight to Lisbon. In another conversation with USADA, I had also mentioned that I felt uncomfortable with a couple of Alberto's massages and noted that he was often drinking while giving them, but I didn't get into specifics. "But he never actually touched you, right?" one of the USADA lawyers asked me.

Without thinking, I responded that his finger went up my shorts twice during a massage, and it had felt wrong.

The words just flew out and once they left my mouth, I couldn't believe that I had said them. It was the first time they'd been spoken, to anyone. The room went quiet. I could see that the lawyers were stunned.

Bock expressed concern that it could be sexual assault.

In March 2017, a new oversight body called the United States Center for SafeSport had been founded, designed to hear and investigate claims about sexual abuse in sports, sanction those who were found to have engaged in wrongdoing, and educate athletes about things like grooming behavior. It had mandatory reporting laws, which can vary by state, but essentially mean that if someone like a teacher or doctor hears of abuse, they need to report it to authorities. In his position at USADA, Bock told me that he was obligated to make a report to SafeSport. He said that someone from SafeSport would then reach out to me.

Hearing the term "sexual assault" was utterly shocking to me in the moment, even if it was the accurate description of what happened. It sounded like something that in my mind, to this point, happened in a *Law & Order: Special Victims Unit* episode, not in my own life. I left the meeting, rattled.

The house of cards had fallen down.

In April, I finally told Adam about the massages.

It was horrible. I felt like I had betrayed Adam by not telling him, tacitly suggesting that I couldn't trust him. I felt dirty, like I had let someone affect me and my marriage without the strength to have told the one person who needed to know. Adam was upset, though not at me. He said that he felt like he had failed as a husband because he didn't protect me. We both cried. I wished that I had told him sooner.

On May 3, the call that I was dreading came through. It was a woman from SafeSport, reaching out to follow up on the sexual assault report. I took the call and sat on my bed upstairs, the door closed so that Adam and Colt couldn't hear me. Once I started talking, I couldn't stop shaking or crying. I told her that I hadn't spoken to a counselor or psychologist about what had happened, that I was so troubled and ashamed about it and nervous about what could transpire if I came forward. Over the ensuing months, she called me back a couple of times and sent me emails, but I didn't answer. I wasn't willing to go on the record. That horrible old guilt, that fear that I was doing something wrong, was still there, holding me back. I thought about Alberto's wife, kids, grandkids. I didn't want to ruin Alberto's marriage. I didn't want to destroy his world. Nothing had happened between us. I still thought more about him than what it was costing me, how it had taxed my marriage, my family, my soul.

On May 4, I called my mom and sisters and told them the bare bones. I said that Alberto had massaged me and touched me inappropriately. I was afraid that the news would leak from the USADA hearings and I wanted them to hear it from me, not on TV or online.

During this whole period, I was a disaster. Everything felt arduous, even things I normally loved like getting Colt his breakfast. Within a week or so, I was functional again in a day-to-day sense, but inside I was ill at ease. I had raging headaches and struggled to sleep. Little things, like seeing Nike shoes on runners on the Boulder trails, or on the feet of kids playing soccer with Colt, drove me mad. Papa was now in his nineties and battling dementia. I'd call him in Minnesota to say hi. Sometimes, he would explain to me that he had a "granddaughter who ran."

On May 21, 2018, Adam and I flew to Los Angeles and checked into the same Marriott in downtown Los Angeles that we had stayed in for the 2016 Marathon Trials. I had been slated to testify in the arbitration on the 22nd, but it was then agonizingly moved back a day. After spending the 22nd trying to kill time, including seeing *Deadpool*, Adam and I woke up early the day of my arbitration and went for a slow, six-mile run to shake off the nerves, part of it on the Trials course that had broken my heart two years earlier. Just as with a big race, I tried to trust the training, ease into the anxiety, take some heart from the music I'd been listening to lately—in this case, Taylor Swift's album *Reputation*—but despite the months of intensive preparation for the arbitration, I still didn't feel ready.

It was Colt's last week of school, my mom was in Boulder watching him, and Adam and I were hoping to fly back the next day in time to be there when Colt got out, but it all depended on how long the arbitration went.

I showered and swapped my running clothes for a starchy business suit, thinking that the last time I wore a blazer was probably the Opening Ceremony at the Beijing Olympics. At thirty-nine, I felt kind of like I was playing dress-up. Adam walked me to the law office in downtown L.A. where the arbitration would take place. He would have to wait outside, but told me that he would have his phone on him and be pacing the streets nearby. *Funny*, I thought. *It's just like a race after all, a thing that I have to do on my own and trust that Adam will be there at the finish line.*

I took the elevator upstairs and was escorted to a seat in the lobby to wait. A door that I could see, further into the office space, opened and Alberto walked out of it, soon followed by other people in suits, at least one of whom looked disconcerted that Alberto had popped out first. Alberto looked tired, older, more stressed than I remembered. For some reason, flustered, I quietly said, "Hi." He looked right into my eyes and said nothing as he walked away.

I was soon escorted to a chair at a large table in a glass-walled conference room. Alberto was seated two chairs away. I wasn't sure why there were so many other people there, but the room was so crowded that people had to sit in window alcoves or lean against the walls. USADA had warned me for months that Alberto's lawyers would do anything in their power to try and discredit me, and I wondered if this was another tactic to make me nervous and say the wrong thing.

I could already feel my teeth chatter and a pool of sweat accumulating in the polyester of my blazer. Alberto now seemed to be his usual, charismatic self, whispering to his half dozen lawyers and passing notes. In a last-minute twist, his wife joined and sat at the end of the table. Not only would I have to describe my abuse to his lawyers, to anti-doping officials, and my abuser, but also to *his wife*? (I was later told that this wasn't allowed, but USADA didn't want it to seem that they were complaining, so they didn't argue it.)

I took a deep breath. I was sworn in. A stenographer began tapping away.

The arbitration began with my testimony, which was done via Bill Bock asking me questions from across the table. I talked about the unethical behavior and actions I'd witnessed at the Nike Oregon Project in the name of results, orchestrated by Alberto with help from Dr. Brown. I spoke of Alberto's attempts to make me and other runners take weight-loss medications, and the humiliating weigh-ins. I mentioned the sexually inappropriate comments and emails about female athletes and their bodies, adding newly remembered details, including that Alberto routinely walked around me and Adam in his underwear. I spoke for more than two hours.

We broke for lunch, and when we came back, it was time for me to be questioned by Alberto's lawyer, Maurice Suh. I found him aggressive and demeaning. Suh used a shrill, whiny, Valley girl tone when reading aloud from letters or comments I had made, which I understood to be a mocking attempt at imitating my voice. He questioned how it could be possible that I would say Galen might have had AndroGel rubbed on him during massages, and I didn't. What did I want people to believe—that half of the Oregon Project was doping, and the other half wasn't? (Yes, exactly.) At one point, the lawyers played the video of me swearing in interviews after the 2016 Marathon Trials for the room, I think with the intention of characterizing me as angry and untrustworthy, or maybe they were just trying to rattle me, but I sat there noticing that I was actually feeling fine. To me, it characterized me as honest. This lasted for about an hour.

Then, Suh asked: "Is there anything else that you told USADA and didn't testify to today?" I told him there was. "But you didn't testify about that here today?" he said again. "No," I responded. He didn't follow up.

We took a break, after which USADA would have the opportunity to question me again on redirect. Bock and his team were debating during the break whether they should ask me about the massages because I had left the door open. I wasn't with them when they discussed this, as they went into another room for their quick conversation. I was told about it later and that they decided not to.

All in all, I felt the arbitration went well. I walked out of the meeting feeling like I had said my piece, and held my head high. As I rode the elevator down from the office, I realized that Adam must have lost his mind waiting for that many hours. I wouldn't have blamed him if he'd walked to the Pacific Ocean by that point, but I found him nearby. "You need a margarita," he said, hugging me tight. We went to a nearby Mexican restaurant, where I filled him in on everything that had happened. I felt my shoulders relax for what seemed like the first time in months. The next morning, we flew home to Boulder, and got there just in time to catch Colt walking out of school.

Not long after, both Adam and I were called by Bock and his team to testify against Dr. Brown. We had little notice and prepared quickly, then went to Houston on June 11. Dr. Brown had a different legal team than Alberto, led by a California-based attorney named Howard Jacobs, but we believed Nike was still footing the bill. I repeated much of what I'd said in my arbitration against Alberto in the one with Dr. Brown, including that he had shared information about me and other athletes with Alberto without seeking consent, flying in the face of medical privacy laws. I did not talk about the massages, as they weren't relevant, and with that, I was done. Adam also testified.

On my fortieth birthday a month later, I walked into a tattoo parlor in Winter Park, Colorado. I'd always admired Adam's interlinked tattoos and the meaning they held for him. He has a map of Portland with a star on the hospital where Colt was born, which connects to a large moral compass that points north with the word "integrity" in the middle, under which is a melting set of Olympic rings—his way of saying that even though the sport is unethical, he got through it with his heart and morality intact. The music was soft and the studio quiet as I told the tattoo artist what I wanted: a simple arrow on the inside of my left wrist. It would point down to the earth when I'm standing, but forward when I'm running. I could just look there and be reminded to do the right thing, to always go in the right direction.

CHAPTER THIRTY-SEVEN
Just Keep Going

I did not retire; I returned to training. I ran the Houston Marathon on January 20, 2019, but dropped out when an old hamstring injury flared up around mile 18.

I kept going, even with the understanding that my goals and expectations could no longer be what they once were. In June, I ran the Leadville Trail Marathon, a grueling and scenic race in Colorado done on old mining trails and dirt roads with a peak altitude of more than 13,000 feet. It was one of the hardest things I'd ever done physically (at various points I hoped that a mountain lion would come and eat me; at another point I literally peed myself while running), but I did it for me, not my sponsor, my coach, or anyone else. It destroyed me, but I loved the feeling of doing something like that again completely on my own terms.

A few days later I was wondering if I might have a 50k race in me—also known as an ultramarathon. I began training for that in earnest and asked Adam to help pace me a couple of times. On September 30, 2019, we had just gotten back to our house from an afternoon run together on the Boulder trails and were getting ready to head out to pick up Colt from school when my cell phone rang.

It was Travis Tygart. It had been nearly six years since I'd first sat down with him and told my story. He said he was calling to let me know that the American Arbitration Association panel had completed its process, and come to a decision in the cases against Alberto and Dr. Brown. Both would be banned from athletics for four years on the grounds of "orchestrating and facilitating" doping, including trafficking testosterone to multiple athletes, and tampering with doping control processes.

I was stunned. Adam was, too. For years, we'd been preparing to be disappointed by the outcome. All the sacrifices we'd made hadn't been in vain.

Travis explained that it was likely that Alberto and Dr. Brown, with

Nike's blessing, would pursue a continued appeals process and do everything possible to challenge this decision. For now, however, they both were prohibited from involvement in the Olympics, World Championships, and elite national competitions.

Within minutes, the news went public. My phone buzzed with message after message.

Four days after the USADA decision was announced, Nike shut down the Oregon Project. Mark Parker announced that Nike would stand by Alberto, and continue to fund his appeal. "A four-year suspension for someone who acted in good faith is wrong," Parker wrote. He called the assertions against Alberto "unsubstantiated" and said the reason the Oregon Project was being shuttered was simply to avoid distractions for athletes who need "to focus on their training." As *The New York Times* reported: "Parker, however, is hardly a neutral source. . . . Parker was looped in [on emails with Alberto and Dr. Brown] on experiments that were conducted to determine the amount of testosterone an athlete could absorb using a lotion without testing positive for the banned substance. . . . [Parker said] that the test was conducted because Salazar was concerned that rivals might sabotage his athletes after a race. USADA officials have disputed that explanation, saying that it is disingenuous and that the goal of the test was to determine how athletes could get away with cheating." I was floored. Parker was never charged with anything.

Darren Treasure made out well for himself and was not hit with any charges. He faced no sanctions or penalties of any kind, and because he was always a private contractor working with the Oregon Project (despite his lofty job titles), he was able to just move on and continue his work. In recent years, I have heard that he has worked as a consultant with runners at the University of Oregon.

Mo Farah was not charged with any wrongdoing. He had left the Oregon Project at the end of October 2017, moved back to London, and continued training under a different coach. When asked about Alberto's ban, he said: "I have no tolerance for anyone who breaks the rules or crosses a line." Yet, he'd stayed with Alberto another two and a half years after Steve Magness, Adam, and I went public in the BBC and ProPublica reporting.

Galen was not charged, either. He had stayed with Alberto right up until the ban was announced and the Oregon Project was shut down. He released a statement. "Since I first met and began working with Alberto 19 years ago, he has always put my health and well-being first and has done the same for his other athletes. I have personally seen him take great care to comply with the WADA Code and prevent any violations of any anti-doping rules. I understand he is appealing the decision and wish him success. From my experience, he has always done his best for his athletes and the sport."

None of the violations that Alberto and Dr. Brown were banned for by USADA made a direct link to them giving performance-enhancing supplements to athletes. Suspicion was rampant, and in my opinion rightly so, but Galen and Mo, who had always tested clean, were not suspended. They both continue to deny any wrongdoing.

However, behind the scenes, Travis told me something that is as close to proof of what was really going on at the Nike Oregon Project as I may ever get. After fighting with Nike and Dr. Brown for years—through what Victor Burgos said he thought was "unprecedented" obstruction, requiring eight legal motions filed by USADA—they did eventually get the key medical records, lab results, and documents on me and other Oregon Project athletes.

These results showed testosterone levels. Though Bock and Tygart weren't allowed to specify to me which athletes they were discussing, they told me that the testosterone levels of "two of my teammates" had changed in a suspicious way over time. Mine had not.

Because their levels had never exceeded the legal threshold, action could not be taken against them. To me, what all this meant was clear, I thought that a crime had been committed. The seeming perpetrators had simply managed to avoid the punishment.

Among the many messages I received in the days after the USADA announcement went out was one on Instagram on October 29, 2019, from Mary Cain, the teenage running sensation who had started working with Alberto in 2012. I had followed her career for years, watching her slay track records left and right and become the youngest American ever to compete on a World Championships team, which she did in her first year at the

Oregon Project, just after turning seventeen. I'd remained nervous about the experience she was having being coached by Alberto, but given the secrecy of the investigation, I'd never felt like I could reach out to her directly. In 2016, I'd started hearing rumors that she was unhappy at the Oregon Project. She left in October of that year.

Now she was twenty-three. In her message, she told me that she was going public with her own story about Alberto and her time at Nike, and it wasn't a good one. I immediately wrote her back and sent her my number. Within minutes, we got on the phone. She told me about weigh-ins, comments Alberto made about her body, the way he policed her food intake. She told me that her physical and mental health suffered so much that she had begun to engage in self-harming behaviors, only to find that when she told Alberto, Darren, and Nike about it, no one would help her. Hearing what Mary went through made my heart hurt. It also deepened the guilt I felt over not speaking up sooner. I wondered if there was something that I could have done to warn her. On November 7, 2019, Mary bravely told her story in a *New York Times* op-ed and corresponding video piece, including the details of her self-harm going untreated. It echoed in and beyond the running world. We've been friends ever since.

While talking to Mary in our first phone call, I also learned something about Darren Treasure that horrified me: he was not a licensed psychologist. On November 13, just a couple of days after Mary published her op-ed, *Sports Illustrated* published an article headlined "Inside the Toxic Culture of the Nike Oregon Project 'Cult.'" As it explained, "On the now-defunct Oregon Project website, his page was once titled 'Darren Treasure, PhD— Sports Psychologist | Oregon Project.'" The article continued, "Treasure, though, is not a licensed psychologist." In a statement he gave to *Sports Illustrated*, Darren said: "'Psychologist' is a term associated with a state-licensed practitioner. I have never been or practiced as a licensed psychologist. There is no such thing as a 'licensed sport psychologist.'" I recall Darren being introduced to me by Alberto as a psychologist, he acted in the capacity of one, and his page on the Oregon Project website had affirmed it. While I was in the Oregon Project, news outlets including *Runner's World* had referred to him as a "sports psychologist," picking up from the website, and nobody from Nike—not to mention Darren himself—had corrected them. It turned out that the PhD he'd listed on the website was in *kinesiology*, the study of movement and muscle function, not psychology. Perhaps it was because he was not in fact a licensed psychologist that he felt unbound by the rules of patient confidentiality and shared what I told him in my sessions with Alberto.

The truth continued to trickle out. The day after the *Sports Illustrated* article was published, Amy Begley told her story to *The New York Times*. "If I had a bad workout on a Tuesday, he would tell me I looked flabby and send me to get weighed. Then, three days later, I would have a great workout and he would say how lean I looked and tell me my husband was a lucky guy. I mean, really? My body changed in three days?" She also talked about a contract Alberto had made her sign stating that she would not be friends with other Oregon Project athletes. "He told me I should think of my teammates as business acquaintances," she said.

Just days after Mary and Amy went public, on November 18, SafeSport called again. This time, I answered. They said that they had two other female athletes who were making SafeSport complaints about Alberto. Their case was building. They asked me if I would commit to testifying. I asked them to give me some time to think about it.

I truly didn't know if I could handle more arbitrations, more prep sessions, more nights of anxiety, more online threats. On October 24, Travis Tygart had called to tell me someone had written a letter to USADA threatening to kill me if I didn't stop talking about doping and Alberto. Travis had already informed the FBI and local police, who were treating it as a credible threat. It was one thing to have people calling me a cunt on the internet (though cowardly and not okay); it was another to feel unsafe in my own home. Adam and I had hired someone to come and teach us self-defense and improve our security systems. Adam had also started to bike with me when I ran.

I didn't want to go forward with the case, but I thought of Mary and the potential harm that could come to other women if I didn't. Two weeks later, I called SafeSport back and said that I was ready to move forward.

The acute fear of the death threat faded a bit, but never totally went away. I returned to running on my own daily. I took Colt to school, Adam went to work, we all ate dinner together at our long table with Freya sleeping nearby, and watched movies together on our couch. If the Olympics were one dream, this—being home with my family, joking around with Adam and Colt, coloring, storytime, the moments of daily happiness—was another. When we could, we loaded up our car and made the drive to Duluth to spend time with my mom, Kelly, Papa, and Grandma Ola Jean. The Russian tea still smelled and tasted delicious and you could set a watch by when Papa and Grandma shared their afternoon Mountain Dew together.

As I got more involved in the SafeSport case, I wanted to find a way to talk to Colt about it without overwhelming him. He was nine, but had already shown he was extremely bright as well as a keen observer. I had started to think more about how to share my story with him in a way appropriate for his age without yet landing on the right words, when one day out of the blue Colt beat me to the punch. "Alberto touched you in your privates," he said.

"Yes," I replied. "That's what happened. It's upsetting and it's not okay." We talked about how there were rules about consent when it came to touching people that had been broken. I wanted him to understand the world. I wanted him to grow into a good man.

In February 2020, it emerged in leaked documents obtained by the BBC that Mo Farah had denied to USADA investigators several times that he had received injections of L-carnitine, but then changed his story shortly thereafter, according to leaked reports. He said he had initially forgotten about the injections—four of them, taken in April 2014—and the name of the supplement, before realizing that someone who had directly witnessed it happening was also being interviewed by the BBC. The dosage was within the 50ml limit, and Farah apologized, but the fact that he'd failed to note taking it on a doping control form, and directly denied doing so to USADA investigators before changing the story, continued to add to the suspicion, despite the fact that he had not failed any drug tests.

When the pandemic hit in March 2020, races were canceled. I was still sponsored by Oiselle, having signed a new four-year deal at a higher annual salary in 2017, and now also had a shoe deal with a company called Altra. I still ran constantly and went to races, but mostly for my brands and for my own joy. One of my goals was to once again break five minutes in the mile. Over Zoom, the SafeSport case was able to progress, which I was thankful for, though I found talking about abuse in front of a screen over and over again even more difficult than doing it in person.

In June 2020, my stepbrother Andy called to say that his father, Tom Wheeler, had died of natural causes. I felt so disconnected from that part of my family. He said that they were planning to wait until Covid was over to hold a real memorial service. While I sincerely appreciated the call, I never heard about anything of the sort happening, virtual or in person.

In September 2020, with Colt's school doing remote learning, we drove to Minnesota to spend three weeks with family. Papa and Grandma Ola Jean were both living in a care facility, with Papa in the memory unit, and Grandma on the independent living side. My mom, Colt, and I were out for a stroll on September 24, the day before Colt's birthday, when my mom got a call that Papa had been diagnosed with Covid. Vaccines weren't available yet, and he was vulnerable. At first, he seemed to be in good spirits and eating well, but a few days later his symptoms became severe. The doctors said our time with him was limited and gave us permission to visit—in masks, goggles, and gloves. It was my turn to offer him soothing words, to tell him to relax, that there was no pressure, that I loved him. We were with him when he passed away the evening of October 6.

As I ran the next day, I wanted to feel my lungs ache to mask the hurt in my heart. Papa had given me the gift of running when I was six years old, and it had become everything to me. It supported me in my grief. It helped me find myself, a clear mind, peace. It had brought me money and fame. It had also brought me pain and suffering. It was my way of interacting with and understanding all of those things, and so much more. It allowed me to touch life in its infinite complexity.

As I ran, I felt the moisture from Fredenberg Lake on my face. I thought about Papa jogging with my mom to help support her after my father died.

My love for the sport of running is what made me come forward against Alberto and Nike. Speaking up is an act of love. But the example that Papa set for me—of integrity, a passion for justice, his insistence that, no matter what, you just keep going—is what allowed me to carry on even when things were tough. What he valued most was the ability to keep getting up, again and again, after falling.

CHAPTER THIRTY-EIGHT
A Call for Change

I did make it to the Tokyo Olympics, but instead of competing, I was traveling there for NBC Sports. They had hired me in May 2021 to join their broadcast team as a commentator on distance events, after I'd made a Trials debut in April and it had gone well. It was an exciting new venture. Though I had still not officially retired from competing, in effect this was my transition to the next phase of my career. It was also bittersweet, remembering my own experiences at the Olympics as a runner. But I was honored to have the chance to approach the Games from a new and different perspective, and communicate to the world from the broadcast booth why running was worth loving.

On July 26, 2021, I was just easing into the flight to Tokyo and trying to sleep when I received a text from Amy Begley, then one from Mary Cain. A decision had been made in Alberto's SafeSport case. I was totally blindsided: no one from SafeSport had reached out to give me a heads-up, as Travis Tygart had done before the USADA ban was announced. I was now learning the news on a long flight overseas, the very situation in which some of Alberto's abuses had taken place. I was also terrified about whether someone had leaked my involvement and the details of my testimony. I still had not, could not, tell anyone about it beyond my family, USADA, and SafeSport. Adam was texting me that he was reading the report, but I couldn't get it to load on the shaky airplane Wi-Fi. A screenshot of the report came through from him, containing the words "digital vaginal penetration." I felt sick; I knew it was about me. I was relieved to see that I was not named, but I wondered if people suspected it. In an eerie way, it felt as though Alberto was still managing to unsettle me before a big competition.

At the same time, I couldn't help but feel the moment's vindication. SafeSport, without going into specifics, had given Alberto a lifetime ban, and an arbitrator said that Alberto's explanation was not credible. He would be permanently ineligible to coach USA Track & Field athletes.

When I landed in Tokyo, I met up with the rest of the NBC running commentating team, none of whom seemed to have heard yet about Alberto's SafeSport ban. I hadn't told anyone there that I was involved in the SafeSport proceedings, but they did of course know I'd been one of the witnesses in the USADA case. Once they got wind of the SafeSport news, we had a production meeting where we discussed whether Alberto's lifetime ban was something that should be mentioned on air. I couldn't imagine having to talk about this with any clarity and calmness to an audience of millions. Sanya Richards-Ross helped refocus me. She did not know the details, but she could tell that I was upset and inferred something was up. She was just the friend that I needed so many miles from home, helping me let it go and focus on what I was there to do. We did not end up talking about Alberto's ban on air. The rest of the Olympics went smoothly and proceeded safely with Covid restrictions and a smaller-than-usual NBC crew.

In the wake of the SafeSport ban neither Nike nor Alberto acknowledged wrongdoing or offered an apology. To the contrary, Alberto and Nike filed an appeal of the decision. When asked during the appeal if Nike was backing him, Alberto first said yes, then quickly said no, he misspoke, and he was paying for the appeal on his own. However, Nike has allegedly spent millions of dollars defending Alberto across the various cases. The largest seller of athletic footwear and apparel in the world, spending all that money to keep my abuser active in the sport. Remember that the next time you see a Nike ad or consider buying shoes or clothing with a swoosh on it.

Mark Parker stepped down as CEO in October 2019, but stayed on as executive chairman, a position he holds to this day. A Nike spokesman said that Parker's decision was "absolutely not" related to Alberto or the Oregon Project, but the culmination of months of working with the board on succession. In a note to employees announcing his move to executive chairman and new CEO John Donahoe, Parker said, "To be clear, I'm not going anywhere. I'm not sick. There are no issues I'm not sharing."

John Capriotti retired from Nike in September 2020, but continued to keep a Nike email address in his role as a consultant. He will "consult and continue to play an important role in our relationship with athletes," Nike said in a statement at the time of his retirement announcement. Numerous agents have told me that Cap is still allegedly in control of deciding which runners Nike sponsors. As one prominent agent said, "He's been the single most influential person in the sport."

As I learned only after leaving the Oregon Project, Cap had arrived at Nike under inauspicious circumstances. He'd abruptly quit as the head coach of the running teams at Kansas State in 1992 to join Nike because he was embroiled in a scandal about paying college athletes. Not only did he say "I knew what I was doing the whole time, and I knew what I was doing was against NCAA rules," soon after resigning, but Phil Knight was aware of what had happened and still allowed him to come to Nike. While the kids at Kansas State's track and cross country programs suffered the consequences, barred by the NCAA from postseason competition and with their programs' scholarships having been reduced, Cap was on his way to becoming a highly paid executive. His history of putting himself above his athletes was a long one, it seemed.

At the Tokyo Olympics, because of an exclusivity contract between Nike and NBC, I had to wear Nike apparel on air when calling Olympic races. When I was first offered the job, NBC was very clear in telling me that they did not want to silence me, but due to their contract with Nike I would have to wear the swoosh on broadcasts, and so they understood if I didn't want to take the position. It gave me pause, but in the end, I felt that allowing Nike to take away more professional opportunities for me than they already had was worse than another protest against a thousand-pound gorilla.

It's a testament to how Nike's financial dominance and influence in the sport of running remain as significant as ever. Since 2014, they have been the top sponsor and main source of funding for USA Track & Field. They're set to remain as such until 2040. Since 2016, they've also been the top sponsor of IAAF. Their millions of dollars a year in support pay the salaries of the people on staff, and their gear is worn by athletes in the world's biggest athletic competitions.

In August 2021, shortly after the news of the SafeSport ban was announced, Nike quietly removed Alberto's name from its building on their campus. However, at the newly remodeled Hayward Field, a project largely funded by Nike money, Alberto's face is still displayed in the lower-level museum and on the stadium walls as part of a tribute to University of Oregon alumni. It was public knowledge that Alberto had been sentenced to a four-year doping ban by USADA when construction was underway. Mary Cain's *New York Times* piece had been out for *two years*. Still, the university featured him.

How am I supposed to feel when I go to Hayward Field to do race commentary? How is Mary supposed to feel when she competes there, or Amy—who is now a great coach—supposed to feel when she goes there to support her athletes?

Alberto is still in the USATF Hall of Fame.

What message does all of this send to men in the sport, and to future generations, about what's acceptable?

———————————

In March 2021, I had to testify again in Alberto's appeal of his four-year ban from USADA. Six months later, Alberto's appeal was denied, further affirming the validity of all that I'd said and all the work that I'd done. Dr. Brown's appeal was denied as well. The panel from the Court of Arbitration for Sport (CAS) that was hearing the appeals determined that Alberto had overseen an "orchestrated scheme" to mislead USADA, and that he had committed anti-doping violations that included the possession of testosterone, complicity in Brown's "administration of a prohibited method," and "tampering with the doping control process with respect to the issue of L-carnitine infusions/syringes."

In October, Mary filed a $20 million lawsuit against Alberto and Nike for abusing her from the time she had started working with Alberto as a teenager. The suit alleged the things she'd told me, about Alberto's obsession with her weight, the public humiliations he put her through about it, and the resulting depression and self-harming behaviors she suffered through. She also alleged that Nike was aware but failed to intervene. Of course, Nike and Alberto have denied wrongdoing and are fighting the suit, while I'm cheering Mary on.

In November, after an extended period during which I'd been struggling with my balance, I was diagnosed by a neurological movement specialist with focal dystonia. I got a second opinion that confirmed it. Focal dystonia is a movement disorder that sometimes plagues professional musicians or artists who work with their hands a lot. Doctors told me they

don't know why it happens, why some people get involuntary muscle reactions; there is no known cause, there is no known cure, but there are
treatments. I'm working with a neurologist to help find a good regimen of
medication and treatment to allow me to run again. I'll never be able to log
the kind of mileage that I did before, but I'm currently working up to being
able to consistently get some longer runs in.

Alberto's appeal of the SafeSport decision meant another round of grueling hearings on Zoom for me in early December 2021. As I offered my
testimony, I saw Alberto there, as a little black rectangle on my screen.
Once again, his lawyer, Maurice Suh, was aggressive and demeaning. The
experience honestly ranks among the worst and most retraumatizing of
my life. "This *has* to be the end," Adam told me. Whatever the outcome,
I felt I had done everything in my power to demand something different,
something better, for my sport.

On December 21, 2021, I received the news that Alberto's lifetime ban
was upheld. Effectively, this means that Alberto is now done. Even once
his four-year USADA ban ends in September 2023, he won't be able to
come back. That said, though he can never coach in the United States at
the Olympic level, conceivably, he could still coach high school kids, at an
NCAA program, or overseas (realms that are beyond SafeSport's jurisdic-
tion), if anyone will have him. I don't think they will.

There's still a lot of change we need to make in sports, and in our culture more broadly, when it comes to supporting those who want to tell the
truth, to ending doping and sexual abuse, and to weeding out subtler forms
of manipulation by the powerful of the less powerful. If I've learned anything, it's that change starts when good people refuse to stay quiet.

Alberto is out of the sport, but I'm still here, running. And the truth is,
despite the heartache it has brought me, and all of the tears, this gift that
Papa handed me has given me purpose. Through training, racing, putting
one foot in front of the other, I've found out how strong a person I truly am.

Running has been my source of inspiration, my religious practice, my
way of interfacing with the world. It has taught me how to move and how
to be in my body. It has nearly killed me. It has saved my life. It's made me
who I am. It's made me happy.

I'm still in love with it.

I always will be.

AFTERWORD

On the evening of March 16, 2023, I found myself walking into a church.

The Longest Race had been on shelves for two days and Mary Pilon and I were arriving for our first in-person book event, in Boulder, Colorado, just a short drive from my home. Colt trotted along the snow-lined sidewalk with me and Mary. Adam wasn't far behind. The event, sponsored by the Boulder Bookstore, was being held at the First Congregational Church—a century-old stone building on Pine Street. Given that *The Longest Race* ends with me talking about running as my "religious practice," it felt oddly fitting to be launching the book there.

As I ascended the church steps to make my way in, I took a moment to appreciate how I felt. Light. Open. Free. This day had finally arrived. The things that I had kept secret for years were now out there. There was a book I could point to and say, "There it is. My story. Take it or leave it." A book is an offering of sorts, an act of creation and inherent vulnerability, particularly in the case of a memoir. Here was my pile of pages, complete with a Library of Congress number.

Publication day had been a surreal blitz. My face had been on not one, but two billboards in Times Square. *Good Morning America* had aired a sit-down interview in which I detailed the abuse allegations against Alberto Salazar. Myriad news outlets around the world then picked up the story, quoting the passages of the book that focused on the abuse, doping allegations, and Nike's role in all of it. My social media feeds had exploded with reactions. For the prior two days, my phone had been chirping with texts every few seconds. I had been trying to balance engagement with sanity, checking my phone but also taking long stretches with notifications off, taking comfort in my routines with Colt, Adam, and our dogs and cats.

Because so much of the book coverage and reaction to it had been unfolding online, it wasn't totally clear to me what impact the book was having. As Mary and I were ushered into a back room of the church, where we killed time joking and drinking seltzers before the event, surrounded by bells and poly-blend robes, I realized how different tonight would be. I wouldn't be looking at numbers on a publisher's spreadsheet or pixels on Twitter, but real people.

Although a few friends had pledged that they would show up that night, Mary and I didn't know what kind of crowd to expect or what the mood would be. When the time finally came to step out on stage, I was completely shocked. The church was *packed*. Adam and Colt sat in the front, and the room had a warm feeling. After the on-stage conversation and question and answer session, hundreds of people lined up, many waiting in the cold, snowy night, to have their books signed. I stayed late, wowed and moved by people's patience, and their stories. They told me about their marathons that went well, and the runs that they had bombed. They told me about getting into the sport as a way to make it through their divorce or to gather the strength to leave abusive relationships. I also heard a lot about loss, specifically the loss of a parent.

In the year since that first event, these experiences have become common. And therein lies the irony. In writing a memoir, I imagined I would be getting something like a final word. In fact, the church event was the start of me recognizing that the opposite was true. A door blew open and the voices of countless other people came in.

In the time since publication, I've been gratified to see that *The Longest Race* has opened up conversations in the running community and beyond. I've heard not only from professional runners and amateurs, including many parents and coaches of high school and college runners, but also from scientists, lawyers, teachers, stay-at-home moms, and countless others who tell me they saw themselves in the pages. These haven't only been women. After an event I did in Beaverton, the belly of the Nike beast, a man approached to tell me that he owed me an apology. He had tears in his eyes as he said that for years, he had seen me as just a woman scorned, out for revenge, but now he understood that there was more to the story. Moments like that have meant a lot to me.

Some of the people who have gotten in touch after reading the book have also opened up about their own experiences with sexual abuse. Their stories have shown me just how wide and pervasive the problem is, and I see that there is still so much work that we as a culture have to do: to ensure safety against abuse, especially as it pertains to women and girls; to cultivate a world that empowers survivors and ceases to protect abusers and their enablers.

Interestingly, I haven't heard anything from Nike. No acknowledgment, no plan to improve the culture, nothing. I didn't write the book for Nike—far from it—but it's disappointing to see an opportunity to change for the better be wasted. The feeling was underscored when I went to the Nike-sponsored Hayward Field in Eugene in July 2023 to call the USATF Outdoor Nationals for NBC Sports and found that Alberto's name was *still* on a brick on a path leading into the venue. A giant picture of him remained in the stands facing the track, impossible to miss. It was infuriating.

Nike may be behind the ball, but I'm seeing via my experience with *The Longest Race* that institutions *can* change, especially when they are compelled by financial incentives. When Mary and I first pitched my story to publishers in 2019, we were frequently told that interest in women's running was "niche" and there was "a limited audience." We called bullshit on that and readers did too. Not only did *The Longest Race* debut at #7 on the *New York Times* bestseller list, books by my friends and fellow runners Des Linden and Lauren Fleshman were published around the same time and also made the bestseller list. I'm so proud of them and grateful to the publishers and the readers who came to these titles and have signaled to the world that these stories have literal worth.

Speaking of Des Linden, we started a podcast together in January 2023 called *Nobody Asked Us*. It's been a blast, and it debuted at #14 on iTunes across all podcasts and #1 for sports. As with our books, we learned that with so much of the women's sports world, it's the *Field of Dreams* axiom: if you build it, they will come.

On the podcast, we spend a lot of our time talking about women athletes. One story that we've discussed hit particularly close to home. Not long before *The Longest Race* came out, my childhood idol Lynn Jennings went public with her abuse allegations against her longtime coach, John Babington. Other athletes came forward describing abuse by Babington as well, who admitted to it when confronted and was given a lifetime ban by SafeSport. As I noted in my book, I had long revered Jennings. After I learned what she had been through, I felt an even greater bond with her.

In addition to committing myself to telling stories that I think are important in writing and on podcasts, I continue my evolution as an athlete and advocate. I'm working to improve the culture of the sport of running, not just on air or in my work with NBC Sports calling races, but behind the scenes, too.

In June 2023, I was pleased to be named the athlete representative board member for USADA, the anti-doping agency that handed Alberto a lifetime ban. Clean sport isn't here yet, but I credit USADA for including athletes in their governance, and I am excited to dig more into the structural issues around doping and fairness in competition.

As for my own running, I'm working with physical therapists to keep building up my mileage steadily and healthily as I learn more about my focal dystonia. I'm also doing more advocacy work to raise awareness of the disorder and help others access treatment. A fundraising campaign I did with one of my sponsors, Altra, raised $50,000 for dystonia research, a check I proudly presented to the Brachman-Strauss Foundation in August 2023.

The process of writing and publishing *The Longest Race* ranks among the most healing of my entire life. I hope that the book continues to function as a mirror by which we examine the system for elite athletes, our purchasing decisions, and who and why we lift certain actors up. And I hope that more people continue to find community in and around these pages. There's so much power in four words: "You are not alone."

I underestimated how speaking my truth, owning my own story—the good, the bad, and everything in-between—would transform me. Calm me. Allow me to have perspective on my career and accomplishments. So often, especially as women, we're told that pride is hubris. (It's one of the seven deadly sins, after all.) But putting my story out there, with the ups and the downs, something shifted in me. There was a newfound pride in how I perceived myself. It felt good.

For years, I had thought of myself as a loser in the biggest moments of my athletic career. I was especially ashamed of my performances in the Beijing and London Olympics, where I felt like I had disappointed my country, coaches, and family. For that reason, I had avoided getting an Olympic rings tattoo, which is a common celebration for people who make the team. Why would I want a constant reminder of that on my flesh? A constant conversation starter for a dialogue I didn't want to have?

Shortly before *The Longest Race* was released, Colt darted into the house after one of his middle school track practices. He asked me why, after all these years, I hadn't gotten an Olympic rings tattoo. He knew that so many other athletes who had made the team had one, including his father.

"Mom," he said. "You should be so proud."

I felt the sucker punch of truth by way of offspring. And I realized he was right. Going to the Olympics was my childhood dream, and I had done it twice in three damn events. I *should* be proud. Instead, I had let other people convince me that I wasn't enough.

Those days were over.

To put it in editor parlance, which I had learned a thing or two about by then, a revision was needed.

The day after our first book event at the church in Boulder, I marched myself to a tattoo parlor. I asked to have those five Olympic rings inked on my left arm. *Yes*, I told the tattoo artist, I was sure.

Once again, a new story had to be told. One in which I now, quite literally, was the author. In fact, I had been all along.

—*Kara Goucher*
Boulder, Colorado
August 2023

RESOURCES

ABUSE PREVENTION AND SURVIVORSHIP

- RAINN (Rape, Abuse & Incest National Network) and the National Sexual Assault Hotline: 1-800-656-4673. Its website, RAINN.ORG, also has a chat feature.
- 988 Suicide & Crisis Lifeline (formerly known as the National Suicide Prevention Lifeline): Call or text 988 to get help. Its website is 988lifeline.org.
- The Army of Survivors, a nonprofit focused on ending abuse of athletes, thearmyofsurvivors.org
- Mothers Against Drunk Driving, its 24-hour victim help line is 877-MADD-HELP (1-877-623-3435)
- The National Eating Disorders Association (NEDA), the largest nonprofit dedicated to supporting those with eating disorders, nationaleatingdisorders.org, call or text 1-800-931-2237

SPORTS

- The Women's Sports Foundation, a nonprofit founded by Billie Jean King that advocates for the inclusion of girls and women in sports, womenssportsfoundation.org
- Girls on the Run, a nonprofit devoted to coaching girls in sports and life, girlsontherun.org
- Black Girls RUN! Encouraging and motivating Black women to run and live actively, blackgirlsrun.com
- The U.S. Anti-Doping Agency, the national anti-doping organization for the U.S. Olympic and Paralympic sports, usada.org
- The World Anti-Doping Agency, wada-ama.org

A NOTE ON SOURCES

In addition to hundreds of hours of interviews with Kara, dozens of other sources were incredibly generous with their time, including Adam, Kara's sisters, her mother, and myriad athletes, coaches, and people familiar with the Oregon Project.

Kara made available to me her logbooks, photos, medical records, text messages, emails, and other documents to round out and support her account. I also relied on transcripts and legal documents tied to the USADA and SafeSport cases, and video archives of races, notably those from FloTrack and NBC.

We enlisted the help of an outside fact-checker, Cole Louison, to re view our work as well.

Some emails and documents cited have been cut for length.

—*Mary Pilon*

ACKNOWLEDGMENTS

Kara and Mary both would like to thank their agent, Deborah Schneider at ICM, editor Max Meltzer, along with his colleagues at Simon & Schuster, including Gallery Books' publisher, Jennifer Bergstrom, and publicity director, Sally Marvin, and ace fact-checker Cole Louison for their help in getting the book out there.

Kara would like to thank Mary Pilon, without whom this book would not exist. Additionally, she'd like to thank Adam and Colt Goucher, the absolute loves of her life; her mother, Patty Wheeler, who taught her to be true to herself; her sisters, Kelly Grgas and Kendall Schoolmeester, who have supported her in all aspects of her life; Papa and Grandma Ola Jean, who always made her feel safe; Davorka Grgas, who has been a window to her father; her entire extended family; Dick Skogg; Mark Wetmore; Heather Burroughs; Sally Bergesen; her amazing friends; and the community that has supported her.

Mary is grateful to Sam Wolf, Aviva Slesin, Sarna Becker, Tim Arango, Michael Yang, Susan Goodman, Jeremy Axelrod, Maricor Resente, Reth Eddy, Jim Miller, Elena Ryan, Jen Bagnall, Anna Karingal, Kari Ensor, her friends in New York, California, Oregon, and elsewhere around the globe. She also thanks her awesome family and her puggle intern, Pedro.

ABOUT THE AUTHORS

KARA GOUCHER is an American long-distance runner. She won the silver medal at the 2007 World Championships in the 10,000 meters and is a two-time Olympian. A podium finisher at the Boston and New York City Marathons, she also competed for the University of Colorado, where she was a three-time NCAA champion. After more than a decade as a Nike athlete, Kara is now sponsored by Oiselle and Altra and is a cohost of the *Clean Sport Collective* podcast, promoting fair play in sports. She lives in Boulder, Colorado, with her husband, Adam, also an elite runner, and their son, Colt. Read more about her at karagoucher.com.

MARY PILON is the *New York Times* bestselling author of *The Monopolists* and *The Kevin Show*. She cowrote and cohosted the audiobook *TWISTED: The Story of Larry Nassar and the Women Who Took Him Down*, and co-edited *Losers: Dispatches from the Other Side of the Scoreboard*. She previously covered sports at *The New York Times* and business at *The Wall Street Journal*, and worked as a producer with the NBC Sports Emmy-nominated team at the 2016 Rio Olympics. Her work regularly appears in *The New Yorker, Bloomberg Businessweek, The New York Times, Vice*, and on NBC, among other outlets. She is a story producer on *BS High*, HBO's documentary about the Bishop Sycamore High School football scandal. Find more at marypilon.com.